ALSO BY JESSICA B. HARRIS

Tasting Brazil:
Regional Recipes and Reminiscences

Sky Juice and Flying Fish:
Traditional Caribbean Cooking

Iron Pots and Wooden Spoons:
Africa's Gifts to New World Cooking

Hot Stuff:
A Cookbook in Praise of the Piquant

The
Welcome

JESSICA B. HARRIS

Drawings by Patrick Eck

A FIRESIDE BOOK
Published by Simon & Schuster

Table

African-American
Heritage Cooking

FIRESIDE
Rockefeller Center
1230 Avenue of the Americas
New York, NY 10020

Copyright © 1995 by Jessica B. Harris
All rights reserved,
including the right of reproduction
in whole or in part in any form.

First Fireside Edition 1996

Fireside and colophon are registered trademarks
of Simon & Schuster Inc.

Designed by Edith Fowler

Manufactured in the United States of America

10 9 8 7 6 5 4 3 2 1

Library of Congress Cataloging-in-Publication Data

Harris, Jessica B.
  The welcome table : African-American heritage
cooking / Jessica B. Harris ; drawings by Patrick Eck.
     p.   cm.
  Includes index.
  1. Afro-American cookery.   I. Title.
TX715.H31443   1995
641.59'296073—dc20   94-32487   CIP

ISBN 0-671-79360-8
    0-684-81837-X (Pbk)

Acknowledgments

No researcher is an island. My work is built on the work of others, known and unknown, from the recent studies of historians on the period of African-American enslavement to untold numbers of unknown cooks who struggled and figured out ways to make dandelion greens into salads, didn't hesitate to try the first chittlin', and decided that watermelon rind looked like it would pickle just fine.

Thanks and praises are due to:

Fellow authors and librarians who jumped on the idea with interest and helped track down hot sauces, recipes, folk, and foods. James D. Porterfield; Rolf Swenson, of the Benjamin Rosenthal Library at Queens College; Nashromeh Lindo, of the Schomburg Center; Mabel McCarthy of the Oak Bluffs Public Library; and oh so many others who answered phones and were willing to talk to a stranger with enthusiasm and interest.

Mrs. Poston of the Hampton University Archives, for her help with photographs; Eve Pelligrino of the Bettman Archive, for her enthusiasm; Chester Higgins, for sharing his photo research knowhow; and John Shelhammer, of Martha's Vineyard, for his photo restoration.

Will from Johnson and Wales in Providence for sitting in dusty libraries and used book shops looking for African-American cookbooks.

Beverly Hall Lawrence of *Newsday* and Pat Dennis, for information on black-owned restaurants around the country.

Dr. Dorothy Height and the wonderful women of the National Council of Negro Women, for recognizing that my work captures a piece of our common history.

Karen Hess for setting a standard of excellence.

Bernatta Wake, for her information on slave cooking, her workshop, and the taste of ash cakes.

Jean Andrews, for ongoing aid with chile identification.

Liv and Willlie Blumer; Judy Kern; Toula Polygalaktos, my original editor; Pam Hoenig; Rux Martin; Ellen Rolfes; Barry Estabrook; and other friends in the wonderful world of publishing who encourage me and urge me on.

W. W. Weaver, Nancy Harmon Jenkins, Fritz Blanc, Lora Brody, Judy Faye in Philly, Beth Schluger in Hartford, Johnny Rivers, Clayton Sherrod, and so many others in the food community around the country too numerous to note for allowing me among their number.

Leah Chase, for just being there, and Cleo, for being willing to take up the toque.

Folks at the Seek Program at QC.

Carla Fitzgerald, Agnes, Diane, and Rita Louard, Tanya Holland, Vernice Charles, Charlotte Lyons, June Bobb, Greg and Mona Jones, and Maxine Clair, for allowing me to interview them about their African-American foodways.

My spiritual lifeline, the *filhas* at Casa Branca Ile FunFun in Salvador da Bahia, Brazil.

Patrick Dunn; Peter Patout; Mary Len, Lou, and Lenore Costa; Ann Bruce; Martha Taylor; Hoppin' John Taylor; Roy Guste; Gray Boone—white southerners all who shared recipes, good times, and tales of meals prepared for them by black hands.

Caroline Avelino, who taught me how to pronounce puhcahns (aka pecans) properly.

Daphne Derven, for historical perspective.

Floria Hasselbard, Grace Sells, and Ruth Jones, for family photographs.

Cassandra Webster, for the gift of conversation with her mother, Eva Webster.

Patrick Eck, for illustrations.

Patricia D. Hopkins, my almost daughter, and her children—Charles Anthony and Ja'nie—for giving me another reason to pass it on.

Kerry Moody; Lurita B. Bown; Brenda Berrian, of the African Studies Department, University of Pittsburgh; Helen Disher (ibae)°, Department of Romance Languages, North Carolina A. & T.; Thomas Hammond of North Carolina University; the folk at the Hermann Grima House in New Orleans; Minnie and Herbie Leonard; Helen Rutledge; Chloe King; Charisse Lillie; Alma Whittaker; and the rest of those on the "friendship train," especially those who come, eat, and comment: Pat Lawrence; Jackie Booker Reeves; June, Robert, and Kamau Bobb; Martha Mae Jones; Lynn Eck; Richard Alleman; Yvette Burgess Polcyn and Ifelami; Ayo Fenner; and more.

Mia and Pam and Derrick Wright at White Top, for getting me around.

Ron Cottman, for keeping the rain off.

Carole Abel, who had faith in me from the beginning and who is always there to encourage and soothe ruffled feathers, wiped my tears when my

° *"Rest in peace" in Yoruba.*

beloved cat Obi died, rejoiced when Toby arrived, and just keeps me keepin' on.

Sydny Miner, who, this second go-round after *Sky Juice,* knew what to expect and kept my nose pressed to the grindstone with applications of encouragement and luncheon meetings and friendship.

And to Jennifer Griffith, her able assistant.

Finally to my mother, my culinary secret weapon, who stays up nights to read manuscripts, debates the placement of each comma, tests recipes, and sees her dreams of culinary involvement come to fruition in my work. She truly is the wind beneath my wings and always keeps me going with liberal doses of love and encouragement.

To all of these and to The Supreme One, without Whom nothing would ever be written by me.

THANK YOU.

Dedication

For my great-grandparents: Samuel Philpot and Rhoda Cobbs Philpot, Charles Jones and Martha Jones, and Harriet Hornbeak (ibae), all of whom journeyed from "can't to can" and brought their families from slavery to freedom.

For the memory of my grandmothers, Bertha Philpot Jones and Ida Irene Harris (ibae), who surrounded me in my childhood with the succulent tastes of roasted fresh hams and savory homemade pickles, and who told me they loved me by preparing pots of pungent chitterlings and aromatic collard greens.

For my father, Jesse Brown Harris (ibae), who ate nothing that wasn't covered in either salt or hot sauce, but who fervently believed that all meals, whether bologna and crackers or caviar and Champagne, should be the occasion for celebration and communion.

For my mother, Rhoda Alease Jones Harris, who taught me to love food, to set the table with fine silver and heavy damask or with paper plates and plastic forks, to respect my guests by always presenting the best I could offer, and most important, to cook with my mouth, so that what was prepared would taste wonderful no matter how humble the ingredients.

It is also for those who went before my great-grandparents, whose names I do not know, and for African-Americans everywhere. May their legacy of the tastes of okra and beans and collard greens remain with us and with those generations yet to come.

Contents

Introduction   15

Appetizers   37

Soups and Salads   57

Condiments   81

Vegetables and Other Side Dishes   101

Main Dishes   143

Breads and Baking   181

Desserts and Candies   199

Beverages   225

Lagniappe   235

Menus   237

Appendices   243

   Glossary   245

   A Cook's Dozen: Some of My
   Favorite African-American Cookbooks 262

   African-American Restaurants
   Around the Country   264

   Local and Mail Order Sources   271

Index   275

Introduction

Folks by the log cabin fireplace, circa 1900.

It's gotta have taste.

HAMPTON UNIVERSITY ARCHIVES

AFRICAN-AMERICAN HERITAGE COOKING

African-Americans have a love affair with food perhaps unequaled in the history of this country. For centuries we've brought the piquant tastes of Africa to the New World. With particular relish we eat, *nyam*, "grease," and "grit" whether it's a bologna sandwich and a peanut patty tucked into the bib of a pair of overalls for a workman's snack or a late-night supper of chitlins and champagne eaten off the finest bone china. Some of us delight in a sip of white lightning from a mason jar in a juke joint while others delicately lift little fingers and savor minted iced tea or a cool drink while fanning and watching the neighbors on the front porch. Good times or bad, food provides a time for communion and relaxation.

It's so much a part of our lives that it seems at times as though a Supreme Being created us all from a favorite recipe. There was a heaping cupful of cornmeal to signal our links with the Native Americans, a rounded tablespoon of biscuit dough for southern gentility, a mess of greens and a dozen okra pods for our African roots, and a good measure of molasses to recall the tribulations of slavery. A seasoning piece of fatback signals our lasting love for the almighty pig, and a smoked turkey wing foretells our healthier future. A handful of hot chiles gives the mixture attitude and sass, while a hearty dose of bourbon mellows it out and a splash of corn liquor gives it kick. There are regional additions such as a bit of benne from South Carolina, a hint of praline from New Orleans, and a drop from at least twelve types of barbecue sauce. A fried porgy, a splash of homemade scuppernog, wine and a heaping portion of a secret ingredient called love fill the bowl to overflowing. When well mixed it can be either baked, broiled, roasted, fried, sautéed, or barbecued. The result has yielded us in all hues of the rainbow from lightly toasted to deep well done.

With a start like that, it's not surprising, then, that we have our own way with food. We've called it our way for centuries and incorporated our wondrous way with food and eating into our daily lives. We have rocked generations of babies to sleep crooning "Shortenin' Bread," laughed to the comedy of "Pigmeat" Markham and "Butterbeans" and Susie, danced the cakewalk, tapped our feet to the rhythms of "Jelly Roll" Morton, shimmied with wild abandon to gutbucket music in juke joints or sat down with friends and "chewed the fat." We've had the blues over the "Kitchen Man," longed to be loved like "Lilac Wine," and celebrated with "A Pigfoot and a Bottle of Beer."

In short, we've created our own culinary universe: one where an ample grandmother presides over a kitchen where the pungent aroma of greens mixes with the molasses perfume of pralines, and the bubbling from a big iron gumbo pot punctuates her soft humming. This is a universe where Aunt Jemima takes off her kerchief and sits down at the table, where Uncle Ben bows his head and blesses the food, and Rastus, the Cream of Wheat man, tells tall tales over a "taste" of whiskey. It's the warmth of the kitchen tempered by the formality of the dining room and the love of a family that extends over generations and across bloodlines. With the improvisational genius that gave the world jazz, we have cooked our way into the hearts, minds, and stomachs of a country.

Our way with food is a way with a long history. It is a way that has deep roots extending back over millennia to ancient and almost unknown civilizations, one that found its way through the kitchens of the royal houses of Kush and Meroë, sat down to dine with the Askias of Mali and supped with the princes of Songhai. It is a way with food that at times produced meals so sophisticated that they astonished travelers who recorded them in their accounts. Our culinary odyssey is one of survival and evolution. It took to its hearths the new foods that came from the West and adapted them to its tastes and needs. It survived the privations and sorrows of the Middle Passage and indeed triumphed over them, creating a style of cooking that is immediately recognizable to the taste buds, one that has left an indelible imprint on the cooking of another hemisphere.

It is a way with food that marked the cooking of the plantation Big Houses throughout the United States and, indeed, throughout the hemisphere, one that migrated from the American South to the West in the saddlebags and stew pots and iron skillets of the Buffalo soldiers and chuckwagon cooks. It rode the burgeoning railroads north and west into the consciousness and palates of the entire country, where many still retain fond memories of meals served by black hands to the accompaniment of rackety-clackety train wheels. In many cases, unbeknownst to the diners, these meals were also prepared by black hands. It marked the tastes of many Americans in the late nineteenth and early to mid-twentieth centuries through the foods that housekeepers prepared for charges in homes North and South and in meals prepared by unheralded family cooks. Finally, in the sixties and seventies, it came out of family kitchens to be celebrated as survival food or soul food, and derided at the same time as the food of enslavement. The eighties and nineties see our way with food being transformed once again, from daily bread to festive fare, as many people change their diets for health or religious or time concerns. Yet, our way with food endures. It endures because it is a microcosm of our history. It combines the improvisational impulses that gave the world jazz with the culinary techniques of the African continent. It combines the African taste for the piquant with the American leftovers from sorrow's kitchens. It combines the bite of hot sauces with the mellow savor of barbecue, and a sweet tooth with a special touch for baking that has enhanced generations of church tea tables, captured more than one husband, and changed untold sylphlike silhouettes into more matronly contours.

This constantly evolving transformation from *tchingombo* (the Umbundu word for okra) to gumbo brings with it all the recollections of a heritage where survival depended on the ability to make the best of a bad lot, where a desire to live higher on the hog kept more than one person going, and where generations of African-American cooks both female and male helped us all to survive with their ability to quite literally transform a sow's ear into something wonderful.

Addina du ceere way des na ko lalo.
Life is a bowl of couscous so it must be seasoned.
—*traditional Wolof proverb*

It all began in Africa, in the area near Al Fayyum in Egypt, where there is evidence of grain cultivation that can be dated as far back as 4000 B.C. This eventually led to the domestication of wild grains, which would become several varieties of the plant that we know today as millet. Recent discoveries in the area sixty miles west of Abu Simbel on the Nile River in today's Egypt, near what is the Sudanese border, may push that date back even farther, to 6000 B.C. Sesame was also developed and was being exported to other civilizations as early as the second millennium B.C. Vegetables, too, were domesticated. Historian Robert L. Hall postulates that the cultivation of wild yams may date back as far as 5000 to 4000 B.C. Yams became so important in Africa that they took on mythical proportions, with festivals marking their planting and harvesting in countries like Ghana, even today.

It is difficult to reconstruct the foodstuffs that were cultivated in sub-Saharan Africa prior to European contact, but from archeological evidence and early Arabic chronicles, it is possible to make some deductions. From them we learn that while the African larder was significantly smaller prior to the Columbian Exchange, there was nonetheless a sufficient variety of foods to provide a varied diet. Certainly there were grains. They were prepared as fritters, porridges, mashes, and couscouslike dishes, much as they are throughout the continent today. One of the grains of preference was indigenous pearl millet (*Pennisetum typhoideum*). The botanical origins of this grain become clear when given its names in French and German, where it is known respectively as *millet Africain* and *negerkorn*.

Other grains included sorghum (*Sorghum vulgare*) and an African variant of rice (*Oryza glaberrima*), a wet rice that was cultivated in what is today the Casamance region of lower Senegal and in the area that would later become known as the Grain Coast.

Other foods indigenous to the African continent and eaten prior to European arrivals were pumpkins (*Telfairia pedata*), and calabashes and gourds (*Lagenaria vulgaris*). They are reported by the chroniclers as being eaten in Timbuktu, in Gao on the Niger, and in other areas within the Niger basin. By the fourteenth century, there were turnips (*Brassica rapa*), which were probably imported from Morocco to the north; cabbage (*Brassica oleracea*), which probably arrived earlier from Morocco and Muslim Spain; eggplant (*Solanum melongena*), and cucumbers (*Cucumis sativus*), which some scholars feel may have originally come from central Africa. In addition, there were onions and garlic.

Okra is indigenous to the continent and was used to thicken sauces. Available, too, was a wide range of leafy greens. A number of legumes existed, including black-eyed peas (*Vigna sinensis*), broad beans or fava beans (*Vicia faba*), and more than likely chick-peas, kidney beans, and lentils. During his journey in 1352 through the area between Iwalatan and Mali, Ibn Battuta observed African women selling a type of bean flour.

There were fruits. There was tamarind, which was and still is consumed as a cooling beverage called *dakhar* in today's Senegal. It is also used medicinally for its prodigious laxative qualities. Wild lemons and oranges were available in parts of the Sahel; the Portuguese traveler Diego Gomes found lemon trees in Senegabmia in 1456. Certainly there were dates (*Phoenix dactylifera*) and figs (*Ficus carica*).

Other more unusual foods included ackee (*Blighia sapida*), which today turns up in Jamaica's national dish, and the fruit of the baobab tree (*Adansonia digitata*), which is eaten as a vegetable. Its seeds are ground into a powder used to thicken sauces. Leo Africanus also records that there were truffles, some of which were so large that a rabbit could make his burrow in them. These were peeled and roasted on coals or cooked in a fatty broth.

For cooking there was the oil of the oil palm tree (*Elaeis guineensis*), which also provided palm wine. It was a beverage that could be cooling and refreshing or, if allowed to sit and ferment, could pack the kick of a country mule. (Our first varieties of white lightning no doubt!) Sesame oil was also used for cooking, as were vegetable butters like shea butter, or *karité*, as it is known in French.

For cooling off from the hot sun, there were melons, including watermelon (*Citrullus lanatus*), which has been cultivated in Egypt for millennia. In a wild form it seems to be indigenous to some parts of tropical Africa. There were other beverages as well—mead, and millet beer, and drinks prepared from tree barks and from the deep red flowers of a bush of the hibiscus family known in the Caribbean as sorrel (*Hibiscus sabdariffa*).

Meat was used sparingly, mainly for seasoning. At times of feasting, though, meat was important. In coastal areas, natives enjoyed the bounty of the sea and the lagoons and rivers. Dishes tended to be soupy stews served over or alongside a starch. To spice things up there were native peppers that went under the names of grains of paradise or *melegueta*, or Ashanti or guinea pepper (*Afronum melegueta* and *Piper guineense*). These were so prized that they were traded with Europe in limited competition with pepper from the East (*Piper nigrum*). They were used in conjunction with ginger. Salt was highly prized and was used mainly as a preservative. For an extra buzz, there was kola (*Cola acuminata*) which was chewed.

These ingredients were prepared according to time-honored recipes in time-honored manners. Cooking and eating utensils were made from earthenware or metal, and many of the dishes and food storage vessels were prepared from calabashes and gourds, a habit that would be duplicated in the new American life.

The late anthropologist William Bascom researched the cooking of the Yoruba people of southwestern Nigeria and found six basic cooking techniques that can arguably be extended to much of West Africa. These can also, with few reservations, be assumed to have been known to West Africans before Columbus. They are:

1. Boiling in water
2. Steaming in leaves
3. Frying in deep oil
4. Toasting beside the fire
5. Roasting in the fire
6. Baking in ashes

These techniques are important because, even allowing for the varying emphasis placed on specific methods in different areas, they provide a fairly good indication of African culinary techniques. They also point the way to the African-American culinary future.

To Bascom's culinary techniques, it is possible to add seven culinary tendencies that traveled from Africa to America and are emblematic of African-inspired cooking in the United States, and indeed throughout the hemisphere. They are:

1. The preparation of composed rice dishes
2. The creation of various types of fritters
3. The use of smoked ingredients for flavoring
4. The use of okra as a thickener
5. The use of leafy green vegetables
6. The abundant use of peppery and spicy hot sauces
7. The use of nuts and seeds as thickeners

With the arrival of Europeans, the larder grew and expanded to include New World foodstuffs such as tomatoes, corn, and chiles, which rapidly became integral parts of the cooking of the African continent. Who today can envision Ethiopian food without *berbere* or Senegal's *thiébou dienn* without tomatoes? What would Nigerian food be without cassava meal? Africa and American had come together for the first time.

The results were a cuisine that drew praise from travelers. Frenchman Rene Caillé, who traveled overland from Morocco through Mali into Guinea, repeatedly mentions the foods he ate in his 1830 travel account. He notes "a copious luncheon of rice with chicken and milk" that he ate with delight and that filled the travelers for their journey. He also speaks of a meal offered to him by the poor of a village he was visiting that consisted of a type of couscous served with a sauce of greens. The hosts ate only boiled yam with a sauce prepared without salt. Theophilus Conneau, another Frenchman, fared better in matters culinary and records that on December 8, 1827, he partook of an excellent supper

> . . . of a rich stew which a French cook would call a *sauce blanche.* I desired a taste, which engendered a wish for more. The delicious mess was made of mutton minced with roasted ground nuts (or peanuts) and rolled up into a shape of forced meat balls, which when stewed up with milk butter and a little *malaguetta* pepper, is a rich dish if eaten with *rice en pilau.* Monsieur Tortoni of Paris might not be ashamed to present a dish of it to his aristocratic gastronomes of the Boulevard des Italiens.

High praise indeed from a Frenchman!

"Voyage through Death to life upon these shores."
—*R. Hayden*

While Caillé was a traveler and a chronicler, Conneau was on the continent in connection with an infamous trade: the triangular trade that wrenched some forty million souls from their African home, enslaved them, and sent them to a new and unknown world. An estimated half a million of them came to what is now the United States. In creating this largest forced migration of people in the history of the world, Conneau and thousands of others like him transformed the face of Africa and changed the complexion and palate of the New World forever. They would rule over the trade in human misery for almost four hundred years.

The period of the slave trade was marked by a second trade in food, for the necessity of feeding the slaves so that they could survive the journey was one of prime importance to the traders. These men were more sagacious about West African cultures and habits than many think. James A. Rawley in his work *The Transatlantic Slave Trade* states that slavers noted that captives from the Bight of Benin (the Niger Delta) were accustomed to yams, while those from the Windward and Gold coasts (the region from Senegambia to Ghana) were accustomed to rice. Slaves were also said to "have a good stomach for beans."

Each nationality of slave trader had rules and regulations to follow. As early as 1684 Portugal enacted rules limiting the number of slaves and regulating the amount of provisions and the size of ships. North American slavers commonly fed their slaves rice and corn, both of which were available in Africa and in America, and gave the slaves black-eyed peas. The rice was boiled in iron cauldrons and the corn was fried into cakes. The beverage of choice was water, occasionally flavored with molasses, though some slavers noted an African taste for the spicy. They offered rice wine made fiery with cayenne pepper to slaves to numb them into submission. More often, wine and spirits were used only for medicinal purposes. British ships fed their cargoes horse beans, which were brought from England and stored in vats. They were later mixed with lard and turned into a pulpy mash. William Richardson, in *A Mariner of London*, speaks of his experiences aboard a slaver:

> Our slaves had two meals a day, one in the morning consisting of boiled yams and the other in the afternoon of boiled horse beans, and slabber sauce poured over each. This sauce was made of chunks of old Irish beef and rotten salt fish stewed to rags and well seasoned with cayenne pepper.

Others claim that the infamous slabber sauce was a mixture of palm oil, flour, water, and chile. The allowance of water was one-half pint per meal, unless the ship was put on short rations. This was the period of trial, one in which the human will to survive triumphed over the impossible.

Many have told tales of slaves bringing with them okra and sesame seeds in their ears, hair, or clothing, thereby transplanting them to the New World. The truth, though, is that in most cases the men and women on the ships had little idea of their ultimate fate. What seeds were brought with them may have been in amulets or transported unknowingly.

The arrival of African foodstuffs in this hemisphere is probably the result of a harsher reality. The economics of slavery were such that it made sense for slavers and plantation owners to feed slaves a diet on which they could work. There was much written during the slave centuries on how to feed slaves inexpensively and in a manner that would allow for survival. The peanut, which originated in Brazil or Peru, was transported to Africa by the Portuguese. It returned to the northern Americas aboard slave ships along with its African name from the Kimbundu word *nguba,* from which comes our word *goober.* As came the peanut, so came indigenous African plants such as okra and black-eyed peas and watermelon. Once rooted in the United States, these African plants grew to become emblematic of the food of the South and particularly of the African-American South.

True yams did *not* come; they were replaced in African-American diets by sweet potatoes. In many parts of the South these deep orange tubers are still called by the name of the vegetable they replaced (yam), thereby leading to eternal confusion.

American slaves came from diverse regions of Africa, but mostly from the region stretching from the coast of Senegal in the north to Angola in the south. Their areas of origin changed throughout the history of the trade. In *Africanisms in American Culture,* Joseph E. Holloway reminds us that the first slaves in South Carolina were Wolofs from Senegambia. He adds that the upper Colonies, including Massachusetts, Connecticut, and the Mid-Atlantic states down through Virginia and North Carolina, were mainly populated by slaves from Western Africa, while those in the lower colonies of Georgia through Florida were mainly inhabited by Africans from Central Africa. Virginians also showed a preference for Senegambians, including Wolofs, Fulani, Bambara, Malinke, and Mandingos, who were prized as house servants and frequently served as cooks. Yoruba, Fon, and Fanti slaves were also preferred by North American slaveholders as house servants and their foods are reflected in many dishes of the antebellum South. In addition to these preferences, many of the early slaves came through the shipping trade with the Caribbean and had spent time on one of the islands.

Contrary to many opinions, slaves from many regions in Africa arrived with skills that were valuable to planters, including notions of agriculture and animal husbandry that made or saved many a planter's fortune. As Karen Hess proves so ably in her landmark *The Carolina Rice Kitchen,* it is to African ingenuity that South Carolina owed much of its rice fortune, as well as a great part of its rice cooking. It is equally to Africa that the South owes much of its knowledge of the cultivation of sweet potatoes, corn, yams, and millet.

"I've Been in Sorrow's Kitchen and Licked the Pots Clean"

It all began in the area that would become the first thirteen colonies. A Dutch man-of-war wandered up the James River in Virginia seeking provisions in exchange for twenty-three and odd Negroes. In 1619, one year prior to the landing of the Pilgrim fathers at Plymouth Rock, the die was cast for the country's racial future. For the first decades, Africans were treated much as were the indentured servants from Europe, but by the 1660s a subtle change was taking place. Africans were stigmatized by color and by law enslaved for life. By the time the English Royal African Company entered the slave trade in 1672, defying the monopolies held by the Portuguese and Spanish, the change of the complexion and the palate of the country had already begun.

The growth of slavery in Colonial America was slow at first, but by the end of the seventeenth century there were enough Africans enslaved in the young country that they were able to begin to bond and maintain some form of African-American communal life. There was, however, no monolithic slave experience, in the same way that there is today no monolithic African-American one. Experiences varied from situation to situation, whether in South Carolina's malaria-ridden Low Country working on an indigo plantation with only a few overseers, toiling on a Virginia tobacco farm, laboring on a small Southern spread with only a few slaves, chopping sugar cane on a plantation outside New Orleans, or picking the stereotypical cotton on a Georgia spread. A new American order was being created, one in which slave labor would be the defining factor and one in which slave tastes would have a pervasive influence.

Much ink has flowed over the diet of slaves, both in the slave centuries and more recently as historians battle over the importance of the nutritional value of rations allowed. There was great variety in the slave diet, as attested to by the recollections of the former slaves themselves. Testimonies from the massive collection of slave remembrances solicited under the WPA recount how slaves on one plantation felt sorry for those of a neighboring owner, as he was so stingy with food. They also detail foodways on some plantations. (These testimonials, however, must be judged with the knowledge that they were recorded at the height of the Great Depression. The respondents were older folk, and for many of them the privations of the Depression certainly equaled those of slavery.)

My marster was a good feeder, always had enough to eat. . . . We had plenty of what was the rule for eating in them days. We had homemade molasses, peas, cornbread, and home-raised meat sometimes. We killed rabbits and possums to eat, and sometimes went fishing and hunting.

Zack Hendon was 93, but recalled in 1937:

> Rations was given out every week from the smokehouse. On Saturday, us get one peck of meal, three pounds of meat, and one-half gallon of black molasses for a person. That's a lot more than they gets in these days and times.

Hendon's memories notwithstanding, the basic diet for most slaves consisted of vegetables. This ironically duplicated what one historian has called the basic vegetarianism of the West African diet.

The slaves worked not only to produce the plantation's cash crop, but also to grow many or all of the agricultural necessities for the smooth running of the plantation itself. Some plantations had large communal gardens, while others allowed slaves a small plot of land to cultivate according to their tastes. Some slaves even managed to obtain their own chickens and, on rare occasions, hogs. During their infrequent times off, they hunted and fished. One reason that possum figured so prominently in slave menus is that it is a nocturnal creature and could be hunted when the slaves weren't working.

In parts of South Carolina, rice, especially cracked rice, was a major part of the slaves' usual ration. It was frequently served combined with salt pork, fish, or game and vegetables. In other parts of the South, corn was king. Planters claimed and their records agree that they gave a "peck of cornmeal weekly per slave." This averages out to about a pound a day. Much of it was consumed as hominy with fatback, perhaps seasoned with molasses, or in mashes and porridges, cornbreads, ashcakes, and the like.

Many slaves prepared the meals individually in their cabins after their long day's toil, but on some larger plantations, there were communal dining facilities. Then morning and evening meals were usually taken in the cabin, while the midday meal was consumed either in the eating room or in the fields. Whatever the system, meals were a time of communion and of getting together. Slave cabins were crude at best, frequently one- or two-room affairs set away from the big house on a street with other like buildings. The heart of the home was the hearth, which served for heating as well as for cooking. In the summertime, when no fire was required for heat, cooking was done outdoors. Open-hearth cooking defined the slave diet as much as did the rations, in that the only cooking methods that were available were those that could be achieved by various uses of the flame, charcoal, and ash.

Archaeological evidence shows that slaves maintained Africanisms in their cooking utensils as well. They made their own pottery in many cases.

Today shards of these clay pots and jugs and dishes offer archaeologists new insights into plantation life. Slaves also wove baskets in the African mode and made various other cooking implements. Calabash gourds were used for storage and as dippers and wooden spoons were occasionally carved. Cast-iron pots—either griddles, skillets, cauldrons, tripod "spiders," or Dutch ovens—were used for boiling, frying, or baking. Spits were used for roasting when fowl or meat was available and vegetables like sweet potatoes and breads like ashcakes could be cooked in the hot embers that were raked out onto the hearth. These cooking methods recalled African ones and undoubtedly allowed for the retention of several dishes. Slaves also retained African habits of eating stews and thick soups: one-pot meals accompanied by a starch.

Thus, South Carolina slaves when confronted with cracked rice, tomatoes, and vegetables came up with a red rice that is a close New World cousin of the thiébou dienn of Senegambia, and when asked to mix rice and black-eyed peas, approximated that region's thiébou niébé in the Low Country's Hoppin' John. In good times, there was kush, cornbread cooked on a griddle and mashed with raw onions with ham gravy poured over it. Anna Wright, a former slave, recalled that her master felt "de culud folks raised de food an dey's 'titled to all dey wants." Fried chicken, ashcake, ember-roasted sweet potatoes, fish dipped in cornmeal and fried, greens, cabbage, slow-cooked snap beans with dumplings, and jelly cakes and two-crust pies were all part of her memories. Others were not as fortunate and remembered only, "we were so hongry we were bound to steal or perish."

Whatever their lot, slaves did not simply cook for their own nourishment. They also cooked most, if not all, of the meals for the Big House, and their cooking in this arena resulted in the subtle but very real transformations of the tastes of the American South. The position of Big House cook was a prestigious one, although it carried with it a great deal of responsibility. It often resulted not only in massive amounts of work, but also in a loss of (already almost nonexistent) personal time and space as a result of the necessary proximity to the master's family.

Meals at the planters' tables were lavish and copious. Scholar Sam Hilliard's study of antebellum southern eating habits suggests that Low Country planters might find at a single meal such delicacies as turtle soup, boiled mutton, turtle steaks and fins, macaroni pie, oysters, boiled ham, venison, roast turkey, bread pudding, ice cream, and fruit. Wine was usually served with dinner and ranged from Madeira to sherry to Champagne. Following the dessert, cordials would be served. Whew! Breakfast was another meal where planters brought new meaning to the term *groaning board*. When William Howard Russell visited a Louisiana plantation, the morning meal consisted of grilled fowl, prawns, eggs and ham, fish from New Orleans, potted salmon from England, preserved meats from France, claret, iced water, coffee and tea, varieties of hominy, mush, and African vegetable preparations.

Spicing took on a heavier hand as Africa's taste for highly seasoned food became part of everyday fare. Chiles and hot sauces were served out of cut glass cruets on the planters' tables. Composed rice dishes, such as South Carolina's Hoppin' John, as well as dishes using such African ingredients as okra and sesame began to be featured on Big House tables and find their ways into plantation "receipt" books.

By the end of the eighteenth century, in the heyday of Mary Randolph, author of *The Virginia Housewife,* one of the nation's early cookbooks, Africanisms had so marked the cooking of the South that she includes a recipe for gumbs, a buttered okra dish, and another for ochra (*sic*) soup, which is similar to today's gumbo. *The Carolina Housewife,* by A Lady of Charleston, published in 1847 but collecting recipes of an earlier period, includes another recipe for okra soup that was considered a restorative by the grand ladies of that city. There are also recipes for peanut soup and sesame soup and a New Orleans gumbo! These dishes as well as other culinary Africanisms such as the use of smoked meats and fish as seasonings, the use of nuts as thickeners, and the use of okra to prepare soupy stews more often than not called gumbos helped expand the planters' culinary vocabulary. Vitamin-rich pot likker—the cooking water in which vegetables had been slow-cooked—had formerly been discarded by planters; now it was eaten and savored.

These dishes were prepared by slave cooks and imposed on planters in what Eugene D. Genovese, in his work *Roll Jordan Roll: The World the Slaves Made,* aptly calls, "the culinary despotism of the slave cabin over the Big House." They, along with dishes like fried chicken, which calls on the West African art of frying; a host of fritters, which hark back to the African method of frying in deep oil; and a range of nut soups, went on to represent some of the best cooking the South had to offer.

Away from the plantations, urban slavery offered other challenges to the slave population. In areas as disparate as the Moravian community of Old Salem in North Carolina, Huguenot Charleston, South Carolina, and New Orleans under Spanish and French rule, African slaves coped with different realities. Their lives were more closely intertwined with those of their masters, and they often did not have the support of a community of fellow slaves. Under these conditions as well, African culinary knowhow surfaced.

Many urban slaves, in fact, were noted as street vendors; the money from their sales frequently supplemented the income of the mistress of the house. Their goods and their street cries brought life to the towns. A privileged few were able to use a portion of their earnings to purchase their freedom, and by the late eighteenth and early nineteenth centuries there were several noted black caterers in cities up and down the Eastern seaboard. Culinary historian William Woys Weaver states that in Philadelphia in the 1790s Polly Haine, Jean Martin, and Flora Calvil were all noted makers of Philadelphia gumbo or pepperpot. They were all of African descent. In North Carolina, slaves who were African Moravian brethren slept and worked at the tavern in Old Salem. In New Orleans, African-American women owned most of the coffee stands scattered through the town, including those in front of the cathedral and those in the French Market. They also sold pralines and other Creole confections in the square in front of the cathedral and hot rice fritters called *cala* door-to-door. Raw ingredients from she-crabs and porgies to sweet potatoes and sugar peas were not all that was sold door-to-door. Hot ready-prepared foods were also available, particularly cakes and candies. The cries of the waffle man and the *cala* woman, the pie man and praline ladies, all with their baskets, punctuated the mornings.

Their street cries have been immortalized in everything from children's games to the literature of Langston Hughes to the music of George Gershwin. Throughout the nineteenth century and in some regions of the South well into the twentieth century, streets in residential neighborhoods would ring with the cries of various vendors hawking their wares from kitchen door to kitchen door. The watermelon man's cry:

> *Watermelon! Watermelon! Red to the rind,*
> *If you don't believe me jest pull down your blind!*
> *I sell to the rich,*
> *I sell to the po';*
> *I'm gonna sell to the lady*
> *Standin' in that do' . . .*
>
> *I got water with the melon, red to the rind!*
> *If you don't believe it jest pull down your blind.*
> *You eat the watermelon and preee-serve the rind!*

His colleague in Charleston sold his shrimp to the patter of:

> *And a Dawtry Daw!*
> *And a swimpy Raw!*
> *An' a Dawtry Dawtry*
> *Dawtry raw Swimp!*

In southern cities like Charleston, Savannah, and the culinary queen of them all, New Orleans, cooks of African descent were making their mark.

Charles Gayarré, writing in *Harper's New Monthly Magazine* in the 1880s, wrote a praise song to African cooks:

> Pierre or Valentin, the colored cook . . . had not studied the records of roasting, baking, and boiling. . . . He could neither read nor write, and therefore he could not learn from books. He was simply inspired; the god of the spit and the saucepan had breathed into him: that was enough . . .

"No More Peck o'Corn for Me"

The Emancipation Proclamation was issued in September 1862 and became effective on January 1, 1863. Word was slow in getting to many areas of the South. In Texas, many slaves did not hear until June 16, after the crops were harvested! Most slaves were unskilled and unlettered. The privations of the war had decimated the southern homes of most African-Americans and whites alike, and had also taught more than one fancy southern family how to live and eat just as their former slaves did. "Us took the best care of them poor white that us could under the circumstances that prevailed," recalled one former slave. Irish potato tops were cooked for vegetables, blackberry leaves were used for greens, and salt came from rinsing the dirt from the floor of the old smokehouse.

The widespread starvation and shortages in clothing and shelter following the war simply maintained that lifestyle. As a result, this is also the period that has led to the hopeless confusion among the foodways of African-Americans, poor southern whites, and the general South.

"I Am Bound for the Promised Land"

The West represented the promised land to many African-Americans after Emancipation. After being denied their promised reparation of forty acres and a mule, they set out to make lives for themselves. While other settlers were fearful of Native Americans, a long history of alliances between Africans and Native Americans had reduced that fear for former slaves. During the period of slavery, settlements of maroons—escaped slaves living in communities—had grown as Native Americans sheltered escaped slaves; by the 1800s, there were black Seminoles, black Creeks, black Choctaws, black Cherokees, and other mixtures within the tribes up and down the Eastern seaboard.

Looking for a way out of sorrow's kitchen, many thousands of African-Americans headed west and took their foodways with them. Texas's cowboy stew, sometimes called "son of a gun stew," is a descendant of the long, slow-cooking, one-pot meals of the slaves. The addition of innards and other lowly ingredients speak to eating habits acquired during slavery. Certainly, Texas barbecue and the 'cueing of Missouri speak also of these migrations. As fully one-third of all cowboys were African-American, many of them cooks and expedition guides like Jim Pierce, it is fairly safe to believe that their African-American cooking styles began to spread to a wider audience.

While some went west, others (many former house servants among them) found their way to prosperity through the new Pullman and dining cars that were first instituted on trains at about the same time as the end of the Civil War, and remained in use through the first half of the twentieth century. A photograph of the crew of the dining car on a first-class train of the Baltimore and Ohio Railroad in the 1920s shows a staff of eleven people, ten of whom are recognizably black. James D. Porterfield, in his history of railroad cuisine, *Dining by Rail,* reveals that out of sixty-three railroads surveyed in a 1921 poll, fifty-one had African-American cooks! Joseph Husband, writing in 1917, felt that "the Pullman Company was the largest employer of colored labor in the world." As had happened in the antebellum South, an Africanization of the railway menus occurred very subtly. This happened particularly on the railroads of the southeastern regions that attempted to highlight regional cusine. The ham with pineapple fritters, plantation beef stews, biscuits, cream of peanut soup, baked sweet potatoes, and scalloped oysters that are shown on their menus all reflected the culinary origins of the cooks.

My great-uncle, Jack Philpot, who appeared at my grandmother's house to dazzle us with his spats and tales of his travels, his ability to carve with aplomb and style, and a love for the very best food, was a veteran of the Norfolk and Western line. He and his hundreds of colleagues were instrumental in bringing the tastes of African-American foods to the rest of the country and, in a parallel exchange, of bringing new ideas of European service and foods home to African-American families like my own. I still serve fresh asparagus every spring off the gold-edged Limoges china asparagus plates that were his.

In the South and in the North, many African-American women found work as housekeepers and cooks, and in other forms of domestic service. These jobs, while usually demeaning, afforded a close, oftentimes unbearably intimate look at how the other half lived. Throughout the country, these women fed their charges with homemade soups and fried chicken and freshly made African-American foods from their own family recipes. With lavish applications of food and love, they generally served as the domestic glue that soldered together countless white American families and raised more than one white child. Their culinary knowhow is largely unsung, but traces of it can be found in early community cookbooks, where recipes praise the culinary skill of Jane Smith's Lucy, Margaret Ford's Ida, and Irene Jones's Bertha. Well into the twentieth century, African-Americans were still working in the countrywide equivalents of Big House kitchens and still influencing the taste of a nation. New foods came home to African-American homes with leftovers from "Miss Ann's" table.

Others also headed North, following the same drinking gourd (as the constellation of the Big Dipper was called) that had led their ancestors to freedom. They walked, rode trains, and followed the mighty Mississippi, ending up in the towns and cities of the Eastern Seaboard and the Midwest. Just as sure as the Delta Blues became the Chicago Blues, and as many would say, just as sure as "grits is groceries," rapidly migrating African-Americans took their foods with them.

Traditional African-American neighborhoods could (and indeed still can) be told by their markets. Vegetable merchants display a wide range of leafy greens including collards, mustards, kale, turnip, and dandelion greens. Butcher shops featured a seemingly endless array of pig parts, from snouts to feet to tails and innards. They also have thick slabs of head cheese, and not only chickens but their gizzards and feet and backs and other bony pieces. Sweet potatoes and root vegetables abound, and in summer, there is always watermelon.

These enclaves became the new northern slave streets as African-Americans journeyed from can't to can. The cooking their forbears brought from Africa continued as a reminder of abandoned southern homes. My grandparents were among those who followed this trend, migrating from the plantations of Virginia, where my maternal great-grandfather, Samuel Philpot, had served as a house slave up until the age of thirty. Stories he told my mother of his enslavement centered around how he had served President Lincoln at a meal.

On my father's side, I, like one out of every three African-Americans, share ancestry with Native Americans. My great-grandmother, Harriet Hornbeak, was a member of the Cherokee nation. Two of her grandchildren, Johnny and Bill, became cooks, and used their earnings to bring their mother and younger brothers north to Brooklyn, New York, from hard times in Napier, Tennessee.

Food has always played an important role in my family life. My childhood is punctuated with vivid memories of Grandma Harris pulling up peanuts in her small garden plot behind the housing projects in Jamaica, Queens. She brought the South north with her and grew not only peanuts but also black-eyed peas, purpley blue-tinged leafy collard greens, and bushes that yielded tiny pods of slimy okra (the only food I never had to eat as a child). There was usually a pot of something simmering on the back of the stove in her tiny apartment kitchen when she wasn't boiling up a batch of laundry or making her own lye soap. She used Bell's poultry seasoning, Calumet baking powder, and Indian Head white cornmeal. Grandma Harris wasn't a particularly good cook, though all of her sons (except my father) worked wonders in the kitchen. However, her beaten biscuits, her skillet cornbread, and her collard greens were ambrosial.

My maternal grandmother, Grandma Jones, had attended a women's seminary in turn-of-the century Virginia. Even after she'd raised a family of ten children to adulthood and learned to cut corners and pinch pennies, she still had the culinary airs of the descendant of house servants that she was. Her table featured roasts and heaping platters of fried chicken. She saved money, though, by knowing her grocer and bringing home bags of slightly spoiled bananas to transform into crisp fritters, and tiny seckle pears and overripe peaches to pickle as condiments or just "put up." Nothing went to waste; even watermelon rinds reappeared pickled. Every Saturday, she'd prepare industrial quantities of hot rolls. There was always good eating at her house.

At home, my childhood meals were bracketed by my mother's sophisticated tastes (learned at her mother's table and honed as a dietetics student at Pratt Institute) and my father's steadfast refusal to eat anything his momma hadn't cooked in his youth. At parties there were rolled sandwiches with olives and multihued cream cheese, silver platters of delicately fluted hors d'oeuvres, and grapefruit bristling porcupinelike with skewered orange-cheese morsels, rosy shrimp, and tangy anchovies. On weeknights, there might be lamb chops and broccoli or neckbones and white potatoes, or, as a special treat for my father, okra.

When African-American cooking came out of the closet in the sixties, I, like most African-Americans, was not surprised at its savory delights. After all, only its name had changed. At my grandmothers' houses, it hadn't been called soul food, it was simply dinner. It was only later—*much* later—that I realized that it was also survival food, the food that took African-Americans from slavery to the present.

And now, in the last decade of the twentieth century, there is a new influx of immigrants into the United States. People of African descent arriving from the Caribbean, Brazil, and from the many countries of Africa itself are adding new African-inspired foods to the mix. African-American food has taken on an international outlook: Our meals can be as sophisticted as leg of lamb pré-salé preceded by a ragoût de truffes or as down-home as pig's feet and potato salad.

As African-Americans look to the twenty-first century, religious constraints and health concerns have given us a new dietary awareness. Yet we still revere the foods that got us through. We may not eat them every day, but the tastes of okra, corn, and tomatoes, of hot sauce and hog meat, of chicken and greens, remain on our tongues. They are a part of our history and a part of us all.

African-American Cuisine and Today's Diet

My desire in *The Welcome Table: African-American Heritage Cooking* is not to preserve African-American heritage cooking in amber as a dead fossil, but rather to press it gently between the pages of the cookbook as a fond remembrance of a living tradition, one that is still growing and one whose growth and diversity will be as much a part of future records as its history. For this reason, the recipes are presented in the most authentic form possible. That means that numerous recipes call for bacon drippings, the traditional African-American seasoning. However, if health or religious concerns preclude using bacon drippings, any oil or smoked meat or fish may be substituted, depending on the recipe and the use. As with all recipes, the ones assembled here are memory aids to be embroidered on in your own manner and fine-tuned to your own individual taste. Used in this manner, *The Welcome Table: African-American Heritage Cooking* is a springboard for cooks, one that will bring back the tastes of the past and enable you to keep them for future generations.

Hypertension is no joke!

According to the *Black Women's Health Book*, edited by Evelyn C. White, hypertension, or high blood pressure, affects one out of three African-Americans, making it one of our major medical problems. Not only is hypertension more prevalent among us, it begins earlier and has greater consequences. The result is that we have a 60 percent greater risk of death and disability from stroke and coronary disease. To those who love traditional African-American food that would seem to be very bad news.

Indeed, while the recipes in this cookbook celebrate the vast history of the cooking of African-Americans, it is clear that some aspects of our cooking, although they are delicious, evocative, and nurturing, should probably be transformed into holiday events, and some dishes should be eaten seasonally or even annually and not daily.

Our traditional diet, although glorious and delicious, was evolved by a group of people who were up at dawn to plow the back forty before having breakfast. Now many of us ride cars and buses and subways to workplaces where we sit at desks exerting little if any physical energy. Certainly our diets should change as well. However, we do not have to turn our collective back on our culinary heritage.

Historically African-Americans have and still abuse the saltshaker. Many of us have let our eating habits lapse shamefully into packaged foods and junk foods, chips, and ice cream. *Shame!* Our tradition is more creative than that. Try adding other spices or even an extra dash of hot sauce instead of reaching for the saltshaker. Make a vow not to salt until you've tasted. Cut down on purchasing prepackaged foods, in which the salt content is invariably higher.

The recipes presented in *The Welcome Table* are presented in their traditional manner with full use of pork and bacon drippings. Most, though, are easily transformed into dishes with which no nutritionist would quarrel with the addition of a few herbs or spices or a drizzle of a polyunsaturated oil. We have a cuisine that traditionally makes abundant use of healthy root vegetables, seasonal produce, and leafy greens and that delights in the freshest of ingredients that can be obtained. It is up to us to use it healthily.

Appetizers

A bumper-crop peanut harvest, Richmond, Virginia, circa 1870.

Me getting ready to cook, age one.

OVER THE GENERATIONS: MOMMA COOKS AND DAUGHTER COOKS

African-American cooking is a generational pursuit. This was well proven by Agnes Louard and her two daughters, Rita and Diane, last summer during a conversation around the old oak table of my mother's country cottage in Oak Bluffs.

Mrs. Louard, a retired professor from the Columbia School of Social Work, recalls, "I was born in Savannah, Georgia. My parents were on their way from Shorterville, Alabama, to Philadelphia, which they thought was the promised land! I would go back down South to stay with grandma every summer (until I got old enough to have to pay half fare) but in Philadelphia, my mother cooked. I remember that my mother was one of the best cookers of fried chicken in the world. She cooked a dry chicken, crisp, and then made gravy. You couldn't have chicken without gravy and rice. I pride myself that I too am one of the best chicken cookers in the world . . . but my children informed me that I had gone through a 'dry period' with my chicken. I cooked fried chicken again last night and my son told me between bites, 'This is good! I hope you're back on track.'

Louard continues, "You don't realize how much effort goes into frying chicken. How much work goes into cooking in general. I grew up with chicken with rice and gravy and porgies and fish on Fridays and pigs' feet and the like, including okra stew with meat in it and even okra placed on top of a pot of greens and steamed while the greens were cooking. (I was never an okra eater though; it's too slimy for me. But I love greens. I always put a pinch of sugar in my greens.) We also had string beans cut up and slow-cooked with a piece of meat and other one-pot vegetable dishes with meat in them and we were glad to get them.

"On holidays we had two meats; frequently the second meat was a ham. For Thanksgiving, there was turkey with cornmeal stuffing. On New Year's Day, chitterlings were on the table along with black-eyed peas. We used simple seasonings. Salt, pepper, and I cook a lot with garlic powder, but salt and pepper were it for my mother. Of course, there was hot sauce. I still bring it out with every meal. The food that I grew up with was simple, basic, and well seasoned.

"My mother used to bake also. She'd make deep-dish peach pies and apple pies. I only made pound cake. I was a working mother. I remember when my daughter Diane was about eight she wanted me to bake some cookies to take to school. I told her I'd go to the store and buy some cookies, but I really couldn't bake them. She then decided to bake them herself and she did. She was making brownies and didn't realize that they were going to be moist so that each time she tested them as for cake, they didn't seem done. She finally cooked them for two hours. She said that the brownies were so hard they were awful. She does much better now. "

Diane, who today is an urban planner with a specialty in the area of homeless housing issues, maintains some of her mother's culinary traditions, but has modified them to reflect her concerns with time and with health issues. "I'm not a momma cook," she says, "I'm a daughter cook. All of mom's dishes are ones that take time and preparation. I don't do that. I'll spend a lot of preparation time that doesn't mean I have to stand at the stove. I just don't have that kind of patience. Where mom fried, I don't. She made roasts; I was too poor to buy a roast; I cut my culinary teeth on pasta. However, I've kept her desire to season things well and her ability to be very liberal with seasonings."

Sister Rita, who is Chief and Director of Diabetes and Nutrition at Medical College of Georgia, doesn't have time to do much cooking anymore. "I'm not a cook, but when I do cook, I'm a good cook. I don't fry. I still have a taste for pork, but I don't cook it. I cook vegetables. I keep collard greens and string beans with the ham hocks and I keep ham and turkey for festive occasions. Mom's legacy is even when I don't have time to cook I can't buy premade things. I still cook fresh, but I cook fresh and fast. Collard greens have to be simmered for hours and I just don't have the time so I do other things."

Mrs. Louard counters, "I think that the girls will take up traditional African-American food when I go to the great beyond. Now they don't really have to cook that way . . . they simply come to my house for their favorite dishes."

Roasted Peanuts

Peanuts are emblematic of African-American food. Although the peanut itself is a plant of New World origin, it was transported to Western Africa fairly early in the Columbian Exchange and became a favorite food there. In fact, many scholars believe that the peanut actually came to the United States via Africa, brought here by slave traders looking for an inexpensive way to nourish slaves. It seems somehow only appropriate that one of the country's great botanists, African-American George Washington Carver, devised multiple uses for the peanut, ranging from food to uses in agriculture and industry. African-Americans still seem to prefer peanuts either roasted or boiled as a snack or as a candy, frequently mixed with brown sugar or molasses.

SERVES 10 OR MORE

1 pound raw peanuts in the shell

Preheat the oven to 400 degrees. Arrange the peanuts on a baking sheet and place them in the oven for 10 minutes. Check them occasionally to see if they have reached the color that you prefer. I like my peanuts a deep mahogany shade (this is only one step away from burned), but other people prefer them only lightly toasted.

Spicy Pecans

To me, one of the fascinating things about the food of southern African-Americans is how many times foods that are considered luxuries in the North turn up. The explanation is simple. These ingredients, such as oysters, shrimp, and pecans, were, and in many cases still are, plentiful in the South. Many black Americans had more pecans than they could ever use. In fact, in many northern households with southern roots, a sack of pecans was a traditional Christmas present from relatives in the South.

I'm not fortunate enough to live in such a household, so I must purchase my pecans. I do like them fresh, though, so I head to one of the stores that has a quick turnover. If they are kept too long, the nuts become rancid and sour-tasting. Alternatively, I order them directly from a reliable mail order source (page 271).

Pecans are an ingredient in everything from New Orleans pralines to some turkey stuffings. I like them best just served lightly toasted in butter and then tossed with a mixture of salt and chile powder. They're perfect with hors d'oeuvres or predinner drinks.

SERVES 8 OR MORE

4 tablespoons (¹/₂ stick) butter
1 pound shelled pecan halves
Equal parts salt and chile powder, mixed to taste

Melt the butter over medium heat in a large heavy cast-iron skillet. Pick over the shelled pecans to make sure that there are no bits of shell or other debris. Place the pecans in the skillet with the butter. Cook the pecans for about 3 to 4 minutes, stirring occasionally to make sure that they are all well coated with butter. When the nuts are lightly toasted, drain them on paper towels to remove any excess butter and sprinkle them with the salt and chile powder mixture. Serve warm.

Roasted Pumpkin Seeds

When I was a child, after we carved out the Halloween pumpkin, placed a lighted candle inside it, and sang, "Little Jack Pumpkin-face grew on a vine," I always looked forward to the crispy, crunchy roasted pumpkin seeds that my mother prepared from the seeds. It was a fun "kid" job to make sure that I got all of the pumpkin fibers off each seed and then to place the seeds on the baking sheet. This was long before I realized that pumpkins and gourds had been a part of African-inspired cooking for centuries. I later found out that the same delicious treat could be approximated by simply purchasing dried pumpkin seeds, drizzling oil over them, and baking them in the oven for a few minutes. Either way, the snacking is delicious, though I remain convinced that nothing can match the taste of the freshly prepared pumpkin seeds of my youth. Squash seeds from acorn squash may be used in the same way.

2 cups pumpkin seeds
2 tablespoons vegetable oil
Salt, to taste

Preheat the oven to 350 degrees. Wash the seeds and place them on a baking sheet, spreading them so that they do not overlap. Drizzle the oil over the seeds while rolling them around with your hands to make sure that they are all moistened. Place the seeds in the oven and bake about 10 minutes, or until they are lightly brown on both sides. Remove from the oven, salt to taste, and serve warm.

Yam Chips

According to *The Black Book*, a compendium of African-American knowledge edited by Nobel Prize–winning author Toni Morrison, the potato chip was first introduced to the United States in 1865 by Hiram S. Thomas, an African-American innkeeper. They were originally a variation on the European game chip (potato chips served with game) and were known as Saratoga chips, named for the upstate New York location of Thomas's inn. These yam chips are a modern version using the more traditionally African-American sweet potato, along with their popular name, *yams*.

4 large sweet potatoes
Oil for deep frying
Salt or a mixture of salt and cayenne, to taste

Place the sweet potatoes in water to cover and boil them for 10 minutes. Remove them from the heat, drain, and peel. Using a mandoline or sharp knife, slice the sweet potatoes as thinly as possible crosswise, as for potato chips.

Heat the oil in a heavy pot or deep-fat fryer to 375 degrees. Place the slices a few at a time in the hot oil and fry, turning once, until they are lightly browned and crisp. Remove and drain on paper towels. Serve warm. The chips may be lightly salted if desired, or dusted with a mixture of salt and cayenne pepper if you want them spicier.

Fried Eggplant Galatoire Style

A few years back, while lecturing in New Orleans, I renewed my love affair with Galatoire's restaurant. The reacquaintance was arranged by my friend Kerry Moody, who is one of New Orleans's black Creoles. A frequent visitor to the restaurant, he led me through the menu and regaled me with tales of off-the-menu delights such as fried eggplant lightly dusted with powdered sugar. I thoroughly enjoyed it. I've returned to Galatoire's many times since. Now, when I arrive at the restaurant, I feel like a regular when my waiter, Imre, remembers me after a long absence and brings the eggplant to the table unasked.

The combination of egplant and powdered sugar sounds strange, but the dish is delicious, a perfect beginning to a Creole feast and a subtle reminder of the African traditions of New Orleans cooking. The eggplant on which the dish is based may have originated in Africa and the frying in deep oil is one of the major African culinary methods brought to this country by slave cooks.

SERVES 4 TO 6

1 large eggplant, cut lengthwise into 1-inch strips
¼ cup flour
Oil for deep-fat frying
½ cup confectioners' sugar

Place the eggplant strips in a bowl, cover, and weight with a 1-pound can (a can of soup or vegetables will do). Leave the bowl for an hour or more until the eggplant expresses its liquid. Drain the eggplant and dredge the strips in the flour.

Heat 1 inch of the oil to 350 to 375 degrees in a fryer or in a heavy cast-iron pot. Place the eggplant strips, a few at a time, in the hot fat and fry them until they are golden brown. Drain them on paper towels. Serve hot with a small bowl of confectioners' sugar at the table. Dip the eggplant strips into the sugar, eat, and enjoy.

Cheese Straws

These traditional southern appetizers are not, strictly speaking, a traditional African-American dish. However, they are one of those things that gradually worked its way from European cooks to African-American ones, more than likely as the folk who had to prepare the cheese straws for the parties of others began to prepare them for their own parties. This recipe was given to me by Mary Len Costa, a friend in New Orleans. It is an adaptation of one given to her by her late African-American housekeeper.

SERVES 8 TO 10

1 pound extra-sharp Cheddar cheese
6 ounces (1½ sticks) butter, softened
2 cups flour
1¼ teaspoons baking powder
1½ teaspoons cayenne pepper

Preheat the oven to 300 degrees. In a large bowl cream the cheese and butter together. Sift the dry ingredients together and cut them into the cheese mixture with a pastry blender. Knead the dough lightly into a soft ball. Using a cookie press, pipe a long strip of dough out onto an ungreased baking sheet, cut it into 1½-inch pieces, and arrange them on the baking sheet.

Bake the cheese straws for 10 to 15 minutes; then lower the heat to 225 degrees and continue to bake until the straws are dry, 15 to 30 minutes (depending on the oven). Allow the cheese straws to cool a few minutes on a baking sheet, then transfer them to a cookie rack to dry completely. When ready, the cheese straws can be served with cocktails, nibbled on as snacks, or packed into tins and given as hostess gifts. They will keep for a month, if they last that long.

Blue Cheese Straws

While this is certainly not a traditional African-American recipe, it may grow into one. This is a variation on the classic Cheddar cheese straw, substituting Roquefort cheese for the Cheddar and eliminating the cayenne. These are a perfect accompaniment for fruit such as apples, grapes, and pears, and fortified wines such as ports or sherries.

Prepare the recipe for cheese straws. Substitute an equal amount of Roquefort cheese for the extra-sharp Cheddar. Use only 4 ounces (1 stick) of butter, and eliminate the cayenne pepper. A dash of nutmeg brings out the flavor of the rich cheese.

Pickled Black-Eyed Peas

While it is difficult to be absolutely sure, many ethnobotanists feel that these legumes are African in origin. From their diverse uses in the cooking of the African diaspora, this would seem to be confirmed. They turn up deep-fried as fritters in Brazil and in the French-speaking Caribbean, in soups and as Hoppin' John in the American South, and even pickled as in this recipe, which also goes by the name of Texas caviar. The dish can be prepared with either dried or canned black-eyed peas, or, if you're really lucky and live in an area where they can be obtained, with fresh ones.

SERVES 10 TO 12

1 pound dried or 3 (16-ounce) cans black-eyed peas
¹/₂ small green bell pepper, minced
¹/₂ small red bell pepper, minced
4 scallions, including green tops, sliced thin
¹/₂ cup extra-virgin olive oil
¹/₄ cup red wine vinegar
1 clove garlic, minced
1 teaspoon minced habanero or other hot chile, or to taste

Prepare the dried black-eyed peas according to directions on page 105. If using canned black-eyed peas, simply drain them.

Place the black-eyed peas and all of the remaining ingredients in a nonreactive bowl. Stir well to make sure that all of the ingredients are well mixed. Cover with plastic wrap and refrigerate for at least 5 hours. Serve chilled or at room temperature. They will keep for several days, covered, in the refrigerator.

Classic Head Cheese

The dictum that African-Americans eat everything on the pig but the oink is borne out by this traditional dish. It is very similar to West Indian souse and in fact is occasionally called "souse meat" by folk from Tennessee. A staple at many African-American meat shops, head cheese is cut into large slabs and savored with pickles or with plain old white bread (which is often called light bread in parts of the South). This "cheese" is traditionally prepared from the hog's head, which is seasoned and boiled along with other pig parts. It can also be made with a cow's head.

SERVES 8 TO 10

1 pig's head, cleaned and split, with the eyes, brain, and tongue removed (see Note)
4 pig's feet (see Note)
2 pig's ears (see Note)
1 pig tail (see Note)
2 large onions, quartered
6 stalks celery, including leafy tops
3 bay leaves
1 teaspoon coarsely ground fresh black pepper
¹/₂ tablespoon salt, or to taste
¹/₄ teaspoon Tabasco or other hot sauce, or to taste
¹/₈ teaspoon red pepper flakes, or to taste
1 cup distilled white vinegar (see Note)

Have the butcher quarter the pig's head and remove the brains, eyes, and tongue and most of the fat. Clean the pig parts thoroughly and soak them in cold water for 3 hours to remove the blood. First dip them in boiling water to aid the removal of any hair, then wash it with a soft brush. Place the pig parts in the largest pot you own (preferably a large, deep stockpot that holds at least 10 quarts), add all of the remaining ingredients except the vinegar, and cover with water. Bring the pot to a boil, then lower the flame, cover, and cook over low heat for 2¹/₂ hours, or until the meat falls off the bones.

Remove the pot from the heat and allow the contents to cool slightly. Remove and discard the celery, bay leaves, and onions, pick the meat from the bones, chop it coarsely, and place it in a glass loaf pan. Discard the bones. Skim any residue from the liquid remaining in the pot, and discard. Add the vinegar to the pork stock and pour the mixture over the meat in the loaf pan, discarding the bay leaves. Cover the pan with plastic wrap and place it in the refrigerator overnight, or until the loaf has jelled. When ready to serve, unmold, slice, and serve cold or at room temperature with crackers.

NOTE: Pigs' heads and other parts can be readily purchased at Hispanic and African-American meat markets and special-ordered at most others.

For a more savory head cheese you can use Hot Vinegar (page 91).

Deviled Crabmeat

African-Americans certainly are a "devilish" people when it comes to cooking. Many of our favorite appetizers call for the addition of a touch of the piquant that adds a certain je ne sais quoi to the fare. We also eat what at times may seem to be luxury foods, but what are in reality a reflection of the local bounty. Here is a dish that makes the best use of Maryland's crab while adding a touch of African heat. It can be spread on crackers or toast points or mounded in celery sticks.

SERVES 4 TO 6

1 pound fresh lump crabmeat
1/4 cup finely minced green bell pepper
2 tablespoons finely minced onion
1/2 cup mayonnaise
Red Devil or Louisiana Red hot sauce, to taste
1 teaspoon prepared mustard
1 teaspoon fresh lemon juice

Mix all of the ingredients together in a medium-sized glass or other nonreactive bowl, breaking up the crabmeat thoroughly. Cover with plastic wrap and refrigerate for at least 1 hour. Serve slightly chilled.

Super-Rich Virginia Crab Cakes

When African-Americans live by the ocean, seafood plays a large part in our diets. From New England to the Gulf Coast this is demonstrated by the numerous recipes that we have for everything from shrimp and crab to catfish. In the region around Chesapeake Bay, crab is king and is featured in many different guises. These small appetizer-sized crab cakes are one version of the famous Chesapeake crab cakes from Maryland. People from Maryland and the region have lengthy debates as to whether bread crumbs or cracker crumbs are more authentic. Others claim that any addition is unnecessary and that pure crab and few seasonings are all that is needed. This version calls for fresh bread crumbs and is from the Virginia Tidewater region. These crab cakes are best accompanied by a homemade Hot Sauce (page 89). They can be made larger and served as a main course.

2 DOZEN SMALL CRAB CAKES (OR 8 LARGE CRAB CAKES)

2 cups fresh backfin crabmeat
1 cup fresh soft bread crumbs
2 eggs
$^1/_2$ cup heavy cream
Dash of Hot Sauce (page 89), or to taste
2 teaspoons Worcestershire sauce
2 teaspoons chopped parsley
2 teaspoons grated onion
Salt and freshly ground black pepper, to taste
Butter for frying

Pick over the crabmeat to remove any pieces of cartilage that may remain. Place the crabmeat and the bread crumbs in a bowl. In a separate bowl beat the eggs until light and then pour in the heavy cream. Slowly add the egg and cream mixture to the crabmeat and bread crumbs. Add the remaining ingredients, except the butter, and mix them in well. Correct the seasoning.

Melt 1 tablespoon of the butter in a heavy skillet over medium heat and drop the mixture into the skillet a tablespoon at a time. Cook, turning once, for 4 minutes, or until golden brown on each side. Continue with the butter and ingredients until finished. Serve warm.

Pickled Shrimp I

In the Gulf and coastal regions of the United States, African-Americans revel in shrimp and crab. In this recipe, the shrimp are twice spiced, once while cooking and a second time in an overnight marinade.

SERVES 6

2 pounds medium-sized raw shrimp (fresh or frozen)
2 teaspoons salt
¼ cup Crab Boil spices (page 97)
1½ cups thinly sliced red onion
5 bay leaves
3 branches fresh thyme
3 lemons, thinly sliced
1 tablespoon pickling spices
1 cup extra-virgin olive oil
¾ cup red wine vinegar
Salt and freshly ground black pepper, to taste

Bring 1 quart of water to a boil in a large heavy saucepan. Peel the shrimp and place them in the saucepan. Add the salt and the crab boil spices, lower the heat, and cook the shrimp for 1 or 2 minutes, or until they turn pink. Drain the shrimp and place them in a large bowl.

Prepare a marinade of the remaining ingredients and pour it over the shrimp. Toss well. Cover the bowl with plastic wrap and refrigerate overnight. Serve slightly chilled.

Pickled Shrimp II

This popular southern appetizer has many variations. This version is prepared from precooked or leftover shrimp. Amazing as it may seem to northerners, shrimp is indeed so abundant in some regions that there are leftovers.

SERVES 8

1¼ cups extra-virgin olive oil
1 cup Garlic Thyme Vinegar (page 92)
2 tablespoons fresh lemon juice
1 teaspoon crushed dill seed
1 teaspoon cracked peppercorn mixture
½ small stick cinnamon
1 teaspoon cloves
¼ teaspoon cracked allspice berries
1 branch fresh thyme
1 medium-sized red onion, thinly sliced
2 pounds boiled shrimp, cleaned and shelled

Place the oil, vinegar, lemon juice, spices, thyme, and onion in a small nonreactive saucepan and bring to a boil over medium heat. Lower the heat, cover, and cook for 10 minutes. Remove the marinade from the heat and allow it to cool. Place the cooked shrimp in a serving bowl and pour the marinade over them. Cover with plastic wrap and refrigerate overnight. Serve chilled.

Shrimp Spread

Here is yet another use for the ubiquitous shrimp. This time it turns up as a dip that can be spread on crackers or toast points or spooned into stalks of celery.

ABOUT 1 CUP

3 tablespoons mayonnaise
3 tablespoons fresh lemon juice
1 teaspoon Worcestershire sauce
1 teaspoon Louisiana Red hot sauce, or to taste
Salt and freshly ground pepper, to taste
½ small green bell pepper, seeded and coarsely chopped
1 small onion, chopped
1 pound peeled cooked shrimp

Place all of the ingredients in the bowl of a food processor and blend until a smooth paste forms. (If using a blender, add the shrimp a few at a time so that the works do not jam.) Place the paste in a small bowl, cover with plastic wrap, refrigerate for at least 2 hours, and serve.

Shrimp Fritters

Fritters are a touchstone of traditional African-American cooking, albeit one that is unfortunately dying out. Ethnologist William Bascom, in an investigation of the cooking of the Yoruba people of West Africa, singled out frying in deep oil as one of their main culinary techniques. A cookbook rooted in the creolized African-American tradition of New Orleans, *The Picayune Creole Cookbook*, included no fewer than sixteen recipes for fritters in its second edition in 1901. One that it missed, though, is shrimp fritters. These are a delicious way to use cooked shrimp that you may have on hand.

APPROXIMATELY
2 DOZEN FRITTERS

2 eggs
1 cup flour
1 tablespoon butter, melted
¹/₂ teaspoon salt
1 cup water
2 cups minced cooked shrimp
Oil for deep-frying

Heat 3 inches of the oil to 375 degrees in a heavy saucepan or fryer. Separate the eggs and reserve the whites. Place the egg yolks in a medium-sized bowl with the flour, melted butter, and salt. Add the water and stir until the mixture is a thin paste. In a separate bowl, beat the egg whites until they form peaks; then fold them into the batter. Add the shrimp to the batter and stir to be sure that they are well coated.

Drop the shrimp fritter mixture into the hot oil by the teaspoonful, a few at a time, and fry for 2 minutes on each side, or until they are thoroughly cooked and golden. Drain on paper towels.

Bless this food that we are about to receive from thy bounty, Oh Lord. Amen

Boiled Crayfish

Crayfish (or crawfish as they are pronounced in Louisiana) are bottom feeders that abound in unsavory places such as drainage ditches. This has earned them their rather unappetizing nickname, mudbugs, and the disdain of some fancy folk. However, they are incredibly sweet when boiled, and delicious when sucked out of the shell. They aren't elegant eating, but almost anyone who has ever tasted them falls in love. These proportions are for appetizer servings of 6 crayfish each.

SERVES 4

2 fresh Tabasco chiles, or dried chiles to taste
1 tablespoon salt
2 bay leaves
4 whole allspice berries, cracked
1 teaspoon freshly ground black pepper
2 large onions, quartered
5 stalks celery
24 crayfish

Place all of the ingredients except the crayfish in a large stockpot and add water to cover. Bring the water to a boil over high heat. Add the crayfish and cook for 15 minutes. Turn the heat off, but allow the crayfish to remain in the water for an additional 30 minutes. (This last step gives the crayfish outstanding flavor.) Serve with plenty of napkins.

Smoked Bluefish Spread

It's a well-known fact that the black bourgeoisie have long had many of the same wants and desires for the American dream as others. Less well known is that a handful of folk have managed to attain a small piece of that dream, complete with summer houses (and mortgages). For almost a century there have been enclaves where generations of African-Americans have spent their vacations. Virginia Beach, Virginia; Idlewild, Michigan; Sag Harbor, New York; and Oak Bluffs, Massachusetts, are but a few. In these summer resorts, people from all over the country spend time sunning, socializing, and eating, eating, eating.

It has been my good fortune to summer at Oak Bluffs on Martha's Vineyard since I was nine years old. The summertime is full of memories of cookouts and house parties, of clambakes and five-to-seven get-togethers. A few years ago, smoked foods caught on in the African-American community, with smoked bluefish the fish of preference. The following spread for crackers or vegetables harks back to this period, and variations of it have become Vineyard favorites. If you cannot find or prepare your own smoked bluefish, any cold smoked fish such as whitefish trout, salmon, or herring will do.

SERVES 6 TO 8

1/2 pound smoked bluefish
1 (8-ounce) package cream cheese, softened
2 tablespoons light cream
1 small red onion, minced
Hot sauce, to taste

In a small bowl, crumble the bluefish with your fingers until it is separated into small pieces. In another bowl whip the cream cheese with the cream until well blended and light. Add the crumbled fish and the remaining ingredients, cover with plastic wrap, and refrigerate for 1 hour or longer for the flavors to mix. Serve as a spread with crackers or vegetable wedges.

Ham Biscuits

This is a surefire southern way to use leftover bits of ham and either leftover or freshly baked biscuits. Sometimes the biscuits are large and the ham pieces merely quickly cut chunks. In this case, the biscuits are made the size of silver dollars, the ham bits are thinly sliced and neatly cut, and the biscuit has a tiny dollop of spicy mustard and a tiny bit of freshly ground horseradish. Voilà, the "grab 'em and go" breakfast treat that has been imitated by many popular food chains is transmuted into an elegant appetizer. Large or small, they're mighty good eating.

SERVES 6 TO 8

20 silver dollar–sized biscuits (pages 191–93)
Spicy mustard, to taste
Freshly ground horseradish, to taste
20 pieces thinly sliced Baked Ham (page 151)

Spread the biscuits lightly with the mustard, add horseradish to taste, layer the ham slices between the biscuits, serve, and eat. These can be eaten in two bites.

Mom's Deviled Ham Spread

My mother is a member of a club that meets during the months of July and August on the island of Martha's Vineyard, where we have summered for over thirty-five years. Years ago, the members were compiling a souvenir cookbook and my mother contributed (much to my chagrin!) her recipe for a deviled ham spread that she makes from leftover ham bits. Like deviled eggs, the dish gets its taste from the mixture of the hot and the smooth, in this case the smoky taste of the ham, and like deviled eggs, it's devilishly simple and satanically good. It can be spread into pieces of celery or onto toast points. Those who do not want to use ham for health or other reasons can substitute smoked chicken or smoked turkey with similar results.

SERVES 4 TO 6

1¹/₂ cups minced cooked ham or smoked turkey
¹/₄ small habanero chile, finely minced, or to taste
Dash of Worcestershire sauce
2 tablespoons mayonnaise, or enough to bind the ingredients for
*   spreading*
Salt and freshly ground black pepper, to taste

Mix all of the ingredients together in a small nonreactive bowl. Cover with plastic wrap and chill overnight. The following day, serve on celery or toast points.

Deviled Eggs

No African-American summer picnic, North or South, would be complete without a selection of deviled eggs wrapped in wax paper. I remember that as a child, part of the fun was unwrapping the eggs and seeing just how much of the savory yellow insides had managed to squeeze out onto the paper, in which case you were allowed to lick it off. Years later, I was very surprised to learn that deviled eggs are also a part of the general culinary history of the South. There are even deviled egg plates especially designed for serving this delicacy. To me they'll always be a part of summer fun—hard-boiled eggs taken to the nth power.

SERVES 4

8 eggs
3 tablespoons mayonnaise
1 tablespoon Dijon mustard
2 dashes of hot sauce, or to taste
Salt and freshly ground black pepper, to taste
Sweet paprika for garnish

Boil the eggs for 5 to 6 minutes, until they are hard-cooked. Gently remove the shells, leaving the eggs whole, and slice each egg in half lengthwise. Remove the yolks from the eggs and reserve the whites arranged on a dish (a deviled egg plate, if you're lucky enough to have one).

Place the yolks in a small bowl with the remaining ingredients except the paprika and mash them together with a fork until smooth. Then gently spoon a bit of the yolk mixture back into each egg white. (Fancy folk will pipe this through a pastry bag for effect, but it doesn't help the taste one bit!) Cover with plastic wrap and refrigerate for an hour. Sprinkle with paprika before serving. Serve cold.

Soups and Salads

Soup's good anytime.

A Georgia dream kitchen, circa 1941.

MOM'S A FABULOUS COOK

Charlotte Lyons, culinary buddy and food editor of *Ebony* magazine, grew up in Atlanta, Georgia, in the 1950s and 1960s. She remembers, "My mother and her mother lived in the same neighborhood on the same block in Atlanta when I was growing up and so that meant that I was privy to two generations of culinary influence. I can remember real old-time-y things like sitting on the porch in the glider and shelling peas or peeling peaches with my grandmother, who was a real good cook; she was getting ready to put them up for the winter.

"Growing up, I didn't realize that the food that I was eating was what someone else called soul food. It was simply dinner. In much of the South, blacks and whites eat the same things. I found that out in my first job in Atlanta, when I went into the cafeteria and saw all of the white people eating the same things we'd been eating at home. It was a shock. But the greater shock was when I left the South for my first job in Minnesota. At breakfast, people had hash browned potatoes instead of grits, and if you could find grits anywhere (no easy task), they were the fast-cooking quick grits.

"Food was very special in my family and for most of my childhood we never had anything that was frozen or canned unless we had canned it ourselves. My grandfather had a garden and we had great fresh vegetables all the time. We also had relatives in the country and they would send up things like hams. My mother also fished, and on Fridays we'd usually have some type of fish like mullet or croaker or whiting or occasionally catfish.

"My mother did most of the cooking during my childhood. She would prepare wonderful dishes like fried chicken with rice and gravy (in the South, you're always going to have gravy!), and smothered pork chops, okra fritters, fried green tomatoes, and her special squash casserole. At times she alternated with my grandmother, who made a mean fried corn with white corn, but basically my mother loved the kitchen so much she stayed there. I would get the chance to make desserts, and as a youngster, I specialized in pound cake and peach cobbler. Mother still loves to cook and is very particular about her ingredients. Even today, she brings her own grits and her own self-rising cornmeal in her luggage when she comes to visit me in Chicago.

"I still cook like my mom on special occasions, but for everyday, I must confess that I've been known to heat up a package of frozen spinach in the microwave. On weekends, though, I'll head to the farmers' market and cook up a pot of greens with cornbread. I also love to bake and make things like angel biscuits and cornmeal crescent rolls. I like to think that I'm still a link in the chain of my grandmother's great cooking."

Peanut Soup

Peoples of African descent have been using peanuts as thickeners for centuries, and it is clearly the inspiration for this Georgia soup. The ancestors of this creamy treat can be sampled in a spicier version in several West African countries even today.

SERVES 6

3 tablespoons butter
2 stalks celery, grated
1 onion, grated
1 tablespoon flour
5 cups chicken stock
1 cup chunk-style peanut butter
$^3/_4$ cup milk
$^3/_4$ cup heavy cream
Tabasco or other hot sauce, to taste
Salt and freshly ground black pepper, to taste
$^1/_3$ cup chopped roasted peanuts

Melt the butter in a large saucepan over low heat. Add the grated celery and onion and cook them until they are translucent. Add the flour and stir until the mixture becomes a smooth paste. Cook the paste for 2 to 3 minutes; then add the chicken stock, stirring until smooth.

Raise the heat slightly, and bring the soup to a boil, and add the peanut butter, stirring to make sure that it is well mixed in. Lower the heat and allow the soup to simmer for 15 minutes. Finally add the milk, cream, Tabasco, salt, and pepper, and bring the soup to the boil again. Correct the seasonings and serve hot, garnishing each serving with a few roasted peanuts.

Okra Soup

I first read of okra soup in a decorating book featuring pictures of old Charleston, South Carolina. The author had used the soup to evoke an image of gracious Charleston ladies taking a restorative on their verandas. Years later, I looked for the soup when in Charleston and when I tasted it for the first time, the okra revealed its true origins: The okra that is one of the soup's ingredients is a sure sign of its African ancestry. Still later I would learn that the soup was also known as Charleston gumbo, and is one of a series of gumbo and gumbolike soups that stretch from New Orleans to Philadelphia (where pepperpot was once called Philadelphia gumbo).

SERVES 6

2½ pounds beef soup bones
2 medium onions, chopped
2½ quarts water
2½ pounds fresh okra, topped, tailed, and chopped fine
¼ pound slab bacon, cut into ½-inch dice
5 large ripe tomatoes, peeled, seeded, and coarsely chopped
2 bay leaves
Salt and freshly ground black pepper, to taste

Place the soup bones, chopped onions, and water in a stockpot and bring to a boil. Lower the heat and cook slowly for 2 hours.

Remove the soup bones from the pot, dice the meat, and return the meat and bones to the liquid in the pot. Add the okra, bacon, tomatoes, bay leaves, and salt and pepper, and continue to cook for an additional 2 hours, adding more water if necessary. Discard the bay leaves and the bones and serve hot in fine china bowls.

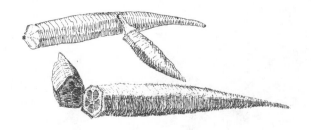

Black-Eyed Pea Soup

The black-eyed pea is one of the African-American culinary staples that seems to have its botanical origin in Africa. Readily available dried, they are also occasionally found fresh in markets in African-American neighborhoods. If you find fresh ones, they're best served simply cooked and lightly buttered. When dried, they're unbeatable in Hoppin' John (page 105), or in this hearty soup that becomes a complete meal when served with cornbread.

SERVES 4 TO 6

2 cups dried black-eyed peas
2 quarts cold water
1 ham bone
1 large onion, chopped
1 bay leaf
Salt and freshly ground black pepper, to taste
Minced ham and freshly chopped parsley, for garnish

Pick over the black-eyed peas to remove any stones and hardened beans, place them in a large stockpot, cover them with cold water, and allow them to soak overnight.

The next day, drain the plump peas, return them to the pot, and add 2 quarts fresh cold water. Add the ham bone and onion. Bring the soup to a boil over medium heat, add the bay leaf and salt and pepper, and lower the heat to a simmer. Cover and cook for 1½ hours, or until the beans are tender and the meat has fallen off the ham bone.

Remove the bone and the bay leaf and put the soup through a food mill until smooth. You may wish to add a bit more water if the soup seems too thick. Return the soup to the stockpot, adjust the seasonings, reheat it, and serve it hot with cornbread. Garnish each plate with a teaspoon each of minced ham and fresh parsley.

Stoup

This is a soup that I remember from my childhood. Its name comes from the fact that when this dish is well made it falls somewhere between a stew and a soup and is a hearty meal all by itself, accompanied only by a piece of freshly made and well-buttered cornbread.

I thought it was a family recipe and had no idea that it might be an African-American staple until one cold winter's day when I dropped in on a friend of my mother's. She apologized for not having anything more to offer and then proceeded to ladle up one of my favorite things, homemade soup, straight from the pot. I was amazed to find that the taste was exactly the same. We compared notes and discovered that she, too, was from Virginia and had also grown up with this dish.

SERVES 4

2 pounds beef soup bones, or 4 to 5 meaty leftover steak bones
4 quarts water
1 teaspoon crushed dry thyme
Salt and fresly ground black pepper, to taste
6 large carrots, sliced
2 cups sliced rutabaga
2 onions, quartered
2 stalks celery, diced
4 medium-sized potatoes, cut into ¹/₂-inch dice
1 (6-ounce) can tomato paste

Place the bones, water, seasonings, carrots, rutabaga, onions, and celery in a large stockpot, cover, and bring to a boil. Lower the heat and cook for 1 hour. Then add the potatoes and tomato paste and continue to cook over medium heat for about 30 minutes, or until the potatoes and rutabagas are fork-tender.

Remove the bones, pick the meat off them, and return the meat to the stoup, discarding the bones. Cook for an additional 5 minutes, then adjust the seasonings and serve hot. If you're feeling fancy, this soup is wonderful with a bit of grated Parmesan cheese sprinkled on the top.

Callaloo

This is a soup that comes into the African-American culinary tradition from the Caribbean, where it is a standard. From Trinidad to the south to Jamaica in the north where it is known as pepperpot, the hearty soup is prepared in numerous ways. Like the African-American way with greens, this recipe develops from the West African idea of stewing greens down to the proverbial "low gravy" and then eating the greens along with the cooking liquid. The constant ingredient in most recipes for southern Caribbean callaloo is the leaf of the taro plant, called *callaloo* in Trinidad and *malanga* in parts of the Spanish-speaking world. But this, like much about African-American cooking in this hemisphere, is up for debate, since different greens are called callaloo on different islands.

This recipe is a version from the French-speaking Caribbean, where callaloo is traditionally whipped into a froth with a three-pronged stick called a *baton lélé*. Here, you can simply use a whisk or a blender.

SERVES 4

1 pound fresh callaloo greens (spinach may be substituted)
1 pound okra, topped and tailed
1 medium-sized onion, coarsely chopped
*1 bouquet garni, prepared from scallions, fresh thyme, parsley, and
    chives*
Salt and freshly ground black pepper to taste
1/2 Scotch bonnet chile, minced
6 1/2 cups water
1 clove garlic, minced
1/2 pound cooked ham, cut into 1/4-inch dice
Juice of 3 limes

Clean the greens thoroughly and remove any woody central stems. Chop the okra and greens into small pieces and place them into a medium-sized saucepan. Add the onion, bouquet garni, salt, black pepper, chile, and water and bring to a boil over high heat. Lower the heat to medium, cover, and cook for 30 minutes.

Remove the mixture from the heat and put it through a food mill until it is a smooth purée. Return it to the saucepan and add the garlic, ham, and lime juice. Cook over medium low heat for 10 minutes while whisking steadily. *Do not allow the soup to come to a second boil or it will lose its texture.* Serve immediately.

She-Crab Soup

This is a classic South Carolina soup, which the fancy folk of Charleston serve in delicate china bowls and savor as a restorative. It is one of the dishes that came into the African-American culinary lexicon through the front door of the Big House. Traditionally prepared in a double boiler, the soup has a creamy consistency, seasoned with a hint of mace and a dash of sherry, that speaks of southern gentility. She-crabs are always called for because they are the most succulent of the crabs and are only available at a premium. If she-crab meat is unavailable, the soup is almost as good if simply prepared from delicate white crabmeat. Some Charlestonians compensate for the lack of she-crabs by crumbling hard-boiled egg in the bottom of the soup plate for added richness.

SERVES 6

3 tablespoons butter
2 teaspoons flour
2 cups milk
1/4 teaspoon mace
Dash of fresh lemon zest
1 pound white she-crab meat
2 cups light cream
1 tablespoon grated onion
Dash of Worcestershire sauce
Salt and freshly ground white pepper, to taste
3 tablespoons amontillado sherry
1/2 cup heavy cream, whipped (optional, for garnish)
Minced parsley (optional, for garnish)
Crab roe (optional, for garnish)

Melt the butter in the top of a large double boiler, add the flour, and blend until smooth. Add the milk, mace, and lemon zest and allow the mixture to cook for 5 minutes.

Pick over the crabmeat carefully to remove any remaining pieces of bone and cartilage and add it to the milk mixture along with the cream, grated onion, Worcestershire sauce, and salt and pepper. Continue to cook for 15 minutes. Add the sherry and cook for 2 to 3 minutes, then serve hot. Each serving may be garnished with a dollop of unsweetened whipped cream and minced parsley and a hint of crab roe.

Quick Seafood Gumbo

The Cajuns and Creoles of southern Louisiana have a running dispute over who created gumbo and whose gumbo is best. Being from the North, I stay out of the dispute and simply take advantage of it by savoring every available type of gumbo I can get my hands on in the interest of objective fairness. Whoever invented gumbo, it is certainly one of the preeminent dishes of African-inspired cooking in this country. The name itself seems to take its origin from one of the Bantu words for okra—*quingombo, tchingombo, kingombo*—which may speak to the dish's origin in Western Africa. In southern Louisiana, the bounty of the Gulf region adds crabmeat, oysters, shrimp, and the like to the heavy gumbo pot. This particular gumbo is not a classic gumbo: It does not call for a roux, is souplike in consistency, and does not take long to prepare.

SERVES 6

5 cups chicken broth
1 teaspoon dried thyme
2 bay leaves
3 cloves garlic, minced
4 large tomatoes, peeled, seeded, and coarsely chopped
1 teaspon dried Italian oregano
2 tablespoons grated onion
$^{3}/_{4}$ cup grated celery
$1^{1}/_{2}$ pounds peeled and deveined shrimp
1 pint fresh shucked oysters
$1^{1}/_{2}$ cups crabmeat
1 cup diced cooked chicken
2 teaspoons crushed dried hot red chile
1 pound fresh okra, topped, tailed, and cut into rounds

Place all of the ingredients except the okra in a large heavy stockpot and bring to a boil. Lower the heat and simmer for 10 minutes. Add the okra and continue to simmer over medium heat for 10 minutes longer (do not allow the soup to come to a boil again).

Remove the gumbo from the heat and refrigerate it overnight so that the flavors will blend. When ready to serve, reheat it, again being careful not to allow it to come to a boil. Remove the bay leaves and serve hot over a scoop of white rice.

Tomato Salad

My maternal grandmother, Bertha Philpot Jones, was a wonderful cook who could make a culinary masterpiece out of virtually anything. She always used fresh ingredients and cooked according to the season. She used to adore fresh tomatoes, which she only served when they were at their peak of ripeness. She treated them as the delicacy they are: plain with their taste heightened only by a tiny pinch of sugar.

In this age of colorless, odorless, tasteless cotton wool tomatoes, I have often thought back to the flavorful red delights that my grandmother brought to the table. And when the late summer farmers' market allows me to have great flavorful tomatoes, I serve them her way.

SERVES 4

4 large ripe tomatoes
2 teaspoons sugar
2 sprigs fresh mint

Slice the tomatoes and arrange them on a platter. Sprinkle the sugar evenly over them, making sure not to oversweeten. Garnish with fresh mint leaves. Serve and savor.

Tomato, Cucumber, and Onion Salad

Lucille Lippman was a neighbor of ours who welcomed us with friendship and food when we first came to summer in Oak Bluffs. The kitchen of her rambling house was one of the centers of island life, and I spent a fair while there as a child listening to her relate island tales and bits of local news each summer.

Several years later my admiration for Mrs. Lippman grew when I found out that she and I shared a fondness for leftover salad eaten the next morning at breakfast. It was years later that I would learn that this is a southern African-Americanism. It's probably an acquired taste, but one thing is sure, when you're going to eat leftover salad, the simplest salad is the best. Mrs. Lippman's salads were usually made up of farm-fresh tomatoes, onions, and cucumbers.

SERVES 4

2 ripe tomatoes, sliced
1 cucumber, peeled, seeded, and coarsely chopped
1 medium onion, thinly sliced
3 tablespoons olive oil
1 tablespoon cider vinegar
Salt and freshly ground black pepper, to taste

Place the tomatoes, cucumber, and onion in a glass salad bowl. Prepare a vinaigrette by mixing together the remaining ingredients. Pour the vinaigrette over the salad and serve. If there's any left over, refrigerate it overnight and serve it the following morning as a breakfast salad. The vegetables will have marinated in the dressing and be even more intensely flavored.

Creole Tomato Salad

Creole tomatoes are a southern Louisiana treat. They only grow in the New Orleans area and they only grow during certain times of the year. Thick, meaty, and immensely flavorful, they are almost an object of veneration in the city that care forgot, as is proven by the French Market's annual tomato festival. The annual auction for the first Creole tomatoes sold is a contest between growers, with farmers and home gardeners vying for the prize of best Creole tomato. They are used in cooking and in the famous Creole sauces of New Orleans, but as far as I'm concerned, they're best eaten raw dressed with a simple vinaigrette.

If you can get your hands on true Creole tomatoes, try this. If not, just get the meatiest, ripest, juiciest tomato that you can find, close your eyes, and pretend that you're sitting near the French Market on a humid day with the sultry New Orleans summer breeze blowing off the Mississippi. One taste and you'll feel like an extra from *The Big Easy.*

SERVES 1

1 luscious, red, ripe, meaty Creole tomato
2 tablespoons Basic Vinaigrette (page 93)
¼ teaspoon minced fresh basil

Core the tomato and slice it onto a chilled plate. Drizzle the vinaigrette over the tomato. Sprinkle with the basil and serve immediately.

Tomato Aspic

Although they have long disappeared from tables in other areas of the country, tomato aspic and Jell-O mold salad still occupy places of pride on many an African-American luncheon table. Surprisingly, these light summer salads are not as awful as one might think. In fact, if you like the taste of tomatoes, and a dash of fire, you'll love this tomato aspic.

SERVES 6 TO 8

½ cup cold water
2 tablespoons unflavored gelatin
3 cups canned peeled tomatoes
⅛ teaspoon Hot Sauce (page 89), or to taste
1 teaspoon sugar
2 tablespooons fresh lemon juice
3 tablespoons chopped onion
1 bay leaf
4 celery stalks with leaves
Freshly ground black pepper, to taste

Place the cold water in a small bowl. Add the gelatin and allow it to dissolve. Place the remaining ingredients in a medium-sized saucepan. Bring them to a boil over medium heat, then lower the heat and allow them to simmer for 30 minutes.

Press the simmered tomato mixture through a food mill to express all of the juice. Pour the gelatin into the hot juice and add enough water to make 4 cups. Pour the liquid into a mold and chill until it has set at least 4 hours, or overnight. Serve cold on a bed of lettuce leaves or as an accompaniment to a chicken or seafood salad.

Cucumber Salad

This cucumber salad is a cooling dish that appeared on my grand-mother's dining table each summer, and even occasionally during the winter months when good cucumbers could be found. The important thing here is to slice the cucumbers as thinly as possible and weight them. Then they will express their own liquid and take on the flavors of the sweet and sour vinegar marinade.

SERVES 6

3 large cucumbers, sliced very thin
2 medium-sized, mild red Bermuda onions, sliced thin
4 allspice berries, cracked
¹/₂ cup cider vinegar
2 tablespoons brown sugar, or to taste

Alternately layer the sliced cucumbers and onions into a medium-sized glass bowl. Heat the remaining ingredients in a small nonreactive saucepan for 5 minutes, stirring occasionally to make sure that the sugar has dissolved. Pour the mixture over the cucumbers. Cover the bowl with a plate that fits inside it, weight the plate with a 1-pound can, and refrigerate for 3 hours. When ready to serve, remove the weight and plate, fluff the vegetables with a fork, and serve chilled.

Avocado and Grapefruit Salad

This salad is a tropical delight and is picture-perfect when prepared with ruby grapefruit and black-skinned Hass avocados. The only trick is to section the grapefruit so that there is no hint of membrane on the pieces. This really only requires a very sharp knife and patience.

SERVES 6

3 ruby red grapefruit
4 Hass avocados
2 teaspoons fresh lemon juice
1 small red onion, thinly sliced
¹/₃ cup Basic Vinaigrette (page 93)
Salt and freshly ground black pepper, to taste

Peel the grapefruit and carefully segment them. With a sharp knife, remove the membrane from each segment, reserving any grapefruit juice. Slice the avocados lengthwise into ½-inch wedges. Arrange the grapefruit segments and the avocado wedges on a serving platter, alternating them for color contrast. Drizzle the lemon juice on the avocado wedges to keep them from turning brown. Arrange the onion slices on the top of the salad and cover with plastic wrap. Refrigerate for 1 hour to chill.

When ready to serve, mix the basic vinaigrette with the reserved grapefruit juice and drizzle it over the salad. Season with salt and freshly ground black pepper, and serve immediately.

Hearts of Palm and Pineapple Salad

This salad is Brazilian in origin. It is best categorized as one of the wonderful new dishes that new immigrants from the African diaspora are bringing to the culinary mix that is black America. It is simple to prepare, uses readily available ingredients, and is delicious as well as pretty to look at.

SERVES 4

1 (1-pound) can hearts of palm
1 cup fresh pineapple chunks (in a pinch you may substitute canned)
¼ cup Basic Vinaigrette (page 93) with 2 tablespoons of pineapple juice added

Drain the hearts of palm, remove any tough outside pieces, and cut crosswise into 1-inch pieces. Place the hearts of palm in a glass salad bowl and add the pineapple chunks and salad dressing. Mix well, cover with plastic wrap, and refrigerate for 1 hour to allow the flavors to blend. Serve chilled on a bed of lettuce.

God is great. God is good. And we thank Him for our food.

Carrot and Raisin Salad

This grated carrot salad with its tangy mayonnaise combination is one that my mother made frequently. The sweetness of the raisins and the carrots mixes well with the tartness of the dressing. Here the salad is made extra special with the addition of a bit of freshly toasted grated coconut.

SERVES 4

6 large carrots
1/4 cup raisins
1/4 cup lightly toasted unsweetened grated coconut
1/4 cup Basic Vinaigrette (page 93) mixed with 2 teaspoons
    mayonnaise

Peel the carrots and grate them, using a food processor or hand grater. Put the carrots in a glass bowl and add the raisins and coconut. Drizzle on the dressing and mix well. Cover with plastic wrap and refrigerate for 1 hour. Place the carrot mixture on a bed of lettuce on a small platter and serve at once.

Wilted Dandelion Greens with Hot Bacon Dressing

Fresh native greens have traditionally been a part of the African-American diet. They are eaten slow-cooked and seasoned with a piece of smoked meat, sautéed, or even raw in salads. During the Depression, dandelions were a source of vitamins for many an African-American family. My father's family, which was poorer than poor in the 1920s and 1930s, has family tales of picking dandelion greens on the lawn of Fisk College campus in Nashville, Tennessee, to survive. Those stewed greens made more than one dinner. Today, dandelion greens have become an expensive luxury item for many, available only in fancy greengrocers' shops. They are still stewed, but they are also served as a wonderful wilted salad with a brown sugar and bacon dressing, a version of the classic spinach and bacon salad, but one with an African-American flair.

1 pound dandelion greens
1 small red onion, thinly sliced
4 strips of sliced slab bacon
2 teaspoons dark brown sugar
2 tablespoons cider vinegar
Salt and freshly ground black pepper, to taste

Wash the dandelion greens thoroughly, spin them dry, and place them in a glass salad bowl. Peel and slice the onion, separating the slices into rings. Cut the bacon into 1-inch pieces and fry them in a heavy skillet until they are crisp. When they have rendered all of their fat, pour off all but 1 tablespoonful of the bacon drippings, return the skillet to the burner, and rapidly stir in the sugar and the cider vinegar. Adjust the seasoning and pour the hot dressing over the greens and onion. Add the salt and pepper and serve immediately.

Potato Salad I

This is a classic African-American salad whose origins seem to be in the meeting of Africa and Europe. Throughout the African culinary diaspora many root vegetables turn up served in various types of salads. This recipe uses white or Irish potatoes. They are called *bukra nyam* by the Gullah people of South Carolina to distinguish them from the more traditional African-American sweet potato.

There is no definitive potato salad recipe; each family stands staunchly behind the way it has been done in their household. There are partisans for the addition of hard-boiled eggs and even those who add sweet pickle relish. I come from a family of purists on this matter, and we want only potatoes, celery, a hint of onion, mayonnaise, and seasonings.

SERVES 6

2¹/₂ pounds white potatoes
2 large celery ribs, minced
1 small onion, minced
1 cup of mayonnaise
Salt and freshly ground black pepper, to taste

Wash the potatoes and place them in a heavy saucepan with water to cover. Bring them to a boil over high heat, then lower the heat and cook until tender but not mushy, about 20 minutes. Drain the potatoes, peel them, and allow them to cool.

Place the celery and onion in a large bowl. When the potatoes have cooled, cut them into ½-inch dice and add them to the onions and celery. Add the mayonnaise a bit at a time until the mixture is well coated, but not too wet. (You may not need the entire cup.) Then add the salt and pepper and mix well. Cover with plastic wrap and refrigerate overnight. Serve chilled.

Potato Salad II

This is a pull-out-the-stops potato salad with all the extras.

SERVES 6

Ingredients for Potato Salad I
¼ cup minced red bell pepper
¼ cup minced green bell pepper
3 hard-boiled eggs, coarsely chopped
2 tablespoons sweet pickle relish

Prepare the potato salad. Place the additional ingredients in the bowl with the celery and onion and proceed as for the plain potato salad. This potato salad is more decorative and seems more festive to many people. However, I'm still a purist and like to taste my potatoes.

Grandma Jones chowing down at a church supper.

Hot Potato Salad

This potato salad, which my mother refers to as hot German potato salad, is a traditional accompaniment to boiled pig's feet in my house. The smoky taste of the bacon mingles with the tart/sweet vinegar-sugar dressing and the onion, celery, and potato to create a salad with enough substance and tang to stand up to the pig's feet. My mother has been making this for so long that she no longer remembers where she learned it.

SERVES 6

5 medium-sized white potatoes
5 strips lean bacon
3 stalks celery, minced
1 medium-sized onion, minced
⅓ cup cider vinegar
3 tablespons sugar, or to taste
Salt and freshly ground black pepper, to taste

Wash the potatoes, peel them, cut them into bite-sized slices, and place them in a medium-sized saucepan. Bring them to a boil over medium heat, then lower the heat and allow them to simmer until tender, about 15 minutes. Drain the potatoes and place them in a heatproof bowl.

While the potatoes are cooking, cut the bacon into small bits and fry it in a heavy cast-iron skillet. When the bacon is almost crisp, add the minced celery and onion and continue to cook, stirring occasionally, until the vegetables are slightly browned and the bacon is crisp. Pour off all but 1 tablespoon of the bacon fat, add the remaining ingredients and the potatoes, and cook for 2 minutes, stirring gently so as to avoid crushing the potatoes. When the potatoes are well coated with the dressing, serve warm—with boiled pig's feet if you like.

Cole Slaw I

Cole slaw is a way of life for many African-Americans. The perfect accompaniment to a North Carolina chopped barbecue sandwich or a fried porgy, it is as much a part of an African-American summer barbecue as the hickory chips and as much a part of a fish fry as the fish. There are probably as many ways with cole slaw as there are folk. As in the case of potato salad, my mother is a purist. Her cole slaw uses only grated green cabbage, mayonnaise, vinegar, and a bit of seasoning. Other cooks add ingredients ranging from grated red cabbage to tarragon vinegar (see Cole Slaw II).

SERVES 6

1 medium-sized green cabbage, cored and grated
¹/₂ cup mayonnaise
2 tablespoons cider vinegar
Sugar, to taste
Salt and freshly ground black pepper, to taste

Place the grated cabbage in a medium-sized glass salad bowl, fluffing it with a fork so that the strips are separated. In a small bowl, mix the mayonnaise, vinegar, and sugar to taste. Pour it over the grated cabbage. Season with salt and freshly ground black pepper. Cover with plastic wrap and refrigerate for at least 1 hour so that the flavors mingle. When ready to serve, adjust the seasonings, and serve chilled.

Cole Slaw II

This is a much embellished variation on the cole slaw theme. Because the ingredients include red cabbage, red and green bell peppers, and grated carrots, it is perhaps more aptly called rainbow cole slaw.

SERVES 6 TO 8

1 small green cabbage, cored and grated
¹/₂ small red cabbage, cored and grated
3 carrots, grated
1 small red bell pepper, minced
1 small green bell pepper, minced
2 celery stalks, minced
³/₄ cup mayonnaise
2 tablespoons buttermilk
1 tablespoon cider vinegar
Cayenne pepper, sugar, salt, and freshly ground black pepper, to taste

Place all of the vegetables in a medium-sized glass salad bowl and toss well to distribute them evenly. In another bowl, stir the mayonnaise, buttermilk, vinegar, sugar, and seasonings together to form the dressing. Pour the dressing over the vegetables and stir it through so that the vegetable pieces are evenly coated. Cover the salad bowl with plastic wrap and chill for at least 1 hour. Serve chilled.

Chicken Salad I

Social reputations have risen and fallen in the South based on nothing more than a recipe for chicken salad. In its most traditional form, this dish includes simply chicken, celery, homemade mayonnaise, and seasonings. For a true southern chicken salad you should only use the white meat. For fancy gatherings and special occasions, the chicken salad is served in cups made from hollowed out tomatoes.

SERVES 6

6 medium-sized firm ripe tomatoes
4 cups minced cooked chicken breast
1¹/₂ cups finely minced celery
¹/₄ cup mayonnaise
Salt and freshly ground black pepper, to taste
Parsley sprigs and fresh basil sprigs, for garnish

Prepare the tomato cups: Place the tomatoes in boiling water for about 30 seconds. Remove and drain. With a sharp knife peel off the skin, hollow out the tomatoes, and remove the seeds. Drain the tomatoes, place them upside down on a plate, cover with plastic wrap, and chill for at least 1 hour.

Meanwhile, mix all of the remaining ingredients except the garnish in a medium-sized bowl. The salad should be neither too wet nor too dry, so add the mayonnaise gradually, stopping when you have reached the consistency you prefer. Cover with plastic wrap and refrigerate for at least 1 hour.

When ready to serve, place several spoonfuls of chicken salad in each tomato and garnish each with a sprig of parsley and one of fresh basil.

Chicken Salad II

For some chefs less is simply not enough. While many a southern grandmother would sneer and talk of seditious behavior, some folk simply like a lot of "stuff" in their salads, adding minced pecans, diced cucumbers, bits of onion, and even a dash of hot curry powder. Here, then, is a no-holds-barred chicken salad for those who dare to be unconventional.

SERVES 6

4 cups minced cooked chicken
1 cup minced celery
1/4 cup minced onion
1/4 cup minced pecans
1/4 cup minced cucumber
2 tablespoons Peach Kumquat Chutney (page 86) or commercial
*   mango chutney*
1/4 cup mayonnaise
2 teaspoons hot Madras curry powder
Salt and freshly ground black pepper, to taste

Mix together the chicken, celery, onion, pecans, and cucumber in a medium-sized bowl. Place all of the remaining ingredients in a small bowl and stir until the curry powder is mixed through and the mixture becomes a mustardy yellow hue. Add the mayonnaise mixture by tablespoons to the chicken mixture. (The salad should not be too wet or too dry—you may not have to use all of the mayonnaise mixture.) Adjust the seasonings, cover with plastic wrap, and chill for at least 1 hour. Serve chilled on a bed of lettuce or mounded in a hollowed-out pineapple half.

Ham Salad

I had forgotten about this salad until the conversation at a ham and baked beans dinner led to a reminder from a friend. Ham is such a frequent meat on many African-American tables that cooks have been particularly inventive in handling leftovers. This one can be used as a sandwich filling or served on a lettuce leaf. (If it is to be served as a sandwich, mince the ingredients finely.)

4 cups minced cooked ham
2 hard-boiled eggs, minced
1 cup minced celery
¼ cup minced green bell pepper
¼ cup minced red bell pepper
¼ cup sweet relish or minced sweet pickles
1 teaspon hot Dijon mustard
Salt and freshly ground black pepper, to taste
¼ cup mayonnaise

Mix all of the ingredients except the mayonnaise together in a non-reactive bowl. Add the mayonnaise slowly, as you may not need the full ¼ cup. Cover with plastic wrap and refrigerate for at least 1 hour. Serve chilled.

Shrimp Salad

This is a classic summer salad that is found on African-American luncheon tables in the Gulf region, where shrimp are plentiful. Instead of serving the classic shrimp cocktail, try this salad, in which the sauce serves as the dressing.

SERVES 4

2 pounds cooked shrimp, peeled and deveined
1 cup minced celery
½ cup minced onion
½ cup mayonnaise
1 tablespoon horseradish
2 tablespoons ketchup
Salt and freshly ground black pepper, to taste
1 small head Boston or Bibb lettuce

Cut the shrimp into bite-sized pieces and place them in a medium-sized bowl. Add the celery and onion. In a small bowl, mix the remaining ingredients together. Spoon the dressing over the shrimp salad and mix it well so that the ingredients are all coated. Cover the shrimp salad with plastic wrap and refrigerate it for 1 hour to let the flavors mingle. Arrange the lettuce leaves on a chilled platter and arrange the shrimp salad on the lettuce leaves. Serve chilled.

Condiments

Blacking the stove was a weekly chore.

Father Divine's kitchens fed thousands for a prayer.

"I GREW UP
WITH GOOD COUNTRY COOKING"

It's a long way from a Russian language and literature major at the University of Virginia to the culinary courses at La Varenne in France, but Tanya Holland has bridged that gap. Growing up in upstate New York played little part in Tanya's love of food. "My father's from rural Virginia and my mother is from northern Louisiana, so I'd call the cooking that I grew up with good country cooking," she states.

"At home, my father was the breakfast man. He'd make home fries, grits, sausage, and salmon and eggs, a special favorite of his. There would always be biscuits, but he'd rarely make them from scratch. Mommy was the everyday cook. She doesn't even own a measuring cup or spoon. There'd always be a pot of beans on the back of the stove, black-eyed peas, or navy beans cooking down with a seasoning ham hock. We had a lot of baked hams at home, as the leftovers could always be used to season the beans. We also had fried chicken at least once a week. Dad always cooked the meats at home; he was the roaster. He also always did the carving. My mom's a chitlin lover; she looks for excuses to cook them and just about anything will do— Super Bowl, New Year's, Christmas, Thanksgiving, or simply those days when she looks up and says, 'I've got a taste for chitlins.' She also makes greens, but only when they're fresh. In her nonmeasuring mode, she'd make desserts like cobblers and banana puddings and other things where you don't have to measure.

"African-American food is a good springboard for invention. It's simple in that there aren't many sauces except gravies and barbecue sauce. It's always concerned with getting as much nutritional value as possible out of the ingredients. It's not complicated in cooking methods and it's not fussy. Presentation isn't an issue, though I think it should be. African-American cooking always uses the freshest possible ingredients and it's always oral—you've got to be quick to follow along. Few recipes are written down. Finally, it's got to be well seasoned. It's not always hot, but it's always spicy. There are always a lot of different flavors going on. It's wonderful."

Watermelon Rind Pickle

The watermelon is a touchstone of African-American cooking. It was a part of the African diet before the Europeans arrived, and during the trials of enslavement, it provided thirst-quenching coolness in the heat of the day.

Actually, I'm not really fond of watermelon. However, I dote on watermelon rind pickles. I spend most summers scheming to beg rind from various friends so that I can have my pickle without having to eat my way through the melon.

MAKES
APPROXIMATELY
4 PINTS

9 cups cubed watermelon rind
¹/₂ cup salt
2 quarts plus 2 cups water
1³/₄ cups cider vinegar
¹/₂ cup balsamic vinegar
2 cups sugar
1 lemon, sliced thin
2 sticks cinnamon, crushed
1 teaspoon whole cloves
2 teaspoons cracked allspice

Prepare the watermelon rind by cutting it into 1-inch squares and removing the green skin and all but a small amount of the red meat. Place the prepared watermelon in a large bowl and soak it overnight in a brine made from the salt and 2 quarts of water.

When ready to prepare, drain the watermelon, wash it with fresh water, and drain it again. Place the rind in a large nonreactive saucepan with water to cover, and simmer it until it is fork-tender. Place the remaining 2 cups of water and the remaining ingredients in another large nonreactive pan, bring them to a boil, and simmer them for 15 minutes or until you have a thin syrup. Drain the watermelon rind, add it to the syrup, and continue to simmer until the rind becomes translucent. Place the watermelon rind pieces in hot sterilized jars, cover them with the (unstrained) syrup, and seal them according to proper canning procedures. The pickle will keep for several months.

Pickled Peaches

Peaches. Peaches. Peaches. Peaches. They're there for the picking when it's harvest time down South. (Why do you think there are so many Peachtree streets, lanes, and avenues in Atlanta, Georgia?) No self-respecting African-American cook would allow any bumper crop to go to waste, so peaches are "put up." They're transformed into chutneys, made into cobblers, and dried for fried pies. They're also pickled. This recipe for pickled peaches is from my maternal grandmother, peach lover and grand mistress of making do.

MAKES
APPROXIMATELY
1¼ QUARTS

2 cups firmly packed light brown sugar
4 cups distilled white vinegar
2 pounds firm, ripe peaches
½ teaspoon powdered cinnamon
¼ teaspoon whole cloves
½ teaspoon powdered allspice
¼ teaspoon freshly grated nutmeg
½ teaspoon grated lemon zest

Put the sugar and vinegar in a nonreactive pot, bring to a boil while stirring to make sure that they are well mixed. While the syrup is coming to a boil, peel the peaches and cut them into large slices. When the sugar syrup is boiling, add the spices and the peaches, lower the heat, and continue to cook for 20 minutes, or until the peaches are fork-tender. If serving immediately, allow the peaches to come to room temperature and serve. If canning a larger batch, place them in sterilized canning jars and prepare according to proper canning procedures.

Peach Chutney

This chutney is a testimonial to the culinary genius of my maternal grandmother, Bertha Philpot Jones, and through her to all the African-American housekeepers who fed folk nightly with food that was delicious and nutritious on very limited budgets. Grandmother Jones had a way with cooking and could "put a hurtin'" on just about everything. She lives in my taste memory as the creator of some of the most fantastic pickles and preserves that I've ever tasted. When peaches are ripe, this chutney is one of my favorites.

MAKES 3 CUPS

12 medium-sized peaches
1 teaspoon minced habanero chile, or to taste
1/3 cup golden raisins
1 medium-sized onion, quartered
2 cloves garlic
1 (1-inch) piece fresh ginger, scraped
1 cup cider vinegar
1 cup sugar

Peel and pit the peaches and place them in the bowl of a food processor with the chile, raisins, onion, garlic, and ginger. Drizzle in the vinegar and pulse until the mixture becomes a thick paste. Pour the paste into a nonreactive saucepan and add the sugar, then cook over low heat, stirring occasionally, for about 30 minutes, or until the mixture has the consistency of jam. Pour the chutney into hot sterilized jars and seal. The chutney is delicious with ham or even spread on ham biscuits.

Peach Kumquat Chutney

This chutney has become a Christmas tradition in my family since the day that I came up with it while looking for a chutney to accompany a baked ham and baked beans supper. The ingredients make it a perfect winter condiment, for it is in winter that the tart/sweet kumquats are available in greengrocers' shops; canned peaches are available at all times. Use only canned peach halves packed in heavy syrup.

MAKES 1 QUART

15 kumquats, seeded and coarsely chopped
6 canned peach halves, drained
1/2 habanero chile, or to taste
1 thumb-sized piece fresh ginger
1/4 teaspoon powdered cloves (grind them yourself)
2 cups granulated sugar
2 cups distilled white vinegar

Place all of the ingredients except the sugar and vinegar in the bowl of a food processor and grind until you have thick paste. Place the paste in a large nonreactive saucepan and stir in the sugar and vinegar. Bring to a boil over medium heat, then lower the heat and cook until the mixture reaches a marmaladelike texture, stirring occasionally to make sure that the chutney does not stick to the bottom of the pot and burn. Spoon the cooked chutney into sterilized jars, or, if you are going to keep it for a while, process it. This spicy chutney is particularly good with baked ham.

Blackberry Jam

Blackberries grow wild in many parts of the South, making this jam virtually a staple. It is simple to make in a relatively short time.

MAKES 2 TO
3 JELLY JARS
(5 OUNCES EACH)

2 cups blackberries
2 cups granulated sugar

Wash the blackberries and pick over them, discarding any bruised and damaged ones. Drain the berries well and place them in a glass bowl with the sugar, mix thoroughly, and set aside for about 10 minutes for the liquid to begin to form a syrup.

Place the berries and sugar in a heavy nonreactive pot. Bring to a boil over medium heat, lower the heat slightly, and cook for 10 minutes, or until the jam has thickened. Pour into jars and process for canning. Try on buttered biscuits or day-old fried cornbread.

Tomato Chutney

Like my maternal grandmother, I love to make chutneys and preserves. For me, though, it's not a frugal way of getting fresh fruits and vegetables ready for the winter. Rather, it's a hobby, a pleasure, a way of keeping the tastes of summer, and I enjoy eating and serving them. Last summer on Martha's Vineyard in the cedar-shingled house where I have spent part of each summer for thirty-seven years, a friend who owns a local restaurant gave me a load of overripe tomatoes and I decided to make a chutney using some of the fresh habanero chiles that are staples in my kitchen. This chutney is particularly good with grilled meats or roasted chicken or turkey.

MAKES 3 CUPS

12 ripe tomatoes
1 (1-inch) piece fresh ginger
1/2 habanero chile, or to taste
2 large onions, quartered
2 cloves garlic, minced
3 sprigs fresh basil, minced
1/2 cup dark raisins
1 cup firmly packed brown sugar
1 cup distilled white vinegar

Peel and slice the tomatoes. Place them, along with the ginger, chile, onions, garlic, and basil in a food processor and pulse until the ingredients are the consistency of a thick liquid. Place it in a heavy nonreactive saucepan with the remaining ingredients and stir well.

Put the saucepan on the stove at medium heat and bring the mixture to a boil. Lower the heat and continue to cook, stirring occasionally, for about 1 1/2 hours, or until the mixture reaches a jam-like consistency. Remove from the heat and pour into scalded 1/2-pint canning jars. The chutney should be served immediately but will keep in the refrigerator for up to 2 weeks. Larger batches can be made for canning for those who have bumper crops of tomatoes, but then proper canning procedures should be followed.

Pickled Okra

Okra, Africa's gift to the cooking of the southern United States, is disliked by many because of its mucilaginous consistency. In other words, folks hate it because it's slimy! However, those who are introduced to okra pickles find that the pod (which is related to cotton and to the colorful hibiscus) is delicious when pickled. The pickles are simple to make and are a perfect addition to almost any menu. I like them with a slice of ham slathered with homemade chutney. This recipe is better if small, tender okra pods are used. Watch out though: These are hot!

1 pound young okra
1/2 small habanero or other hot chile, sliced thin, or to taste
1 small onion, sliced thin
2 cloves garlic, sliced thin
1 cup water
3 cups distilled white vinegar
1 tablespoon pickling spice
2 teaspoons salt

Wash the okra and pick it over, removing any pods that are hard and woody and any with soft spots. Pack the okra into hot sterilized pint canning jars, stem ends down. Place the remaining ingredients in a nonreactive saucepan and bring them to a boil over medium heat. Remove the liquid from the heat and slowly pour it over the okra in the jars. Seal the jars according to proper canning procedures and store them in a cool dark place for 4 weeks, then serve as a condiment with virtually everything.

Hot Sauce

Hot sauce is indispensable to any well-set African-American table. In truth, though, most African-Americans do not prepare their own hot sauces as do our cousins in the Caribbean and Brazil. Instead we rely on commercial brands. However, a few hardy souls like their hot sauce homemade and even grow their own chiles.

Fresh hot chiles, though, are easier to find in markets than ever before, so preparing you own hot sauce is a snap. Here's a recipe that approximates the taste of the sauce in those long thin bottles that are a hallmark of good African-American cooking.

MAKES 1 PINT

24 small hot Tabasco chiles
2 garlic cloves
1 teaspoon grated prepared horseradish
2 teaspoons sugar
1/4 teaspon salt
1/2 cup cider vinegar

Place the chiles and garlic in a small nonreactive saucepan, cover them with water, and cook them until the garlic and the chiles are soft. Press the garlic and chile mixture through a sieve into a small bowl with the back of a fork. (For a hotter hot sauce put the garlic and chile mixture through a food processor, which will allow you to retain the heat of more of the seeds.)

Add the remaining ingredients to the sieved chile and garlic mixture and return it to the saucepan. Bring the mixture to a boil over medium heat, then lower the heat and simmer for 5 minutes, or until the tastes have blended. Pour into hot sterilized jars, seal, and store until ready to serve. Use sparingly.

Garlic Spiced Oil

As African-American tastes become more sophisticated and international in scope, some traditional methods of seasoning are changing. Where once garlic powder and garlic salt reigned supreme on the edge of the stove, now curious and health-conscious cooks are investigating other methods. They are using fresh garlic and even preparing their own vinegars and oils and using them as everything from hot sauce and barbecue sauce substitutes to additions to marinades.

MAKES 1 QUART

6 branches fresh thyme
12 garlic cloves, peeled
2 teaspoons cracked peppercorn mixture
1 quart mild-flavored olive oil

Place all of the ingredients in the top of a double boiler. Allow them to infuse over low heat for 45 minutes. Then allow to cool. When the oil is cool, pour it into decorative bottles and cork. The oil should sit for at least 1 week to mellow fully. It can then be used in salad dressings and even to make a spicy mayonnaise (page 93).

Thyme Oil

The Greene Avenue Grill, a restaurant near my neighborhood in Brooklyn, serves African-American food that takes our culinary tradition into the twenty-first century. They prepare a dish of shrimp grilled in thyme oil that has become one of my mother's favorites. As I live in a neighborhood where thick flavorful branches of fresh thyme are available year-round at the corner greengrocer's, I was inspired to make an oil to use for grilling shrimp and other seafood.

MAKES ABOUT
1 QUART

10 branches fresh thyme
½ habanero chile (or to taste)
3 cups extra-virgin olive oil
3 cloves garlic, peeled
4 Tabasco chiles

Place all of the ingredients except for 2 branches of the thyme, 1 garlic clove, and 1 Tabasco chile into a small nonreactive saucepan and heat over a low flame for 10 minutes. Allow the oil to cool, strain it, and pour it into a bottle in which you have placed the remaining thyme branches, the remaining garlic clove, and the remaining Tabasco chile. Stopper the bottle with a cork and set it on a cool dark shelf for at least 1 week. When ready, the oil can be used for grilling, in salad dressings, and in marinades.

Hot Vinegar

Hot sauces and preserved chiles are among of the hallmarks of African-American cooking. In fact, anyone who heads into an unknown soul food restaurant and doesn't see a long thin bottle of hot sauce on the table should immediately leave, for the restaurant is not authentic. Whether you use the red hot sauces of Louisiana such as Louisiana Red, Red Devil, the ubiquitous Tabasco, which is not authentically African-American, or the newer condiments from the Caribbean, a dash of heat is the perfect way to bring out the flavor in many African-American dishes.

Many African-Americans are finding out that it's easy to make their own hot vinegars and that they're a good substitute for too much salt. This is a basic recipe that is childishly simple to make but astonishingly potent in its heat. It's great on collard greens, and a dash does wonders to stews and soups.

MAKES 1 QUART

1 quart red wine vinegar
5 habanero or other chiles to taste

Remove the top from the bottle of red wine vinegar. Using rubber gloves to protect yourself from chile burns, split the chiles and force them (including the seeds!) into the bottle. If you are using bird chiles, simply put the whole chiles into the bottle. Close with a cork, as the pungency of the chiles may cause the metal bottle top to rust, and allow the vinegar to sit in a cool dark spot for at least a week.

Alternatively, if you're being fancy, the chile vinegar can be prepared and served in a cut-glass cruet that won't embarrass you when it is brought to the table. This vinegar makes a good Christmas gift when placed in a good-looking bottle, sealed with red sealing wax, and tied with a pretty ribbon.

Garlic Thyme Vinegar

One season on Martha's Vineyard, I went vinegar mad. I infused all manner of herbs and spices into various vinegars on the sunny shelves of our old kitchen. This one, redolent of garlic, is one of my favorite memories of that summer. I now make it and give it to friends as part of a holiday food basket. It is a seasoning vinegar that allows cooks to add flavor to all manner of dishes. It can be made in well-washed empty wine bottles with the labels removed or in the decorative glass jars that can be found in shops around the country.

MAKES
APPROXIMATELY
1 QUART

6 branches fresh thyme
12 garlic cloves, peeled
2 teaspoons cracked Peppercorn Mixture (page 96)
1 quart white wine vinegar

Force all of the ingredients into a decorative bottle. Cork the bottle and place it on a sunny window ledge for at least 2 weeks. The flavors will infuse into the vinegar. When fully mellow, the vinegar can be used in salad dressings and as a marinade in dishes like Pickled Shrimp (page 50).

Basic Vinaigrette

This recipe is not yet a traditional one in the African-American community. However, when folk begin to realize just how easy it is to prepare a fresh salad dressing for each salad, perhaps it will catch on.

MAKES ¾ CUP

¼ cup Garlic Thyme Vinegar (page 92)
Salt and freshly ground black pepper, to taste
Pinch of sugar
½ teaspoon Dijon-type mustard
½ cup extra-virgin olive oil

Combine the vinegar, salt, pepper, sugar, and mustard in a small nonreactive bowl and whisk them well with a fork or wire whisk. Gradually drizzle in the olive oil, continuing to whisk until the dressing is well mixed. Serve immediately on any salad.

This dressing can be transformed into a blue cheese dressing with the addition of a tablespoon of mayonnaise and 2 tablespoons of crumbled Roquefort cheese.

Mayonnaise

There is no doubt that the best mayonnaise is homemade and prepared with the freshest ingredients available. However, if that is not possible, remember that the only "store-bought" mayonnaise really considered acceptable by southern ladies is Hellmann's. That's not an endorsement, that's simply the truth.

With this recipe, which can be used in any recipe in this book calling for mayonnaise, you can make infinite variations by your choice of olive oils and vinegars. It calls for a simple white wine vinegar, but a flavored vinegar or oil will give you a flavored mayonnaise. Leah Chase of Dookey Chase's restaurant in New Orleans, the empress of African-American Creole cooking, would think me amiss if I didn't inform you that in that town the *only* way to pronounce this condiment is May-oh-Naize. Anything else is just plain wrong.

MAKES
APPROXIMATELY
1 CUP

1 egg yolk
$1/2$ teaspoon salt
2 tablespoons white wine vinegar
1 cup extra-virgin olive oil
Dash of fresh lemon juice

Place the egg, salt, vinegar, and lemon juice in the container of a blender, then immediately add $1/2$ of the oil while blending at high speed. Slowly drizzle in the remaining oil while continuing to blend. When all of the oil has been added, *stop blending*; the mayonnaise is ready.

Cocktail Sauce

In the African-American world of seafood, variations of this thick red sauce are found wherever shrimp cocktail turns up. It also makes occasional appearances alongside fried seafood platters and in the company of boiled crab claws. All too many folk simply open a jar of cocktail sauce and pour it out, thereby giving cocktail sauce a bad name. However, when prepared from freshly grated horseradish and given just the right bite, it is a delicious counterpoint to the briny taste of shellfish.

MAKES 1 CUP

1 cup tomato ketchup
$1/2$ cup fresh lemon juice
$1/4$ cup freshly grated horseradish
2 tablespoons Worcestershire sauce
Louisiana Red hot sauce, to taste
Salt, to taste
Freshly ground black pepper, to taste

Mix all of the ingredients together in a serving bowl, cover with plastic wrap, and chill in the refrigerator for at least 2 hours. Serve chilled to accompany fried and boiled seafood.

Creole Seasoning

While I make it a point of honor to use only the freshest seasonings in the kitchen, I also use many dried seasonings that I squirrel away in a variety of containers on shelves next to the stove. One of my favorites for seasoning grilled chicken is a mixture I called Creole seasoning in my first cookbook, *Iron Pots and Wooden Spoons: A Cookbook in Praise of the Piquant.* I keep refining it; this is a slightly different recipe.

MAKES
APPROXIMATELY
1/3 CUP

1 tablespoon salt
1 tablespoon dried hot red chile
1 tablespoon chile powder
1 tablespoon dehydrated garlic
1 tablespoon dehydrated onion flakes
2 teaspoons black peppercorns
1 teaspoon white peppercorns
1 teaspon allspice berries

Place all of the ingredients in a spice mill (or a coffee grinder that you use to grind spices) and pulverize until the mixture becomes a coarse powder. Pour into a screw-top glass jar and store. A rub with this mixture will add a taste of sunshine to your grilled meats.

*Mom and Dad, Uncle Bill and Aunt Edna
—and me, as a "bun in the oven."*

Peppercorn Mixture

This is not the usual black pepper that is found in most traditional African-American recipes. That is the tinned variety that usually comes already ground. However, as peppercorns are readily available, more and more African-Americans are discovering the joys of freshly ground black pepper and with it the pungency of taste that recalls the traditional pepper of West Africa.

This mixture of black, white, and green peppercorns and allspice berries evokes those tastes and is a welcome addition to any dish. It has made a believer out of everyone who has tried it. Like all good peppers, it should be ground just prior to use as it will lose its pungency if allowed to sit for too long.

MAKES 1 CUP

¹/₂ cup black Tellicherry peppercorns
¹/₄ cup white Muntok peppercorns
3 tablespoons freeze-dried green peppercorns
1 tablespoon allspice berries

Mix all of the ingredients together in a bowl and pour them into a 1-cup corked storage jar. (This pepper mixture also makes a good gift along with a good peppermill.) Simply place in a pepermill and grind as needed.

Lamb Rub

Lamb is a recent addition to the diet of many African-Americans, but it is one that we have taken to with great delight. Perhaps our taste buds remember the *mechouis* and lamb stews of West Africa. Lamb is a dish that doesn't really yield a good gravy—a hallmark of African-American cooking. My paternal grandmother used to say, "Lamb gravy goes to sleep early." It was her way of saying that the lamb fat congealed on the gravy rapidly. Instead of gravy, I usually prepare a leg of lamb with a crust of pepper and salt and serve it with homemade chutney. No one has ever asked for gravy. The trick is in the lamb rub, a mixture of spices that are rubbed onto the lamb before cooking.

¹/₄ cup salt
¹/₂ cup coarsely ground Peppercorn Mixture (page 96)
¹/₄ cup herbes de Provence (a mixture of basil, fennel seed, sage,
*   lavender, thyme, summer savory, rosemary, and marjoram)*

Place all of the ingredients in a spice grinder and grind them until they are well mixed. You may find that you have a personal preference for rosemary with lamb. If so, add a tablespoon or so more. If you have a problem with salt eliminate some of it, or use a salt substitute. You get the idea. The mixture will keep in a sealed jar for several months. I'm not really sure how long—my jar is always empty before the rub goes bad.

Crab Boil

From Maryland to Georgia, crabs in some form or another are a prized part of the African-American diet. Whenever they have to be boiled before other steps in preparation, they're usually boiled with the addition of a commercial crab boil such as Maryland's Old Bay. For the lucky few, though, there's homemade crab boil.

This is an all-purpose crab boil and can also be used for cooking shimp and crawfish. It will keep for several months in the refrigerator in a tightly stoppered container.

MAKES 1 CUP

¹/₄ cup commercial pickling spice
2 tablespoons mustard seeds
2 tablespoons black peppercorns
1 tablespoon celery seeds
2 tablespoons crushed red chiles
2 teaspoons minced dried ginger
5 bay leaves
2 teaspoons dried oregano
1 tablespoon minced dried chives
¹/₄ cup sea salt

Mix all the ingredients together in a food processor and pulse until you have a coarse powder. Then stir the boil to make sure that there are no large unprocessed bits and that the ingredients are well mixed. Pour the mixture into a glass jar that can be tightly stoppered. It will keep for several months in a cool, dark place.

Cornmeal Stuffing

Each African-American family has its own traditions when it comes to stuffing the holiday turkey. The stuffings run the gamut from cornmeal stuffing through oysters all the way to sausage and sage, and mixtures of all of the above. In my family, cornmeal reigns supreme. By the way, when it's passed around the table, it's called dressing not stuffing.

ENOUGH FOR
A 10- TO 12-POUND
TURKEY

4 cups coarse dry bread crumbs
2 cups yellow cornmeal
1½ cups minced celery, including the leafy green parts
½ cup chopped onion
½ cup butter or bacon drippings
2½ tablespoons Bell's poultry seasoning
Salt and freshly ground black pepper, to taste

Place the bread crumbs, cornmeal, celery, and onion in a large mixing bowl. Add the butter and seasonings and mix well so that the ingredients are evenly distributed. Place the stuffing in the neck and interior cavities of the bird, sew it up with coarse thread, and roast it.

Molasses Butter

During my childhood, when I watched my father eat Sunday breakfast or when I watched my Uncle Johnny eat at my Grandma Harris's house, I was treated to a ritual that I've never seen duplicated elsewhere. Prior to eating the flaky home-baked biscuits that my mother and grandmother inevitably placed on the table (mom's were flaky and light and grandma's were, I would later learn, the glazed-looking beaten type), each man would methodically pour out a plate of syrup. Karo dark was the syrup of choice, but this was only because Alaga, the traditional cane syrup of the African-American South, was hard to find. They would then proceed to cut bits of butter into the syrup, transforming it into a marbleized swirl of dark syrup and creamy yellow butter. Only then did they begin to sop their biscuits.

I was reminded of this taste when, many years later, at an African-American food symposium, I was treated to a taste of molasses butter. The creator, Carolina Avelino, a food consultant originally from Arkansas, informed me that this was simply her mother's answer to the butter and molasses ritual I had known as a child. My family ritual was just another long-standing African-Americanism that they had held onto. This molasses butter captures the memory of all that wonderfullly. It's simple to prepare and keeps well in the refrigerator.

MAKES ABOUT ½ CUP

¼ pound (1 stick) unsalted butter
2 tablespoons dark molasses, Karo dark syrup, or Alaga syrup

Soften the butter. With a whisk beat the molasses into the butter until thoroughly blended. Pack the butter in a mold or container and refrigerate until ready to serve with hot biscuits.

Pecan Butter

Once I discovered molasses butter, the whole horizon of various seasoning butters opened up. I tried peanut butter butter, but not only was that awkward to say, the taste was only good, not super. Then came pecan butter, which is perfect on toast with a sprinkling of brown sugar.

MAKES ABOUT ⅔ CUP

¼ pound (1 stick) salted butter
⅓ cup shelled pecan halves
1 tablespoon olive oil

Soften the butter and place it in a bowl. Place the pecan halves in a food processor with the oil and pulverize them until they are a thick paste. Combine the pecan paste with the butter, stirring to be sure that they are well mixed. Pack the butter in a mold or container and refrigerate until ready to serve.

Vegetables
and
Other Side Dishes

Stringing beans is a communal activity for former slaves at an almshouse.

It wasn't soul food; we just called it dinner.

"I'M A VEGETARIAN;
IT'S JUST WHAT I DO"

Maxine Clair, professor of English at George Washington University in Washington, D.C., and author of *Coping with Gravity,* a collection of poems, and *Rattle Bones,* a collection of short stories, was born and raised in Kansas City, Kansas, into a family that had been Midwesteners for four generations. She recalls, "There were nine in my family and I'm the second eldest. When I was growing up, my family would probably have been considered the 'working poor.' We didn't eat very much meat. Two or three times a week we'd have one-pot meals of greens, cabbage, beans or green beans cooked with bacon skin and slab bacon. These meals were usually served with cornbread and cole slaw on the side. We ate a lot of vegetables. On Sundays, there was frequently chicken and a chuck roast now and then. We had things like pork chops rarely because they were expensive and there were a lot of us.

"My father worked in construction and in the winter when he wasn't working, he hunted, so there were also rabbit and squirrel and quail. We ate rabbit every way—stewed, baked, barbecued, and fried. Later on, as I grew up, he also fished in the summer. My mother was a canner who would put up fresh vegetables in the summer so that we could have them in the winter. When she got a freezer, she would freeze things, too. We didn't have a garden, but we always had some tomato plants. My mother would bake rolls and she made wonderful pies and cakes, and during the winter holiday season she'd make cookies. My parents were very strict about what we ate and drank; we couldn't have things like Kool-Aid, and when we did have soda, we were only allowed a half a bottle and then she'd water that down.

"When I married, my husband was from Florida, so that I got to see some of the differences in how we ate. We ate potatoes, where his family ate rice, and we didn't know about things like cracklin' cornbread, we just had cornbread. We also didn't eat a lot of hot sauce; our main seasonings were salt and pepper, and for a treat we'd have sage in the dressing of the turkey at holidays. We did have traditional African-American things like chitlins, but my mother would cook them with potatoes in them, so they became a one-pot meal, and there was succotash, which to us meant tomatoes, okra, and fresh corn cut off the cob and seasoned with bacon.

"These tastes changed as I grew. Recently, when I visited my parents, I noticed that they now eat no pork. I find that many African-Americans are giving up pork for fat and health reasons. I too gave it up over fifteen years ago when my children were born, for health concerns. Now, in fact, I am a vegetarian. I'm not a strict one, and I may have fish or chicken one or two times a month, but I just find that on a vegetarian diet, I feel healthier—it's just what I do. In a funny way it's almost like going back to childhood, for although they're cooked a different way now, I'm still eating a lot of vegetables."

Black-Eyed Peas

This African-American dish harks back directly to West Africa, where black-eyed peas, according to work done by some culinary historians, were eaten prior to European arrival. Noted art historian Robert Farris Thompson informs me that the Yoruba word for black-eyed pea, *ewa*, is a pun on the origins of life. Certainly for many African-Americans, black-eyed peas were and are still the staff of life. They turn up with rice in Hoppin' John, the traditional New Year's dish that has spread from South Carolina to the rest of the South, and in other parts of the South as a main dish or vegetable with the addition of a ham hock or bits of ham.

This is a basic recipe. The black-eyed peas may also be cooked with a leftover ham bone, a precooked ham hock, or with olive oil instead of the bacon fat. The latter sacrifices the smoky traditional taste to contemporary concerns about cholesterol. Whatever way they're served, they're delicious.

SERVES 6 TO 8

1 pound dry black-eyed peas
1 quart cold water
2 tablespoons bacon fat
1 small onion, peeled

Pick over the beans, removing any stones, broken beans, or other debris you may find. Then place them in a a heavy stockpot with water to cover and leave them overnight to plump.

When ready to cook, drain the beans and put them back in the stockpot with the quart of fresh cold water, the bacon fat, and the onion. Cover and simmer for 30 to 40 minutes. If more water is needed during cooking, add only boiling water. Otherwise the beans will be tough.

Hoppin' John

No one seems completely sure where the name Hoppin' John comes from. Variations run from the clearly apocryphal suggestion that this was the name of a waiter at a local restaurant who walked with a limp, to the plausible, a corruption of *pois pigeon* (pigeon peas in French). Culinary historian Karen Hess in her masterwork, *The Carolina Rice Kitchen: The African Connection*, offers a twenty-plus-page dissertation on everything from the history of the dish to recipe variations to a number of suggestions for the origin of its name, ranging from Malagasy to ancient Arabic. The only thing that all seem to agree on about Hoppin' John is that the dish is emblematic of South Carolina and is composed of rice and black-eyed peas.

Many years back I was amazed to discover a startlingly similar dish on the luncheon table at the Dakar home of Senegalese friends. There, the dish was prepared with beef and not smoked pork, but the rice and black-eyed peas were the same. The name of that dish was given as *thiébou niébé*.

There seem to be two variations on Hoppin' John: One calls for the rice to be cooked with the peas. The second calls for the peas and rice to be cooked separately and then mixed together at a final stage prior to serving. I prefer to cook my rice and peas together.

SERVES 4 TO 6

1 pound dried black-eyed peas (cow peas)
1/2 pound salt pork
1 quart water
1 sprig fresh thyme
Salt and freshly ground black pepper, to taste
1 1/2 cups raw long-grain rice
3 cups hot water

Pick over the black-eyed peas to remove dirt and stones. Soak them in water to cover at least 4 hours or overnight. Fry the salt pork in a large heavy casserole to render the fat. When the salt pork is crisp, add the black-eyed peas and the quart of water, the thyme, salt, and pepper, cover, and cook over low heat for 40 minutes. Adjust the seasonings and continue to cook until the peas are tender. Add the rice, cover with the 3 cups hot water, and simmer over low heat until all of the liquid has been absorbed and the rice is tender. Serve hot.

On New Year's Day, in some families, a dime is placed in the Hoppin' John to ensure special good luck throughout the year for the person who gets it. However, the thought of cracking a tooth makes me think that this may not be the best idea. Try it if you wish.

Red Beans and Rice

Anyone who has been to the Crescent City knows that this dish is the traditional Monday dish. If pressed, many will give the story that this is so because Monday was wash day and the dish was cooked in advance so the washing could be done. However, few have thought about just who *did* the washing and about who *did* the cooking. In this way many African-American dishes are absorbed into the general culinary tradition of a region. Red beans and rice are very much a part of black New Orleans. In fact, legendary jazz trumpeter Louis Armstrong, a Big Easy native, would sign his letters to friends, "Red beans and ricely yours." So for Monday or any day, here's a dish that can stand on its own as a full meal.

SERVES 6 TO 8

1 pound dried kidney beans
1 ham bone
1 cup ham chunks
1 medium-sized onion, coarsely chopped
1 clove garlic, minced
1 bay leaf
1 quart cold water
Salt and freshly ground black pepper, to taste
4 cups cooked rice

Prepare the beans according to the directions for Black-Eyed Peas on page 105. Place the plumped beans in a pot with the ham bone, ham chunks, onion, garlic, and bay leaf. Add the quart of water and cook until the beans are fork-tender (*not* mushy), about 30 minutes.

Drain the beans, reserving ½ cup of the cooking liquid. Add the rice, mix well, and season to taste. Return the beans and rice to the stove. Add the reserved cooking liquid and cook over low heat until warmed through. Remove the bay leaf and serve hot.

Bless the table. Bless the food. Bless the hands that prepared it, oh Lord, and give food unto those who have none.

Plain White Rice

Rice is important for many African-Americans, so important, in fact, that it may be eaten at all three daily meals if the folks hark from the coastal areas of South Carolina or Georgia. A form of rice was grown in West Africa before the Europeans arrived, and agricultural knowhow from enslaved African labor contributed mightily to the rice industry in South Carolina's Low Country, making true Carolina rice some of the world's finest.

Plain white rice is one of those painfully simple dishes that separates the women from the girls and the cooks from the novices in many an African-American household. I'm afraid that I rank among the novices in my household. My mother, who prefers Carolina rice, cooks it each time until "each grain stands up on its own"—perfection. There are two methods of rice preparation in my family, and in many other African-American families. My more traditional mother is a steamer, first boiling the rice and them steaming it until fluffy. This is the old-fashioned way and indeed still the way in many South Carolina households. I doggedly follow the package directions in hope that one day I will obtain her perfect results. This method has worked well for me.

SERVES 6 TO 8

3¹/₃ cups water
1¹/₂ cups uncooked rice
1 teaspoon salt
1 tablespoon butter

Bring the water to a boil in a medium-sized saucepan. Stir in the rice, salt, and butter. Cover, lower the heat, and simmer for about 20 minutes, or until fork-tender. Remove the rice pot from the heat and allow it to stand, covered, for 5 minutes, until all of the water has been absorbed. Serve hot with butter or gravy.

Thank you for the world so sweet.
Thank you for the food we eat.
Thank you for the birds that sing.
Thank you, God, for everything.
—*Child's Grace*

Charleston Red Rice

This rice is one of the links between the food of West Africa and that of African-Americans. Several years ago, on my first trip to Charleston, South Carolina, I noticed that all the restaurants featured red rice on their menus. When I lunched one day with a group of friends who had spent time in Senegal, we all decided to sample the red rice. When the dish arrived, we all looked down and said in a rousing chorus, *"Thiébou dienn!"* Indeed, the red rice struck each and every one of us as being very much like the red rice that accompanies fish and other ingredients in the Senegalese national dish. The link becomes clearer when one realizes that the Casamance region of southern Senegal is a rice-growing area and slaves were taken from there to work in Carolina's rice fields. This is not a pre-European African dish, for there were no tomatoes in West Africa before the Columbian Exchange. Also, in Muslim Senegal there would be no bacon in the dish. In spite of this, the dish definitely reflects the tastes of West Africa in the New World.

SERVES 4 TO 6

6 strips lean bacon
1 medium onion, chopped
3 scallions, minced, including the green parts
2 cups coarsely chopped seeded and peeled ripe tomatoes
1 cup uncooked long-grain rice
¾ cup minced cooked ham
Salt, pepper, and hot sauce, to taste

Preheat the oven to 350 degrees. On the top of the stove, heat a heavy cast-iron skillet, add the bacon strips, and cook them until crisp. Remove the bacon strips and drain them on paper towels. Cook the onion and scallions in the remaining bacon fat until translucent. Crumble the bacon and add the bacon bits, tomatoes, and the remaining ingredients to the skillet. Reduce the heat to low and cook for 10 minutes. Place the seasoned rice and tomato mixture in a greased 1½-quart ovenproof casserole. Adjust the seasonings, cover the dish, and bake the red rice for 1 hour, stirring every 15 minutes.

Dirty Rice I

Composed rice dishes are one of the hallmarks of African-American cooking in the New World. They range from Charleston's Hoppin' John to the Caribbean's rice and peas, peas and rice, congris, and moros y cristianos, to the red beans and rice of New Orleans that Louis Armstrong loved so much. These dishes are ours. New Orleans's dirty rice is just another addition to the list.

Chopped chicken innards and savory seasonings give the rice its "dirty" appearance.

SERVES 6 TO 8

1½ cups raw long-grain rice
3 tablespoons vegetable oil
1 large red onion, chopped
1 clove garlic, minced
½ pound chicken livers, minced
4 ounces chicken gizzards, minced
2 scallions, green tops included, chopped
2 stalks celery, including leafy parts, minced
¼ cup minced green bell pepper
1 sprig parsley, minced
2 preserved bird pepper chiles, or to taste, minced
Salt and freshly ground black pepper, to taste

Cook the rice according to the directions on page 108 until almost done, about 15 minutes. While the rice is cooking, heat the oil in a heavy skillet and brown the onion and garlic. Add the minced chicken livers and gizzards to the onion and garlic mixture and sauté them until they are cooked and crumbly, about 4 minutes. Add the remaining ingredients and the drained rice and continue to cook over medium heat, until the rice is thoroughly cooked. Toss gently until the ingredients are well mixed, and serve at once.

Dirty Rice II

This version of the New Orleans classic includes not only the traditional chicken innards but also ham, sausage, and chicken necks. It demonstrates the thriftiness of the Creole cooks.

SERVES 6 TO 8

6 chicken necks
6 chicken gizzards
1/2 pound chicken livers
1 pound hot sausage meat
1 medium onion, minced
3 scallions, including the green tops, minced
1/4 cup minced green bell pepper
2 celery stalks, minced
1/2 cup minced cooked ham
4 cups cooked white rice (page 108)

Place the chicken necks, gizzards, and livers in a large saucepan with water to cover. Bring them to a boil, then lower the heat to medium, cover, and cook until the meat of the chicken necks is falling off the bones. Remove the meat from the cooking liquid, and reserve the liquid. Pick the chicken meat from the bones and chop it, along with the gizzards and livers.

In a large, heavy cast-iron skillet, cook the sausage meat, turning it frequently to make sure that it is well browned. Remove the sausage to paper towels and drain all but 3 tablespoons of the sausage fat. Fry the onion, scallion, bell pepper, and celery in the retained fat for 20 minutes over low heat. Add the sausage, ham, and chopped chicken parts to the mixture and moisten with 1/4 cup of the liquid reserved from the chicken. Continue to cook over low heat for 10 minutes, then add the rice, stirring well to make sure that all of the ingredients are well mixed. Serve hot.

Limpin' Susan

Ask most folk about the cooking of South Carolina and they will tell you something about rice. If they're a little more knowledgeable, they'll tell you about Hoppin' John. If they're really expert, they'll tell you about Hoppin' John's little known cousin, Limpin' Susan.

Limpin' Susan is a local Carolina name for one of the region's rice pilaus, or purloos. These composed rice dishes are the jewels of the cooking of the region. Many of them have definite links to the cooking of other areas of the African Atlantic world and to that of West Africa itself.

This dish is prepared with okra and seasoning pieces of bacon. Occasionally, tomatoes are added to this pilau, but the classic dish simply calls for rice, bacon, okra, and seasonings. It requires, as do many South Carolina rice dishes, a rice steamer, which is an excellent gift to ask for at the next holiday. If you don't have a rice steamer, you can approximate one with a colander and a covered saucepan.

SERVES 4

5 strips lean bacon
3 cups thinly sliced okra
1 small onion, minced
1 cup washed raw long-grain rice
1 cup water
Salt and freshly ground black pepper, to taste

Cut the bacon into 1-inch pieces and fry it in a heavy skillet until it is crisp and has rendered most of its fat. Add the okra and onion and sauté them in the bacon drippings, stirring occasionally, until the onion is translucent and the okra is tender. Add the rice, water, and salt and pepper and continue to cook for 5 minutes, making sure that all of the ingredients are well mixed.

Transfer the rice and okra mixture to the top section of a steamer, add water to the bottom, cover, and cook until the rice is fluffy and dry. The cooking times will vary depending on the type of rice, but this should take between 45 minutes and 1 hour. Serve hot and use a rice spoon, if you have one. In the rest of the world, this is a long-handled stuffing spoon. In rice-eating Charleston, it's a rice spoon.

Basic Okra

Okra is one of Africa's gifts to the cooking of the New World. In Africa, it's prized for its slipperiness and is used to add body to soups and stews. Perhaps the most traditional way to eat this vegetable pod is boiled. It's certainly the preferred way for those who really love it. Those who are afraid of the vegetable's characteristic "texture" will be pleased to know that much of that can be eliminated by adding a bit of lemon juice or vinegar to the cooking water just after the okra is cooked.

SERVES 4 TO 6

1 pound small okra pods, topped and tailed
2 cups water
Salt and freshly ground black pepper, to taste
1 tablespoon fresh lemon juice

Wash the okra and cut it into $1/2$-inch rounds. Bring 2 cups of water to a boil in a nonreactive saucepan. Place the okra rounds in the saucepan, lower the heat, and cook for 5 minutes. When the okra is fork-tender, remove from the heat, add the salt and pepper and the lemon juice, drain, and serve hot.

Fried Okra

Okra is the Rodney Dangerfield of vegetables. It gets little respect from cooks and diners alike. Fried okra, with its crunch of cornmeal, is perfect for those who are normally leery of the mucilaginous pod.

SERVES 4 TO 6

1 pound small pods fresh okra, topped and tailed
1 cup yellow cornmeal
Salt and freshly ground black pepper to taste
$1/2$ cup bacon drippings for frying (see Note)

Wash the okra, cut it into $1/2$-inch rounds, and place it in a small brown paper bag or plastic bag. Add the cornmeal and salt and pepper and shake to coat the okra with the cornmeal and seasoning mixture. Heat the bacon fat in a large, heavy skillet. Drop in the okra pieces a few at a time and fry until golden brown, turning frequently so that they are browned on all sides. Drain on paper towels and serve warm.

NOTE: You can substitute olive oil or a low-cholesterol vegetable oil. The taste, while delicious, will not be authentically African-American.

Okra Purloo

Africa's okra and South Carolina's rice come together again in this classic rice dish. This time the rice is precooked and fresh ripe tomatoes and a hint of tomato paste are added to create yet another variation on this popular southern theme.

SERVES 4

4 slices slab bacon
1 cup okra, topped, tailed, and sliced
2 ripe tomatoes, peeled, seeded, and coarsely chopped
2 cups cooked long-grain white rice
1 tablespoon tomato paste
Salt and freshly ground black pepper, to taste

Fry the bacon in a heavy skillet until it has rendered all of its fat and is crisp. Remove the bacon with a slotted spoon, crumble it, and reserve it on paper towels. Add the okra and the tomatoes to the drippings and cook them over medium heat, stirring constantly, for 5 to 7 minutes, or until they are fork-tender. Add the rice, tomato paste, and salt and pepper and continue to cook until all of the ingredients are well mixed and heated through. Stir in the drained bacon and serve hot.

Okra and Rice

This mixture of okra and rice could turn up on a South Carolina table or on any table in Guadeloupe. Its roots are pure African. Indeed, the dish is a close Caribbean country cousin of Limpin' Susan. This version I learned from Carmelita Jeanne, one of Guadeloupe's famous *cuisinières,* and it is pure Creole magic. It, like other composed rice dishes, is returning to the United States with African-Americans from other areas of the hemisphere to expand our culinary vocabulary.

SERVES 6 TO 8

2 teaspoons olive oil
¹/₂ pound fresh okra, topped, tailed, and cut into rounds
1 quart water
3 scallions, minced
1 tablespoon minced fresh parsley
1 teaspoon minced fresh thyme
2 cloves garlic, minced
1 teaspoon minced habanero chile
Salt and freshly ground black pepper, to taste
2¹/₃ cups raw long-grain rice

Heat the oil in a heavy saucepan over medium heat and lightly brown the okra for 3 minutes. Add 1 quart of water, the scallions, parsley, thyme, garlic, chile, and salt and pepper. Bring the mixture to a boil over medium high heat and boil for 5 minutes. Add the rice, lower the heat to medium, and allow the rice to continue to boil gently for 8 to 10 minutes.

Drain the mixture and place it in a large sieve or colander or the top of a rice cooker over a pot of boiling water. Cover and steam for 7 minutes, or until the rice is tender. Fluff the rice, adjust the seasonings, transfer to a serving bowl, and serve the dish hot.

Okra Fritters

African okra and the African technique of frying in deep oil come together in these okra fritters. They are another perfect way to introduce the wary to the delights of okra.

SERVES 6

Oil for deep frying
1½ cups water
1 pound small okra pods, topped
Salt and freshly ground black pepper, to taste
2 eggs
2 teaspoons baking powder
¼ cup flour
Hot Sauce (page 89, optional)

Preheat 3 inches of oil to 375 degrees in a heavy saucepan or fryer. Place 1½ cups of water in a medium-sized saucepan and bring it to a boil. Drop in the okra and cook it for 10 minutes. Drain it and place it in a food processor. Pulse until you have a paste.

Scrape the paste into a medium-sized bowl and beat in the salt and pepper, eggs, baking powder, and enough flour to make a thick batter. Drop the batter a tablespoonful at a time into the oil and fry until crisp and golden brown, about 5 minutes, turning the fritters once. When ready, drain the fritters on paper towels, and serve piping hot with spicy hot sauce as a snack or as a vegetable.

Okra, Corn, and Tomatoes

This is one variation of the many southern black dishes that combine three ingredients basic to much African-American cooking: okra, corn, and tomatoes. The attraction of this dish is that it can be prepared in the summer from the freshest of ingredients, or in the winter from frozen ingredients and canned whole tomatoes. Either way (although in truth the fresh version is unbeatable!), the surprise is the hot bite of the habanero chile that is pricked and placed in the vegetables for the entire cooking time. When I am serving this dish to African friends who like things *really* hot, I mince half of another habanero chile and stir it into the vegetables.

6 large ripe tomatoes, peeled, seeded, and coarsely chopped or 3
*   cups canned peeled tomatoes, seeded and coarsely chopped*
2 cups fresh or frozen corn kernels
1 pound fresh or frozen okra, topped, tailed, and cut into ¹/₂-inch
*   rounds*
1 habanero chile

Place all of the ingredients in a medium-sized saucepan and add 2
cups of water. Bring to a boil, then lower the heat, cover, and cook
for 20 minutes. Serve hot.

Southern Succotash

For most Americans, succcotash is the Native American dish that
combines lima beans and corn. Not so for African-Americans. Okra
succotash is one of the classic ways that the black South has with
okra and corn. Some variations add the ubiquitous seasoning piece
of smoked pork and others call for other vegetables such as lima
beans.

  This variation on the classic theme uses okra, corn, and tomatoes, and is much milder than its chile-heated cousin in the preceding recipe.

2 medium-sized onions, chopped
1 cup fresh corn kernels cut off the cob
1 tablespoon vegetable oil or bacon fat
4 ripe tomatoes, peeled, seeded, and coarsely chopped
¹/₄ pound fresh small okra pods, topped, tailed, and sliced into
*   ¹/₂-inch rounds*
Salt, freshly ground black pepper, and a pinch of sugar

Place the onions and corn kernels in a heavy saucepan with the oil
or bacon fat and sauté them until the onions become translucent.
Then add the tomatoes and the okra. Cover with water. Season with
salt, freshly ground black pepper, and a pinch of sugar and cook
over low heat for 1 hour, adding more water if necessary. Serve hot.

Corn on the Cob

New World corn arrived in Africa after the European discovery of the New World. However, it is a vegetable that African-Americans took to their hearts. Fresh, served on the cob, it is a must at many a southern barbecue if corn is in season. Slathered with butter and a pinch of salt, there's nothing to match it. Some of today's varieties, like milk and honey corn, are so sweet that you can even forgo the butter and salt.

SERVES 4

4 ears fresh corn
Salt, butter, and freshly ground black pepper, to taste

Fill a heavy stockpot with water and bring it to a boil over high heat. Shuck the corn, removing the green husk, the corn silk, and the bottom stalk. Place the cleaned corn in the boiling water and boil for 5 minutes. Remove and drain. Serve hot with butter and salt or plain.

Corn Fritters I

The Yoruba of southwestern Nigeria have traditionally made fritters and fried food in deep oil, culinary practices that predate the slave trade. These cooking methods came to the States with slaves, where they met up with other culinary traditions and with corn, the primary grain of much of the South.

African-Americans have traditionally placed much emphasis on breakfast as an important meal, and certainly to those who worked in an agricultural setting, it was, for it afforded the much-needed energy to get on with the work of the day. Today, though they may no longer work the soil, African-Americans still eat hearty breakfasts. The breakfast table may include everything from chicken and waffles to grits and ham and red-eye gravy to corn fritters and bacon. On festive occasions, there's likely to be all of the above and more. These light corn fritters are a perfect breakfast dish and can be served alone or with a breakfast meat.

Oil for deep frying
1 cup flour
1 teaspoon baking powder
2 cups whole fresh corn kernels, cut from the cob
2 eggs, separated
1/2 cup heavy cream
Salt and freshly ground black pepper, to taste
Cane or maple syrup (optional)

Preheat 3 inches of oil in a deep heavy skillet or fryer to 375 degrees. Sift the flour and baking powder into a medium-sized bowl, add the corn, and mix them together with a spoon. Place the egg yolks in a small bowl and whisk them, stir in the cream, and pour the liquids into the corn and flour mixture; season to taste. In a separate small bowl, beat the egg whites until they hold stiff peaks, and fold them into the corn mixture.

When the oil is hot, drop the fritters into the oil a few tablespoonfuls at a time. Cook them for about 4 minutes, or until golden brown, then turn them and cook on the other side until done. Drain the fritters on paper towels and serve hot with syrup.

Corn Fritters II

Fritters play a major part in the African habit of snacking and a large part in the African-American way with vegetables. Prepared from everything from legumes (as in black-eyed pea fritters) to corn to bananas, they grace the table from the appetizer course straight through dessert. These corn fritters can be served at breakfast with bacon or sausage or at lunch or dinner as a vegetable.

SERVES 4

Oil for frying
2 eggs
1/2 cup milk
1 cup sifted flour
1 teaspoon baking powder
1/2 teaspoon salt
1 teaspoon melted butter
1 1/2 cups cooked corn kernels

Preheat 3 inches of oil to 375 degrees in a deep, heavy skillet. In a medium-sized bowl, beat the eggs while drizzling in the milk. Add the flour, baking powder, salt, and melted butter. Finally, stir in the corn. Drop the batter by the spoonful into the hot oil and fry for 2 minutes, or until golden brown. Serve hot.

Creamed Corn

In my family we could never understand why my father preferred this way of eating corn to all others. Mom and I were chomping away madly on corn on the cob while dad requested that his corn be creamed. Only later in life would I learn that he was being true to the tastes of his southern youth and maintaining an African-American tradition.

Creamed corn is easy to make. The hardest part is cutting the corn off of the cob and reserving all of the succulent corn liquid that comes from each ear.

SERVES 4

6 ears fresh yellow corn
1 tablespoon sugar
¹/₂ cup light cream
1 tablespoon butter
Salt and freshly ground white pepper, to taste

Shuck the corn and remove all corn silk. Wash the ears and slice the kernels off into a bowl or a rimmed plate with a sharp knife, saving any liquid that comes from the corn. Place the corn kernels, reserved liquid, and remaining ingredients in a medium-sized saucepan and cook over low heat for 5 minutes, or until the corn is tender. Serve immediately.

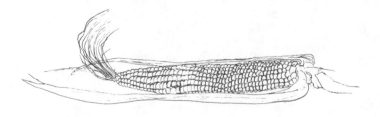

Fried Corn I

Corn means summertime to African-Americans in much the same way that fall means greens. Corn is served as succotash, mixed with okra and tomatoes, as sliced corn, and as fried corn nearly as often as it is served on the cob. There are, as with most classic African-American recipes, as many ways to prepare fried corn as there are African-American cooks. This preparation is one of the simplest and depends on the sweetest, freshest, most succulent corn. As farm cooks know, corn is best and sweetest when it is cooked just after being picked. If you don't live next door to a cornfield, head for the nearest farmers' market or roadside stand. If you can't find truly fresh corn, think about trying the following recipe, which doesn't depend as much on the sweetness of the corn.

SERVES 4

7 ears fresh corn
3 tablespoons bacon drippings
1 tablespoon flour
1 tablespoon sugar
1 cup half-and-half
Salt and freshly ground black pepper, to taste

Slice the corn off the cob in such a manner that the kernels and the juice are all retained. Heat the bacon fat in a heavy skillet. When the fat is hot, add the corn and the remaining ingredients and stir thoroughly to be sure that they are well combined. Lower the heat and cook the corn for 7 to 10 minutes. Raise the heat and brown the corn mixture slightly on the bottom. Stir to mix it well, so that the brown bits are evenly distributed throughout the corn mixture. Adjust the seasoning and serve hot.

Fried Corn II

This is a more substantial way with fried corn, calling for pork sausage, red and green bell pepper, onion, and garlic in addition to the corn. It's a good way to use corn that is not fresh enough for simpler preparations.

SERVES 6

12 ounces hot bulk pork sausage
¹/₂ cup chopped green bell pepper
¹/₂ cup chopped red bell pepper
1 large clove garlic, minced
¹/₃ cup chopped onion
2¹/₂ cups corn kernels, cut from the cob
¹/₄ teaspoon chili powder
Salt and freshly ground black pepper, to taste

Cook the pork sausage in a heavy skillet, crumbling it into pieces as it cooks. Add the bell peppers, garlic, and onion and continue to cook, stirring occasionally, until the sausage is cooked and the onion is translucent. Drain off all but 1¹/₂ tablespoons of the fat. Then add the corn and seasonings and continue to cook for an additional 5 minutes, or until the corn is thoroughly cooked. Serve hot.

Coosh Coosh

Like maquechou, coosh coosh is a Louisiana specialty. (It is sometimes spelled cush cush.) Here the corn is yellow cornmeal (unusual for the South), which is cooked over a slow fire into a mush. Again, the origin of the name is perplexing. Some say that it comes from the North African semolina dish couscous, others think that it is a Native American term, and still others relate it to West African starches and porridgelike mashes. Take your pick. The dish is delicious and is occasionally served as a breakfast treat as well.

SERVES 6 TO 8

3 tablespoons bacon drippings
4 cups yellow cornmeal
2¹/₂ cups cold water
Salt, to taste

Heat the bacon drippings in a heavy saucepan or dutch oven. In a medium-sized bowl, add the water to the cornmeal, stirring to make sure that they are well mixed. Pour the moistened cornmeal into the saucepan, cover, and lower the heat. Cook, covered, for about 40 minutes, stirring occasionally.

NOTE: Do not stir too often, as the coosh coosh should form a crisp crust on one bottom.

Maquechou

No one is really sure of the origin of this southern Louisiana specialty but it is probably one that African-Americans inherited from their Indian neighbors, as it is a variation on the traditional succotash. Indeed, some think that the name should be applied to a dish composed of corn and lima beans. Others opt for a corn, bell pepper, and tomato mixture.

The name is equally problematic. Some scholars feel that the name *maquechou* is from the French, meaning that it is a mock cabbage dish. But frankly, this just doesn't seem to make sense. Why bemoan a lack of relatively available cabbage? Others suggest that the word and the dish originated in South America and were brought to Louisiana by the Native Americans or even perhaps by the Spanish, who borrowed it from the Native Americans there. Whatever its origin, it's a treat.

SERVES 6 TO 8

¼ cup vegetable oil
1½ cups minced onion
2 cloves garlic, minced
4 cups corn kernels, cut from the cob
1 small green bell pepper, minced
1 small red bell pepper, minced
1 pound ripe tomatoes, peeled, seeded, and coarsely chopped
½ cup water
Salt and Tabasco, to taste

Heat the oil in a heavy saucepan and sauté the onion and garlic until the onion is translucent. Add the remaining ingredients and bring the maquechou to a boil over high heat. Then cover the pot, lower the heat, and continue to cook for about 5 minutes, or until the corn is tender. Serve hot.

J'ai bien mangé. J'ai bien bû. J'ai la peau du ventre
bien tendu. Merci petit Jesus.
—*West African Child's Grace*

I have eaten well. I have drunk well. The skin of my
stomach is well stretched out. Thank you little Jesus.

Mixed Greens

Greens are a direct part of African-Americans' African heritage. Dishes using leafy greens abound in the cooking of the African Atlantic world. They turn up as *couve* in Brazil, as callaloo in the Caribbean, as *sauce feuilles* in French-speaking West Africa, and simply as greens in the southern United States. The African-American twist with greens is in the manner of cooking. We cook 'em long and slow—down to the proverbial "low gravy"—(but then again that was the way all vegetables were cooked in much of the past). The real innovation is in the eating: We savor not only the greens but also their cooking liquid or "pot likker," a rich source of vitamins and iron.

SERVES 6

4 pounds mixed collard, mustard, and turnip greens
8 strips bacon
6 cups water
Salt and freshly ground black pepper, to taste
Hot sauce (optional)
Chopped onions (optional)
Vinegar (optional)

Wash the greens well, picking them over to remove any brown spots or blemishes. Drain well. Discard the discolored outer leaves and cut out the thick ribs. Tear the greens into pieces. Place the bacon strips in a large heavy saucepan and cook over medium heat until it is translucent and the bottom of the pot is coated with the rendered bacon fat. Add the greens and the water and bring to a boil over medium heat. Reduce the heat to low and continue to cook until the greens are tender, about 2 hours. Add the seasonings and serve hot.

Traditionally greens are accompanied by a hot sauce, chopped onions, and vinegar. You can also serve your own homemade Hot Sauce (page 89) or Hot Vinegar (page 91). In some parts of the South, cooks add a pinch of sugar to the greens to take away a bit of their bite.

Turnip Greens with Turnips

Samuel Clemens Floyd III was a dear friend of mine from North Carolina who taught me many things about cooking and entertaining. One of his favorite dishes was turnip greens, to which he would add small purple and white turnips as well. The greens were delicious, slow-cooked in the traditional southern manner, and the tasty tangy bites of turnip were just perfect with them.

SERVES 6

3 strips bacon
3 pounds turnip greens, with turnips (if possible)
6 small purple and white turnips, topped, tailed, and cut into
     1-inch chunks
1 cup cooked ham chunks
Pinch sugar
Hot Sauce (optional, page 89)
Hot Vinegar (optional, page 91)
Chopped onions (optional)

Cook the bacon strips in a large, heavy saucepan until the bacon has rendered all of its fat. Wash and drain the greens thoroughly. Discard any brown or yellow leaves and cut out any blemishes you may find. Tear the greens into bite-sized bits and place them in the pot with the bacon and the rendered fat. Add the turnip pieces, ham, and sugar, and cover with water. Bring the greens to a boil over high heat, then reduce the heat to low, cover, and cook, stirring occasionally, for 2 hours. Check to make sure that there is enough water, and add more if necessary. Serve hot, with the optional condiments if you like.

Quick Greens, Brazil Style

This Brazilian-inspired recipe is an example of one of the ways that new healthier versions of old foods are entering the African-American culinary lexicon. Cooked as couve, sautéed in olive oil and garlic, the traditional accompaniment to feijoada, collard greens lose none of their familiar taste. This time-saving method is perfect for those who cannot or do not eat pork.

2 pounds fresh collard greens
3 tablespoons extra-virgin olive oil
5 cloves garlic, minced, or to taste
¹/₄ cup warm water
Salt and freshly ground black pepper, to taste

Wash the collard greens thoroughly to remove any dirt or grit. Drain well. Pick over the greens, discarding any that are old and cutting out any discolored spots and the fleshy ribs. Then place the leaves in a pile, roll them into a thick cylinder, and cut them into thin strips crosswise. Fluff the cut greens into a bowl. Heat the olive oil in a heavy skillet, add the garlic, and cook until it is slightly browned. Add the greens and cook, tossing them frequently to make sure that they are coated with the olive oil and the garlic. Add the water, season, cover, and cook for 5 minutes. Remove and serve warm.

Wilted Spinach

Some days there just ain't no greens! When African-Americans moved north and greens were simply not available on some occasions (no garden plot, no nearby grocery store selling greens, or only kale or turnip greens instead of collards and mustard), there was always spinach. So it was cooked and served with a variety of hot sauces as well.

3 pounds fresh spinach (fresh leaves, please, not *the kind in plastic bags)*
2 tablespoons water
Butter to taste
Salt and freshly ground black pepper, to taste

Wash the spinach thoroughly, picking it over to remove any blemished spots and making sure that there is absolutely no grit remaining. Rinse it. Wash it again. Rinse it. Do not drain it the second time, but shake it, place it in a heavy saucepan, add the water, cover, and cook it over low heat until the spinach is tender and wilted. Add the butter, salt, and pepper and serve.

Baked Sweet Potatoes

During the period of slavery, sweet potatoes were an occasional treat for the slaves. Because the only source of heat for both warmth and cooking in most slave cabins was an open hearth, these sweet potatoes were frequently baked in the ashes of a fire. The taste of those ash-baked potatoes is approximated by baked sweet potatoes; which are candy-delicious when eaten with a pat of butter or even plain. These potatoes can be prepared when the oven is on for a roast and then placed in plastic bags, stored in the freezer, and microwaved, so they're available anytime.

SERVES 4

4 medium-sized sweet potatoes
2 tablespoons extra-virgin olive oil or other shortening
4 metal skewers

Preheat the oven to 400 degrees. Wash the sweet potatoes, pat them dry with paper towels, and grease them with the oil or shortening. Force the skewers through the potatoes. (This will conduct the heat and shorten the cooking time.) Place on a rack in the oven and bake for 1 hour. Serve hot with a pat of butter. They are a perfect accompaniment to roast or fried chicken, and can even be served for dessert with a sprinkling of brown sugar.

French-Fried Sweet Potatoes

While french fries seem to be the classic American accompaniment to almost anything, they could be quickly replaced by french-fried sweet potatoes, an African-American delicacy that is gaining widespread national acceptance. Frequently eaten in many parts of West Africa, where they go by a variety of names, these crunchy fries are slightly sweet.

SERVES 4

Oil for frying
4 medium-sized sweet potatoes

Preheat 3 inches of oil in a heavy saucepan or fryer to 375 degrees. Place the unpeeled sweet potatoes in a saucepan with water to cover and bring them to a boil. Lower the heat and allow them to simmer for about 10 minutes, or until they are fork-tender but still slightly firm. Remove them from the heat, peel them, and cut them into lengthwise strips as for french fries. Dry them well. Place the sweet potato strips a few at a time in the oil and fry for 2 or 3 minutes or until they are lightly browned. Drain them on paper towels and keep warm in a low oven. Continue the process until all of the potato strips have been fried. Serve hot.

Sweet Potato Pone

The South is noted for its baked mushes, which are called pones. The word comes from the Algonquian word *apan,* meaning baked. Traditionally, these pones are made from corn. But in some areas, sweet potatoes are also used. This sweet potato pone is a perfect substitute for candied sweet potatoes. You can also add a bit more sugar and serve it as a dessert.

SERVES 6 TO 8

3 tablespoons butter, softened
1¹/₂ pounds sweet potatoes, peeled and grated
¹/₂ teaspoon ground allspice
¹/₄ teaspoon ground cinnamon
¹/₂ teaspoon vanilla extract
Grinding of fresh nutmeg
1 teaspoon fresh lemon juice
1 tablespoon sugar
1 egg, beaten

Preheat the oven to 350 degrees. Grease an 1¹/₂-quart ovenproof dish with 1 tablespoon of the butter. Place the remaining ingredients, including the remaining butter, in a large bowl and stir until they are well mixed. Then spread the mixture into the baking pan. Bake uncovered for 30 minutes, or until a toothpick inserted into the pone comes out clean. Remove from the oven, cool, and serve in slices.

Mashed Sweet Potatoes

On the African-American table sweet potatoes are served in just about every way imaginable and in every course from appetizer right on through dessert. In this recipe they're cooked like mashed potatoes, with butter, and seasoned with a grinding of nutmeg and grated cinnamon. For a special treat you may wish to add a dash or two of dark Caribbean rum for an extra spark.

SERVES 6

5 medium-sized sweet potatoes
¹/₂ cup light cream
4 tablespoons (¹/₂ stick) butter, softened
¹/₃ cup firmly packed dark brown sugar
2 teaspoons grated cinnamon
Grindings of freshly grated nutmeg
Barbadian, Jamaican, or Haitian dark rum, to taste

Wash the unpeeled sweet potatoes and place them in a saucepan with water to cover. Bring them to a boil and then lower the heat and simmer until they are fork-tender, about 20 minutes. When the potatoes are done, remove them and allow them to cool slightly. Peel them and put them through a ricer or food mill into a large bowl. Gradually add the remaining ingredients, whipping constantly with a wire whisk until the sweet potatoes are a smooth, heavenly mixture. Serve warm.

Fried Green Tomatoes

Despite their recent popularity due to the book and movie of the same name, this traditional southern dish has long been a perfect addition to any breakfast table. Unfortunately it's only available to those who grow their own tomatoes or frequent farmers' markets, for it must be prepared from unripe green tomatoes. My father, who adored fried green tomatoes, would wait for the tomato season and literally had to be physically restrained from picking all of the tomatoes off the vines when they were green. I usually prepare them right after frying bacon, so they are fried in the drippings remaining in the skillet, but they're almost as tasty when cooked in polyunsaturated canola oil.

SERVES 4

4 large green tomatoes
¹/₄ cup flour
2 tablespoons yellow cornmeal
Salt and freshly ground black pepper, to taste
Bacon drippings or oil for frying

Wash the tomatoes and cut them into thick slices. Mix the flour, cornmeal, salt, and pepper in a small brown paper bag or a plastic bag. Heat the bacon drippings in a large, heavy skillet. Place the tomato slices in the bag and shake them gently until they are coated with the flour and cornmeal mixture.

Place the tomato slices in the skillet and fry them a few at a time, turning them often so that they do not stick and are browned on both sides. Drain the slices on paper towels, adjust seasonings, and serve hot with bacon or sausage.

Baked Tomatoes

On the African-American table, fresh vegetables always appear in their appropriate season. Sometimes they appear several times in different guises in one meal. Nowadays, with many more vegetables and fruits readily available year-round, what began as the necessity of purchasing whatever was least expensive in the market, or of harvesting what was growing in the garden, has become a hallmark of good taste.

Vine-ripened red tomatoes are one of the best tastes in the world. This simple dish can only be prepared with the freshest, ripest, firmest tomatoes. These tomatoes are usually cooked as an accompaniment to a roasted meat, and are cooked at the same time.

SERVES 6

6 firm ripe tomatoes, cored
3 tablespoons olive oil
Salt and freshly ground black pepper, to taste

Preheat the oven to 350 degrees. Place the tomatoes in a baking dish and drizzle the olive oil over them. Place them in the oven for 20 minutes. Season with salt and pepper and serve hot.

Grilled Tomatoes

Many culinary historians feel that tomatoes may have been introduced to the southern United States by slaves from Africa or from the West Indies. They were used in these two areas long before they became popular in the United States. If slaves did not introduce the tomato, they certainly savored it when they could. Tomatoes are a major ingredients in many African-American soups and stews. They are also served grilled or broiled as a vegetable accompaniment to hams and roasted meats.

SERVES 4

4 firm ripe tomatoes
Butter
4 blades chives, chopped
Salt and freshly ground black pepper, to taste

Preheat the broiler. Core the tomatoes and place them in a heat-proof dish. Dot a small amount of the butter on the top of each tomato and sprinkle it with the chopped chives, salt, and pepper. Place the tomatoes in the broiler and cook for 10 minutes, or until the tomatoes are slightly blackened on the top. Serve hot. You can add bread crumbs and a dash of any grated cheese to the tomatoes for a fancier dish.

Butter Beans

Butter beans are the achingly tender tiny versions of lima beans that are served throughout the South. They can be slow-cooked with a ham hock or a seasoning piece of smoked meat into a traditional African-American southern specialty or, if you can get fresh ones, they can be cooked with just a bit of bacon drippings (or olive oil) for taste. In this recipe, while you don't have the smoky traditional taste of the African-American South, you have the fresh, almost sweet taste of the young beans.

SERVES 4 TO 6

2 pounds fresh butter beans
1 tablespoon bacon drippings
3 scallions, minced
4 cups water
Pinch brown sugar
Salt and freshly ground black pepper, to taste

Shell the butter beans, wash them, and place them in a bowl. Heat the bacon drippings in a heavy saucepan, add the scallions, and cook until they are lightly browned. Add the remaining ingredients and cook the butter beans uncovered over medium heat for 40 minutes, or until tender. Drain and serve.

Creamed Onions

Creamed onions are a typical Thanksgiving dish on many an African-American table. In my home, it has become a family joke. It began on a Thanksgiving when my Aunt Ethel and my Uncle Richard ate at our house. Uncle Richard spent the entire dinner whining because we did not serve creamed onions. From that day onward, all anyone in my family has to say is, "Where are the creamed onions? What, no creamed onions?" to send the others into gales of laughter. So that you will never be without creamed onions, here's how to prepare them. You can use globe onions or pearl onions.

6 large globe onions
1 teaspoon salt
1 tablespoon flour
1 cup light cream
4 tablespoons (¹/₂ stick) unsalted butter
¹/₃ cup dry bread crumbs

Peel the onions and cut off the papery skin and tough first layer. Place the onions in a heavy saucepan with water to cover. Add the salt and bring to a boil; lower the heat and simmer for 30 minutes. Drain the onions and place them in a deep, ovenproof baking dish.

Preheat the oven to 350 degrees. Mix the flour and cream together and pour it over the onions. Dot the butter onto the onions and cream, reserving some for the top. Top the onions with the bread crumbs and the remaining butter. Cover with aluminum foil and bake for 30 minutes. Remove the foil and brown the top for 10 minutes. Serve hot and make your Uncle Richard happy!

Minted Green Peas

Few delicacies can match the taste of freshly shelled garden-grown green peas. Those of us who live in the North have almost forgotten that taste, but it's one of the delights of the spring season in the South. The mere thought of them brings back mental pictures of back porches and screen doors, relatives with bib aprons sitting with bowls in their laps, and the particularly satisfying pop a pea pod makes when opened.

3 cups freshly shelled garden-grown green peas (about 2¹/₄ to 2¹/₂
    pounds in the pod)
1 sprig fresh mint
¹/₂ teaspoon sugar
Salt, to taste
Butter

Place all of the ingredients except the butter in a medium-sized saucepan with a small amount of water and cook over medium heat until the peas are mouth-meltingly tender (about 5 minutes). Then serve hot with a pat of country butter. Yum!

Smothered Cabbage

Smothered cabbage was one of the standard dishes in my house and in many other African-American households. The slightly sweet taste of the cabbage mingles perfectly with the bacon fat and the result is ambrosial. Like many African-American specialties, the traditional method of preparation calls for bacon drippings as the cooking fat of preference, however, you can substitute any vegetable oil.

SERVES 6

2 tablespoons bacon drippings
2 pounds green cabbage, quartered, cored, and shredded
1 tablespoon sugar
Salt and freshly ground black pepper, to taste
¼ cup water

Place the bacon fat in a large cast-iron skillet and heat over moderately high heat for about 3 minutes, or until the fat has melted. Add the cabbage, sugar, salt, and pepper, and cook, stirring occasionally, for 10 minutes, or until the cabbage browns slightly. Stir in the water, reduce the heat, cover, and continue to cook for about 8 minutes, or until the water has evaporated and the cabbage is tender. Serve hot.

Slow-Cooked String Beans and Ham

The slow cooking and the seasoning piece of ham are what give these string beans a special African-American flavor. This is a perfect one-pot meal and a good way to use any leftover ham bones. While this is a traditional dish throughout much of the black South, South Carolina cooks like to add a tiny pinch of sugar to their beans. They say that it takes out some of the bite and gives the dish a smoother taste.

SERVES 6

1 leftover ham bone, or a bone-in piece of ham steak
2 pounds fresh string beans
6 small boiling potatoes, cleaned, peeled, and quartered
Salt, freshly ground black pepper, and hot sauce, to taste
Pinch of brown sugar (optional)

Place the ham bone or piece of ham steak in a heavy saucepan or dutch oven with water to cover and bring to a boil. Top and tail the string beans and cut them to 2-inch lengths. Add the beans to the boiling ham bone along with the remaining ingredients. Lower to a simmer and cook for 1 hour. Adjust the seasonings and serve hot with freshly made cornbread.

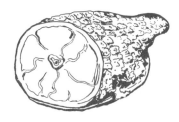

Jerusalem Artichokes

These root vegetables are a staple on many southern African-American tables. They are readily available in the South and are relatively easy to grow in some northern climates (like mine in New York). They are also sold in many large chain supermarkets as sunchokes. They're simple to cook and their slightly nutty taste makes them a perfect foil for roasted meats.

SERVES 4

1 pound Jerusalem artichokes
Salt and freshly ground black pepper, to taste
Butter (optional)

Fill a heavy saucepan with water and bring it to a boil. Wash and peel the Jerusalem artichokes, paring off any discolored or soft spots. Place them in the boiling water and cook for 20 minutes, or until fork-tender. (Cooking times will differ depending on the size and shape of the Jerusalem artichokes.) Serve hot, seasoned with salt and freshly ground black pepper. You may wish to add a pat of butter.

Rutabagas

Throughout the African Atlantic world, root vegetables have great importance. In Jamaica, they're known as ground provisions. In the States, they're simply turnips, parsnips, Jerusalem artichokes, potatoes, sweet potatoes, carrots, and, of course, rutabagas.

This is dish is a Thanksgiving tradition at my house; in fact, it's not a holiday if there aren't rutabagas. The puree is slightly sweet because the sharpness of the rutabagas is tempered with the addition of potato and the faint smoky taste of bacon drippings. This dish is perfect with pork, or, of course, turkey.

SERVES 6 TO 8

6 strips bacon
1 large (about 2 pounds) rutabaga, peeled and cut into 1-inch
   chunks
2 large baking potatoes, peeled and cut into 1-inch chunks
Pinch of sugar
Salt and freshly ground black pepper, to taste

Fry the bacon strips in a heavy saucepan until they begin to brown and the fat is rendered. Add the rutabaga pieces and water to cover. Bring the rutabaga to a boil and then lower the heat to medium and cook for 20 minutes. Add the potato pieces to the saucepan and cook for an additional 20 minutes, until the potatoes and rutabagas are very tender. Drain the vegetables and reserve the bacon. Place the vegetables in a food mill and purée into a bowl. Finely mince the bacon and add it to the bowl. Add the sugar, salt, and pepper and stir well. Transfer to a serving bowl and serve hot.

Macaroni and Cheese

Although I'd be hard-pressed to trace its African heritage, macaroni and cheese has become a classic soul food dish. It is served steaming hot from glass casserole dishes North and South at Sunday dinners and family reunions. It turns up at family feasts such as Thanksgiving and Christmas, and is even brought to bereaved households as a token of friendship during a period of mourning.

Macaroni and cheese can be prepared from almost any Cheddar-type cheese, but extra-sharp Cheddar is my cheese of preference. I've added a bit of zing here with a half a cup of freshly grated Parmesan cheese, but the classic recipe is Cheddar all the way.

SERVES 6

1¹/₂ cups medium elbow macaroni
2 tablespoons unsalted butter
2 tablespoons flour
1 cup milk
1 cup freshly grated extra-sharp Cheddar cheese
¹/₂ cup freshly grated Parmesan cheese
Salt and freshly ground black pepper, to taste
¹/₄ cup fine dry bread crumbs

Preheat the oven to 350 degrees and lightly grease a 1¹/₂-quart ovenproof baking dish. Cook the macaroni according to the package directions until tender but still firm. Drain it and place it in the greased casserole dish. Melt the butter in a small saucepan and whisk in the flour. Cook for about 2 minutes or until the mixture is thick and pasty. Gradually add the milk, whisking constantly, and cook for 7 to 8 minutes, or until the sauce has thickened. Remove the sauce from the heat and keep warm.

Combine 1 tablespoon of each cheese in a small bowl and set aside. Add the remaining Cheddar and Parmesan cheese to the white sauce and stir until smooth. (You may have to return the pan to the stove over low heat to melt the cheeses.) Season to taste. Pour the sauce over the macaroni in the casserole and stir it well to make sure that everything is well mixed. Add the bread crumbs to the reserved cheese and mix well. Sprinkle over the top of the macaroni. Bake for 35 to 40 minutes, or until hot, bubbly, and lightly browned on top. Serve hot.

◀ *Formal dances were a hallmark of urban life.*

Hominy Grits

Hominy is one of the dishes that comes to African-Americans and to southerners in general from Native Americans. The process by which it was prepared is still followed by some in the South today. Roasting ears of corn are boiled for hours with lye (or simply hickory ash from the cooking stove) until the corn softens, loses its yellow shell and kernel, and fluffs up into the hominy. This large-grain hominy is still used today by many southerners and is referred to by some black southerners as samp. The same hominy is available canned or dry in Latin American stores as white hominy. It is also used in Mexican cooking, where it is known as *pozole*.

Hominy grits are cracked pieces of hominy. Traditionally mixed with water and cooked into a thick porridge, hominy grits are one of the hallmarks of a true southern breakfast. Lye-processed hominy came into being only in the nineteenth century. Before that there were simply grits. Confusion about their name has arisen from the fact that hominy grits are also simply called grits. However, grits is simply the name for the size and texture of the corn. During the period of slavery, African-Americans pounded dried corn in a mortar, then sieved it. The coarsest pieces were bran, and were fed to the animals; the next coarsest were the grits; and the finest were cornmeal. The grits were slow-cooked with a seasoning piece of fatback and taste much like today's hominy grits.

In much of the South, hominy grits are traditionally served with ham and red-eye gravy. In New Orleans they're served with veal grillades. In other places they come to the table with bacon or sausage. Nowadays, they find themselves transformed into fancy dishes like grits cheese soufflé and cheese grits, but for many African-Americans the best way is the simplest one, just plain grits.

There are two basic methods to cooking grits, the slow-cooked one, which adds more and more liquid (either water or milk) and cooks them until they are a creamy mixture, and the quicker one given here, which leaves the grits with a bit of a grainy consistency Today, instant grits are also available; they should be prepared according to package directions. I enjoy grits and have even served instant ones. However, after receiving a gift of stone-ground white hominy grits from Hoppin' John Taylor, in South Carolina, I've become a convert to the delicious, slightly nutty-tasting, grainy stone-ground grits that are available via mail order from his Charleston, South Carolina shop. (See mail order sources, page 271.)

SERVES 4 TO 6

3½ cups water
1¾ cups grits
Salt and freshly ground black pepper, to taste
3 tablespoons butter

Place the water in a large, heavy saucepan and bring it to a rolling boil. Gradually pour in the grits, slowly stirring the mixture with a wooden spoon until it thickens. Lower the heat so that the grits are simmering and continue to cook for 20 minutes, stirring occasionally so that they do not stick. Season to taste, add the butter, and serve hot.

Cheese Grits

The most authentic version of cheese grits should probably use Velveeta or processed American cheese. This version, however, calls for the addition of one cup of grated extra-sharp Cheddar cheese to the cooking grits.

SERVES 4

1 recipe Hominy Grits (preceding recipe)
1 cup grated extra-sharp Cheddar cheese

Prepare the grits according to the recipe for hominy grits. When the grits have become a thick porridge, but before they are completely cooked, pour in the grated Cheddar cheese and continue to stir until the cheese has melted into the grits. Continue to cook until the grits are done. Serve hot.

Fried Grits

There are never any leftovers in any African-American cook's kitchen. Everything is transformed into something else, a bit different, but just as delicious. Here, leftover grits are formed into cakes or cut into strips and fried in hot fat (either bacon fat, after cooking the breakfast bacon) or any vegetable oil. If you are using a grainier grit (like Hoppin' John's grits), be careful to use a cover, as the grits may pop like popcorn.

SERVES 4

2 cups leftover cooked hominy grits
2 tablespoons fat or vegetable oil

Press the congealed grits into a ½-inch slab and cut it into strips 1 inch wide and about 2 inches long. Alternatively, press the grits into small patties. Heat the fat in a heavy skillet, and when it is hot, put the grits strips or patties in the skillet. Fry until they are lightly browned at the edges. Serve hot with syrup or breakfast meats.

Pepper-Cheese Grits Soufflé

The history of African-American cooking didn't stop with the Great Migration. No indeed! As folks moved north they became acquainted with new tastes and added other seasonings and techniques to their cooking. The late years of the nineteenth century and the early years of the twentieth century brought increasing sophistication to African-American southerners and the ability to indulge in some of the dishes that before Emancipation had only been served on the master's table.

The later half of the twentieth century saw African-Americans develop into some of the most innovative chefs in the country. This recipe is a culinary history of African-Americans in itself, an amalgam of Native American hominy grits, contemporary Monterey Jack pepper cheese, Africa's taste for the hot, and France's soufflé. I've cheated a little and used instant hominy grits in this recipe.

SERVES 4

¾ cup instant hominy grits
½ cup grated jalapeño Monterey Jack cheese
3 eggs, separated
2 tablespoons salted butter
⅛ teaspoon cream of tartar

Preheat the oven to 400 degrees. Prepare the grits according to the directions on the package. When the grits are cooked, remove them from the heat and beat in the cheese, egg yolks, and butter. Allow the mixture to cool slightly. Whisk the whites until they are foamy. Add the cream of tartar and continue to whisk until the whites form stiff peaks. Fold the whites into the grits and cheese mixture and pour the mixture into a well-greased 1½-quart soufflé dish. Bake for 30 minutes, or until the soufflé has risen and browned on the top. Serve immediately.

Baked Pineapple

This is a dish that comes to the African-American table from Brazil. It is magnificently simple and is a perfect accompaniment for a baked country ham.

SERVES 4

1 ripe medium-sized pineapple

Preheat the oven to 350 degrees. Remove the leafy top from the pineapple and place the pineapple in the oven on a sheet of aluminum foil. Bake for 1 hour, or until it is fork-tender. Remove from the oven and allow it to cool for a few minutes. Slice the pineapple into quarters, peel it, core it, and serve it warm.

Broiled Peaches

Although these might seem to be more of a garnish than a true vegetable dish, they are frequently served as vegetables in parts of Georgia and other areas of the South where a peach tree in the back yard is a must for good living. These broiled peaches are a perfect foil for baked hams and pork and chicken dishes. They can be prepared from fresh peaches that have been skinned and pitted or from canned peach halves.

SERVES 6

6 firm ripe peaches, peeled and pitted, or a dozen cling peach
  halves
2 tablespoons butter
2 tablespoons light brown sugar
1 teaspoon ground cinnamon
1 teaspoon freshly grated nutmeg
$1/4$ teaspoon freshly ground cloves

Preheat the broiler. Place the peach halves, rounded sides down, in a broilerproof baking dish. Dot a small bit of butter in each peach half. Mix the brown sugar, cinnamon, nutmeg, and cloves together in a custard cup and sprinkle a bit of the mixture on each peach half. Place the dish in the broiler and cook until the peach halves are lightly browned on top. Serve hot.

Fried Apples

When it's apple time, this quintessentially American fruit appears in many guises on African-American tables. Traditionally, fried apples are an accompaniment to grits and pork sausage for a Sunday breakfast, but they are also delicious with roast fresh ham, roast pork, or even baked ham. If cooked for breakfast, they are fried in the drippings from the sausage or bacon and slightly caramelized with a bit of cinnamon sugar.

SERVES 4

6 hard-ripe McIntosh apples
2 tablespoons bacon drippings
1 tablespoon water
2 teaspoons sugar
$1/2$ teaspoon ground cinnamon

Core the apples and slice them, but do not peel them. Heat the bacon drippings in a heavy cast-iron skillet. When the drippings are hot but not smoking, add the sliced apples and the water. Cover, lower the heat, and cook until the apples are soft, about 10 minutes. When the apples are tender, sprinkle them with a mixture of the sugar and cinnamon and serve warm with bacon and/or sausage, and grits. This dish makes it worth getting up for breakfast.

Main Dishes

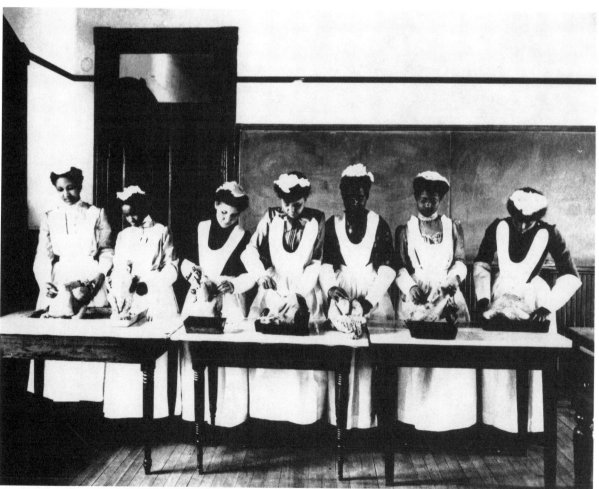

Turkeys always require stuffing.

Hunting possum was hard work in 1902.

"I THOUGHT ALL MEN COULD COOK!"

I was born in Birmingham, Alabama, but I grew up in Los Angeles. My maternal grandfather worked on the railroads as a porter. My paternal grandfather worked on the railroad, too. Basically, though, I come from two different culinary traditions. They were both large cooking families." So says Carla Fitzgerald, a former executive in marketing who has trained as a chef at Peter Kump's in Manhattan.

"My mother's family was more pristine in their foods. They'd make wonderful breads and would can preserves from fresh fruits. On my mother's side of the family, there were specific mealtimes and everyone sat down together. There were things like brains and scrambled eggs, oysters in a jar on Fridays, and my mother's wonderful cornbread. I remember as a child I wanted my wedding cake to be made of cornbread. It was that good.

"My father's family would put a neckbone in a pot with some peas and it would be something tasty. At my grandma's on my father's side, during the week there were too many different shifts so folks would see what was on the stove and then serve a plate and eat. It was informal, but warm and wonderful.

"I thought all men could cook," Carla recalls. "I remember my father in the kitchen cooking and singing. My father had at some point worked in a professional kitchen in some segregated spot in the South. A lot of the things that he did in the kitchen made standard kitchen sense even today after my training. I'll never forget the first demonstration we had of making a roux at cooking school—I could see my father at the stove cooking. Throughout my childhood, my mom made great potato salad and a great pound cake; otherwise, she stepped back in the kitchen because my father loved it so much."

"He didn't bake, but he could barbecue. Just before he died over twenty years ago, he bought a cast-iron barbecue grill that's about four feet wide, with all of the implements that I still use. I'm smoking a salmon over it tomorrow. As a child I never had barbecue from a stand because I thought you were supposed to go out into the backyard and do it yourself.

"There's a special taste to my family's food. It's a taste of love and warmth and the ingredients that you can't always find in California. Whenever I leave to go back home from the South, the family joke goes, 'Cousin Carla's upstairs packing her groceries.' I do carry them home with me; it helps me to recapture the tastes from my past and the memories that go with them."

Possum

Perhaps the most evocative of all of the African-American main dishes from the period of enslavement, possum (short for opossum) is one that has rarely ever been tasted by many urban folk. The meat is quite succulent and indeed many a nineteenth-century stereotype hinged on the assertion that African-Americans, though offered other meats, preferred possum. Possum were the creatures most likely to be abroad after dark when slaves were able to go hunting, so they were a frequent catch. Possum are best caught alive and kept in a pen for several days. They are fed on a diet of bread and spices to clean their systems out and make them tastier.

This recipe simply calls for a ready-to-cook possum. Where you get it is up to you and your hunter or butcher.

SERVES 2

1 ($^1/_2$- to 2-pound) ready-to-cook possum
1 tablespoon salt
$1^1/_2$ teaspoons freshly ground black pepper
Cayenne pepper or hot sauce, to taste
2 medium-sized sweet potatoes
$^1/_3$ cup water
4 tablespoons ($^1/_2$ stick) unsalted butter, melted

Preheat the oven to 350 degrees. Wash the possum thoroughly inside and out and trim off any excess fat. Prepare a mixture of the salt, black pepper, and cayenne pepper and rub half of it in the inner cavity of the possum. Truss the possum and tie its legs together with heavy thread. Place it in an ovenproof dish.

Scrub the sweet potatoes well and arrrange them next to the possum in the dish. Pour the water over the possum and the sweet potatoes, brush them with melted butter, and rub the remaining salt mixture on them. Cover the dish and bake for 1 hour, or until the potatoes are done and the meat is tender. Then remove the cover and continue to cook, basting frequently, until the possum is browned. Serve hot.

Dear Lord, thank you for this food that we are about to receive to strengthen and nourish our bodies, for Christ our Redeemer's sake. Amen.

Rabbit Stew

My Uncle Bill, who was also my godfather, had worked as a cook for many years. In fact, he and his brother John had brought their entire family up from the South, including my father, their younger brother, with their earnings as cooks. It was at his home that I first tasted rabbit. I, like most others, was tempted with the same lie: "It tastes just like chicken." It didn't, but it was delicious. Little did I know then that rabbit was frequently eaten by African-Americans in the South, because it was something that they could catch in the wild and even raise, if there was time. You can get fresh rabbit at a willing butcher, or you may find it frozen at a well-stocked super-market.

SERVES 6

2 medium-sized rabbits, cleaned and dressed
8 cups water
1¹/₂ tablespoons salt
2 teaspoons freshly ground black pepper
2 medium-sized onions, coarsely chopped
1¹/₂ cups cooked corn
12 small new potatoes
2 medium-sized tomatoes, peeled, seeded, and coarsely chopped
2 tablespoons butter
2 tablespoons flour

Wash the rabbits thoroughly, cut them into serving-size pieces, and place the pieces in a heavy stockpot with the water. Add the salt, pepper, and onions and bring to a boil, then lower the heat, cover, and simmer over low heat for 1 hour. Add the corn, potatoes, and tomatoes and continue to cook for 30 minutes, stirring occasionally so that the stew doesn't stick.

In a small saucepan, melt the butter and prepare a roux by mixing the butter and the flour into a paste and cooking it, stirring constantly until it is light brown. Add ¹/₂ cup of the cooking liquid to the paste and stir it well to make sure that there are no lumps, then pour it back into the stew, stirring to make sure that the liquid is well mixed. Continue to cook for 10 minutes, stirring occasionally, until the stew has thickened. Serve hot.

Brunswick Stew

Georgia, North Carolina, and Virginia all claim to be the home of Brunswick stew. Historians tend to believe that the dish originated in Brunswick County, Virginia; some recipes date as far back as the early 1800s. It's one of those Southern one-pot meals that were eaten by poor whites and African-Americans as well, but the use of okra is a hint that it may have its origin in the soupy stews served in West Africa. Today's African-American Brunswick stews are slightly more savory with hot sauce than their white counterparts. Traditionally they are prepared from whatever was on hand and more frequently than not from wild game such as possum, squirrel, and rabbit. Most of the Brunswick stews that find their way to our tables today usually have chicken as the main meat.

SERVES 6 TO 8

1 (3- to 3$^{1}/_{2}$-pound) chicken, cut into serving pieces, including the giblets
$^{1}/_{4}$ pound lean salt pork, cut into $^{1}/_{2}$-inch pieces
3$^{1}/_{2}$ cups water
$^{1}/_{4}$ teaspoon freshly ground black pepper
$^{1}/_{8}$ teaspoon cayenne pepper or hot sauce, to taste
1 pound ripe tomatoes, peeled and coarsely chopped
2 cups corn kernels
1$^{1}/_{2}$ cups cubed white potato
2 stalks celery, including the leafy green parts, minced
1 medium-sized onion, chopped
1 cup fresh lima beans
1 cup okra slices
2 tablespoons flour

Clean the chicken, removing any excess fat. Place the chicken and giblets, the salt pork, 3 cups of water, the black pepper, and the cayenne pepper or hot sauce in a heavy saucepan or dutch oven and bring to a boil. Lower the heat and simmer for 45 minutes, or until the chicken is tender.

Skim the fat from the chicken broth. Remove the chicken from the broth, strip it of skin and bones, and return the meat to the broth. Add the vegetables and simmer for 30 minutes. When the cooking time is almost up, adjust the seasonings. Then, mix the flour and $^{1}/_{2}$ cup cold water together and pour it into the stew. Bring the stew up to boiling, stirring constantly. Cook for 2 to 3 additional minutes, or until the sauce has thickened slightly. Serve hot.

Fresh Ham
with Peach-Sage Marinade

Fresh ham is a typical southern black dish. It is actually a pork roast from the pig's hind leg, usually a portion of the entire leg, but for special occasions, the whole hind leg.

During peach season in the Deep South, the peaches are so abundant that creative cooks come up with all sorts of ways to use them at all stages of ripeness from rock-hard to overripe. This peach-sage marinade is simply another way of seeing to it that nothing goes to waste, using overripe peaches to create the pulpy marinade that seasons the pork.

SERVES 10 TO 15

2 overripe peaches, cored, peeled, and cut into 1-inch chunks
1 tablespoon light flavored vegetable oil
2 teaspoons salt
1 teaspoon crumbled dried sage
Dash of freshly grated nutmeg
1 teaspoon poultry seasoning
1 (7½-pound) bone-in butt-end fresh ham, rind removed

Preheat the oven to 400 degrees. Place the peach chunks, oil, salt, sage, nutmeg, and poultry seasoning in a food processor and pulse until you have a paste. Place the ham in a roasting pan and slather peach paste all over it, coating it well.

Place the ham in the oven and cook for 15 minutes. Reduce the heat to 325 and continue to cook the ham for 23 minutes per pound. If the glaze begins to burn, cover the ham lightly with aluminum foil and continue to cook. (If you are using a meat thermometer, the internal temperature should be between 165 and 170 degrees.) Remove the ham, place it on a serving platter, and allow it to rest for 15 minutes, then carve it into thin slices and serve it with Peach Chutney (page 85).

Baked Ham

The classic recipe for baked ham requires a Smithfield ham or one of the other hams that must be soaked and boiled to remove the salt, or scrubbed to remove the mold. However, this variation using a supermarket ham will do just nicely, thank you. Leftover ham can be sliced for sandwiches, ham bits can be chopped up into omelets or into deviled ham spread, and the ham bone itself can be used to season collard greens, in black-eyed pea soup, in black-eyed peas, or any number of other dishes where a touch of smoked meat adds the southern "je ne sais quoi."

SERVES 8 TO 10

1 (5-pound) precooked bone-in smoked ham
20 whole cloves or more
4 ripe peaches
1 cup fresh orange juice
$1/4$ cup firmly packed dark brown sugar
2 tablespoons Dijon mustard

Preheat the oven to 350 degrees. Cut the skin off the ham. (It can be used as seasoning in other recipes.) With a sharp knife, score the ham fat into squares and place a clove in each square. Peel 3 of the peaches, place them in a food processor, and pulse until you have a thick paste. Place the peach pulp, orange juice, brown sugar, and mustard in a small bowl and mix well. Coat the ham with $1/2$ of the mixture and place it in the oven.

Bake the ham without basting for $1^1/_2$ hours. Remove the ham from the oven. Slice the remaining peach and place the slices on the ham, securing them with toothpicks. Slather the remaining glaze on the ham and return it to the oven for an additional 30 minutes. Slice and serve hot. This ham is delicious when accompanied by Peach Chutney (page 85).

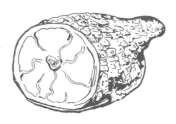

Quick Pork and Greens

This is a variation on the traditional dish of collard greens and pork. I developed it one evening when I discovered that I had unexpected guests for supper, and three pounds of collard greens and two pork chops with which to feed four people. It borrows from Brazil the method of preparing the greens and from West Africa and the American South in the proportion of vegetables to meat. My guests were pleased, and I think you will be too.

SERVES 6

3 pounds fresh collard greens, washed and picked over
¼ cup extra-virgin olive oil
6 cloves garlic, or to taste
¼ cup water
3 loin pork chops or ⅓ pound pork loin
2 tablespoons cornmeal
2 teaspoons lemon pepper
2 tablespoons flour
1 teaspoon poultry seasoning
Salt, to taste

Wash the greens thoroughly, drain, and remove the thick central rib from each leaf. Cut away any blemished spots and discard any discolored leaves. Then roll the greens into bunches and cut them crosswise into thin strips about ¼-inch wide. Set aside. Meanwhile, heat 2 tablespoons of the olive oil in a large, heavy skillet. When the oil is hot, brown the garlic and add the greens, tossing them to make sure that they are cooking evenly. Add ¼ cup water, cover, lower the heat, and continue to cook for 5 minutes, stirring occasionally.

Bone the pork chops and cut the meat into ½-inch cubes. (If using pork loin, cut the meat into ½-inch cubes.) Place the pork cubes and the remaining ingredients in a plastic bag and toss the cubed meat in the bag until it is well covered with the mixture. Heat the remaining 2 tablespoons olive oil in a separate skillet. Add the pork cubes and cook them, stirring occasionally to avoid sticking, for 5 minutes, or until they are cooked through but not tough.

When ready to serve, mix the pork pieces in with the greens and serve with black beans and rice. There should be a cruet of Hot Vinegar (page 91) on the table for those who like their food a bit spicy.

Pig's Feet

Pig's feet have long been a part of the slave legacy that lives in African-American foods. J. D. Suggs, a Mississippi man transplanted to Calvin, Michigan, told a "Master and John" story to folklorist Richard M. Dorson that explains that on hog killing day, the slave in charge of the killing was frequently given the head, feet, ears, and innards, while the master took the choice cuts, giving rise to the slaves' desire to live "higher on the hog."

Nonetheless, pig's feet have become a part of the African-American culinary tradition. Each sticky little bone is savored with hot vinegar or hot sauce. The traditional accompaniment to pig's feet is a hearty potato salad, but some families (like mine) prefer a version of hot potato salad prepared with bits of bacon and sweetened vinegar. These pig's feet are not like the famous grilled ones formerly served in Les Halles in Paris; these are boiled, and though delicious, they are, perhaps, an acquired taste.

SERVES 4 TO 6

6 to 8 whole pig's feet, split
2 bay leaves
6 peppercorns, cracked
¼ cup cider vinegar
Hot Sauce (page 89) or Hot Vinegar (page 91) for serving

With a sharp knife, scrape the pig's feet to remove all hair. (Recalcitrant hairs should be removed by singeing or by cutting off that piece of skin.) Place the pig's feet in a large stockpot, cover with water, and bring to a boil. Allow the feet to boil for 2 to 3 minutes, then pour off the water and the scum that has accumulated. Rinse the feet and the pot. Replace the feet in the pot and cover them with water again. Add the bay leaves, peppercorns, and cider vinegar. Bring the water to a boil, then lower the heat and cook for 2½ to 3 hours, or until the meat begins to fall off the bones. Remove the pig's feet, drain them, place them on a platter, and serve hot with the hot sauce and hot vinegar.

Chitterlings/Chitlins

No African-American cookbook would be complete without a recipe for chitterlings, or chitlins, as they're more commonly called. This dish of innards is a controversial mainstay of African-American cuisine. Some poeple dote on them while others leave the house (and even the neighborhood) while they are cooking, driven away by their earthy, pungent odor. Some folk are so ambivalent that they'll eat them only if they haven't been around while they were cooking. For those of you who haven't encountered them before, chitlins are the small intestines of a pig, and they are deceptively easy to prepare. They must be scrupulously scrubbed. The trick with chitlins is in the cleaning, *not* in the cooking; they're the ultimate test of confidence in the cleanliness of a kitchen. More than one friendship ended when someone refused to eat chitlins at another's house. Chitlins are available in supermarkets in African-American neighborhoods, especially during the holiday season, and can be ordered from butchers. Just remember, no matter how much the bucket (gutbucket—get it?) they're packed in says they're precleaned, don't believe it. Scrub, *scrub*, SCRUB!

SERVES 4 TO 6

5 pounds frozen chitterlings, thawed
2 large onions, coarsely chopped
2 bay leaves
2 teaspoons Hot Sauce (page 89)
2 scallions, including the green tops, chopped
1 teaspoon minced parsley
Salt and freshly ground black pepper, to taste
1 quart water

With a small, soft brush, clean each and every inch, wrinkle, and fold of the chitterlings thoroughly. Rinse them in several changes of water. Cut the chitterlings into pieces about 1½ inches in length. Then place all of the ingredients in a large stockpot, cover, and simmer over low heat for 2½ to 3 hours, or until the chitterlings are tender. Remove and serve hot with additional homemade hot sauce. If there are leftovers, they can be batter-dipped and deep-fried the next day.

Smothered Pork Chops

Slowly cooked meats are standbys at African-American dinners throughout the country. This undoubtedly harks back to the time when blacks could only afford the cheaper, tougher cuts of meat and had to slow-cook them to desired tenderness. Current nutritional information tells us that this may have been wiser than we thought. The less tender cuts of meat have less fat, making them, in many cases, healthier. The only thing that must be done to some of the old traditional recipes to update them is to shorten the cooking time a bit. Who said the old folks didn't know anything?

Smothered pork chops are usually served with rice, so that the sauce from the chops can become the gravy for the rice. The sauce is frequently prepared from ketchup. In this case, however, the sauce is made from ripe tomatoes and spices and is slow-cooked along with the chops themselves.

SERVES 6

6 (1-inch-thick) center-cut pork chops
3 tablespoons bacon drippings
1 lemon, thinly sliced
2 medium-sized onions, thinly sliced
1 small green bell pepper, cored and sliced into rings
1 small red bell pepper, cored and sliced into rings
4 large ripe tomatoes, peeled, seeded, and coarsely chopped
1 cup water
2 tablespoons distilled white vinegar
Pinch of ground clove
Pinch of ground allspice
Pinch of ground cinnamon
Pinch of celery seed
Pinch of cayenne pepper
2 tablespoons sugar
Salt and freshly ground black pepper, to taste

In a heavy skillet, brown the pork chops in the bacon drippings. Add the lemon and the onion and bell pepper slices, and continue to sauté. In a small bowl mix the tomatoes, water, vinegar, spices, sugar, salt, and pepper until they are a thick sauce and pour over the pork chops. Cover the skillet and simmer the pork chops over medium heat for 45 minutes, or until they are tender and the tomato mixture has turned into a thick, gravylike sauce.

Breaded Pork Chops

Sir Pork has marked African-American lives in multiple ways in the New World, and even those of us who revile him today must admit that he had a lot to do with our survival and with the survival of all Old World peoples in the New World. Up until the middle of the nineteenth century, pork was the most readily available, if not the preferred meat, of the entire country.

SERVES 6

6 loin pork chops
¹/₃ cup flour
¹/₃ cup yellow cornmeal
Salt and freshly ground black pepper
6 tablespoons vegetable oil

Wash the pork chops and pat them dry. Place the flour, cornmeal, salt, and pepper in a brown paper bag. Add the pork chops a few at a time and shake well until they are coated with the mixture.

Heat half of the oil in a heavy skillet. When it is hot, add 3 of the pork chops. Cook over medium heat for approximately 3 to 5 minutes on each side, depending on thickness turning once. When they are done, keep the first chops warm while frying the second batch in the remaining oil. Serve hot.

Ham with Red-Eye Gravy

Many an African-American southerner still wakes up on Sunday morning hoping for a breakfast of ham and red-eye gravy complete with grits and hot biscuits. This was once considered a particular treat and living very high on the hog indeed.

SERVES 2

2 ham steaks, each about ¹/₄ inch thick
1 cup milk
Bacon fat for frying
1 cup strong black coffee
Freshly ground black pepper, to taste

The night before, trim the ham steaks, place them in a dish with the milk, cover with plastic wrap, and allow them to soak overnight in the refrigerator. The following morning, heat the bacon fat in a large skillet, drain the ham and discard the milk, add the ham steaks, and fry them over medium heat until they are evenly browned on each side. Remove the steaks and keep them warm. Add the coffee to the skillet and stir it well, scraping up whatever ham bits remain. Season to taste and bring the gravy to a boil. Stir the gravy again and pour it over the ham steaks. Serve hot.

Fast, Cheatin' Barbecue

Now, I know that everyone expects an African-American cookbook to have at least one recipe for barbecue in it. I, however, feel differently. No, I'm not trying to deny the immense contribution made by African-American "cuers" around the country. Rather, I feel that the subject is so vast and so important that it deserves a book of its own. The regionalisms of African-American barbecue, its origins, and its present state are fascinating. To attempt to capture them in a recipe or two would be sheer folly, because African-American pit masters have their secrets that simply cannot be reproduced in most home kitchens. They deserve their respect and their say.

With all due respect to them, then, this is a fast, cheatin' recipe that can be whipped out when you're dying for barbecue in a city that offers scant pickin's. It involves leftover roast pork and a bottle of Ken Davis barbecue sauce (see mail-order sources).

SERVES 1 IN SECRET

¹/₃ pound pulled leftover roast pork
1 teaspoon vegetable oil or bacon drippings
¹/₄ cup Ken Davis barbecue sauce

Place the roast pork in a heavy skillet with the oil. Cook until warm. Then drizzle the barbecue sauce over the pork and continue to cook until the sauce and pork pieces are well mixed and heated through, about 2 minutes. Serve hot and dream of real southern barbecue as you eat the next-best thing.

Neckbones

Neckbones were one of my father's favorite dishes. I remember very little about them except not liking them. My father, however, could not get enough of them. He liked his neckbones cooked with potatoes into a type of stew. As with most of the dishes that my father preferred, this is one that harks back to the rural South and to times when the neckbones of an animal were among the few things that most African-Americans had to eat.

SERVES 4 TO 6

4 pounds neckbones
Salt and cayenne pepper, to taste
4 quarts water
5 black peppercorns, cracked
1 bay leaf
1 stalk celery, coarsely chopped
4 large white potatoes, peeled and cut into quarters

Season the neckbones by rubbing them with a mixture of salt and cayenne pepper. Place the neckbones in a large heavy stockpot and cover them with the water. Add the peppercorns, bay leaf, and celery and simmer for 2 hours. Add the potatoes, adjust the seasonings, and continue to cook for an additional 30 minutes, or until the potatoes are fork-tender. Serve hot with cornbread.

Fried Baloney

When an all-purpose luncheon meat like baloney meets up with breakfast-loving African-Americans, it becomes a substitute for bacon. Baloney (no, if we're eating this, we aren't fancy enough to call it bologna) is a staple in many African-American households. It's used in luncheon sandwiches, cut into chunks, or speared on a toothpick with an olive and passed as an hors d'oeuvre at more than one "fancy" party. It has even turned up in one of my all-time favorite "reading" recipes (I shudder to think how it *tastes*) in a variation on beef Wellington called baloney Wellington . . . prepared with biscuit dough, naturally.

2 tablespoons bacon drippings or other oil
1 pound pork baloney, sliced medium-thick

Heat the bacon drippings in a heavy skillet. Peel the casing off the baloney and make a small cut from the outside to the center of each piece so the slices don't puff up too much. Place the baloney slices in the skillet and cook, turning once, until they are lightly browned. Cooking times will vary with the brand of baloney and thickness of the slice. Serve hot with fried cornbread and eggs.

Roast Leg of Lamb

Lamb was certainly not a traditional dish in most African-American households. However, lamb was and is often eaten in Muslim Africa, and in the mid-nineteenth century, as many African-Americans went to work in the dining cars of the railroads that crisscrossed the country, they brought back to their homes the dining habits of the wider world.

I remember serving a variation of this dish to some friends of my mother and having them wax lyrical. One spoke of his father, who had worked on the railroads and had taught him to slice lamb for maximum tenderness lengthwise parallel to the bone. His technique only enhanced the taste of the lamb.

SERVES 8 TO 10

1 (5- to 6-pound) leg of lamb
3 cloves garlic, slivered
½ cup white wine
8 tablespoons Lamb Rub (page 96)

Preheat the oven to 450 degrees. Place the lamb in a roasting pan, remove all excess fat, and pierce the lamb skin with 15 or so small incisions. Insert the garlic slivers in the slits. Pour the wine over the lamb and rub it in. Put the Lamb Rub ingredients in a spice grinder and grind until they are well mixed. Pat the dry ingredients over the lamb, making sure that the surface is well covered.

Place the lamb in the oven and roast for 15 minutes, then lower the heat to 350 and continue to roast for 1 hour and 5 minutes longer, or until the internal temperature registers 140 degrees for rare, 150 degrees for medium, 160 degrees for well-done. Serve hot. Cooking times will vary according to the shape of the lamb and the heat of your oven, but the lamb should be slightly pink and very tender. Serve it with one of the chutneys on pages 85–87.

Cowboy Stew

This recipe was given to me by Diane Randolph, a New York schoolteacher who attended a lecture that I gave at the Schomburg Center for Research in Black Culture in New York City. She said that it was a family recipe from South Texas, where one of her forbears had been one of the famous black cowboys. Anything that was on hand simply went into the pot, which was placed on the back of the stove and allowed to simmer for the day while the cowboys were out with the cattle. Its diverse ingredients have also earned it the nickname son-of-a-gun stew.

The stew is typically prepared from the innards after a steer has been slaughtered. This hearty, rich stew is definitely an acquired taste (boiled heart, marrow, and kidney are not for everyone!), but it speaks eloquently of the sustaining foods eaten by those men who are some of the West's unknown heroes. I have added the tomatoes to give the traditional stew a bit of color.

SERVES 6

1 beef heart, cut into 1-inch pieces
1 beef kidney, cut into 1-inch pieces v
1 pound marrow bones, sawed into 2-inch pieces
3 medium-sized onions, cut into quarters
3 large white potatoes, peeled and coarsely chopped
6 mild green chiles, cut into rounds
1 hot habanero chile, or to taste
12 cherry tomatoes
Salt and freshly ground black pepper, to taste

Prepare the meat by pulling off any membranes and fatty pieces. Then wash the meat and bones thoroughly. Place them in a heavy stockpot and add water to cover. Bring the meat and bones to a boil, lower the heat, and cook for 15 minutes. Pour off the water and any scum that may have accumulated. Return the meat and bones to the stockpot, add water to cover, add the vegetables and seasonings, and cook for 30 minutes. Add water to cover and cook over low heat for 2 hours. Serve hot with cornbread.

Gospel Bird

Chicken—served stewed, roasted, fried, and baked—has been the traditional Sunday dish in southern African-American households for more than two centuries. Southern fried chicken has its roots in West African foodways and was a favorite in the slaves' kitchens, but roast chicken is a favorite in many households as well. Long before African-Americans had ovens, they were spit-roasting chickens in front of the flames of the fireplaces in their cabins.

SERVES 4 TO 6

1 (3½-pound) roasting chicken
3 tablespoons butter
1 tablespoon fresh lemon juice
1 teaspoon salt
2 teaspoons Bell's poultry seasoning
1 teaspoon freshly ground black pepper
1 large onion

Preheat the oven to 450 degrees. Remove the giblets from the chicken and clean it thoroughly inside and out. Heat 2 tablespoons of the butter in a small saucepan and mix it with the lemon juice and seasonings. Peel the onion and roll it in the butter and seasoning mixture; place it in the chicken's cavity. Rub the remaining mixture on the chicken. Cut the remaining 1 tablespoon of butter into bits, gently lift the chicken skin with your fingers, and place the butter bits under the breast skin of the chicken.

Place the chicken in the oven and roast for 10 minutes. Then lower the heat to 400 degrees and continue to roast for 1 hour longer. Serve hot. (The onion may be removed from the chicken and a slice served to each diner.)

Iron-Skillet Fried Chicken

No southern African-American main dish is as evocative as fried chicken. It turns up everywhere, from country suppers to breakfast. It helped hungry travelers on their way in the days of segregation, when no self-respecting African-Americans would hit the road without a shoebox full of fried chicken and deviled eggs to sustain them. It appears at church suppers and at after-hours joints, nourishing the Sunday "saved" and Saturday night "heathen" as well. By now, everyone knows that the best fried chicken is prepared in a heavy cast-iron skillet, but there are a few more flourishes that can be added. For the truest flavor, the chicken should really be fried in bacon drippings and drained on brown paper. Seasonings should be kept simple—salt, freshly ground black pepper, poultry seasoning, and perhaps a bit of cornmeal added to the dipping flour for crunch. Some folk insist on garlic powder or garlic salt, but for me, this is one of those classics in which less is best.

SERVES 4 TO 6

1 (2½- to 3-pound) frying chicken, cut into pieces
Bacon fat and lard for frying
½ cup flour
½ cup yellow cornmeal
1 tablespoon Bell's poultry seasoning
Salt and freshly ground black pepper, to taste

Wash the chicken parts thoroughly and dry them on paper towels. Heat the fat to 380 degrees in a heavy cast-iron skillet. Place the flour, cornmeal, and seasonings in a brown paper bag. Add the chicken pieces, a few at a time, and shake well to ensure that each piece is coated with the seasoned flour.

Put the chicken pieces in the frying pan and fry uncovered for 20 to 25 minutes, turning occasionally to make sure that each side is golden brown. Remove the chicken pieces and drain them on pieces of brown paper bag. Serve hot.

Gravy for Fried Chicken

Gravy is considered a necessity by many African-Americans. It is ladled over mounds of mashed potatoes or rice and sopped up by dozens of biscuits and cornbread pieces at many meals. This milk gravy is from the Virginia area and is the perfect partner for the biscuits or the rice that are traditionally served with fried chicken.

YIELDS
APPROXIMATELY
1½ CUPS

2 tablespoons pan drippings from fried chicken
3 tablespoons flour
1½ cups milk
Salt and freshly ground black pepper, to taste

After frying the chicken, pour off all but 2 tablespoons of the remaining fat, retaining all of the crunchy brown bits. Then, over low heat, add the flour and stir it evenly into the drippings with a wooden spoon, scraping up the brown bits from the chicken. Slowly pour in the milk and continue to stir until the gravy has thickened. Season to taste and serve hot.

Chicken and Dumplings

While for many people this dish has its origins in the Pennsylvania Dutch region of the mid-Atlantic states, like hot potato salad, it is also an African-American staple and is a typical weeknight dinner in many a home. It is one of the one-pot meals that (except for the dumplings) could be kept on the back of a stove throughout the day while other work was done and then appear at dinnertime ready to eat. This is a purist's version of the dish: a clear chicken broth enhanced only with dumplings and boiled chicken. It is given a bit of extra zing with the addition of a hot Madras curry powder.

SERVES 6

1 stewing hen, cut into pieces (see Note)
3 ribs celery, including the leafy tops
1 small onion, quartered
1 tablespoon hot Madras curry powder
1 bay leaf
Salt and freshly ground black pepper to taste
2½ quarts water, or to cover
1 cup flour
2 teaspoons baking powder
½ teaspon salt
½ cup milk
2 tablespoons melted butter

For the chicken: Place the stewing hen into a deep stockpot and add the celery, onion, curry powder, bay leaf, salt, pepper, and water to cover. Bring to a boil over medium-high heat; then lower the heat and allow the chicken to simmer, covered, for 2 hours, or until the meat falls off of the bones. Remove the stockpot from the heat and allow the contents to cool. When it is cooled, defat the chicken broth; pull the chicken from the bones and cube it.

For the dumplings: Mix the flour, baking powder, salt, milk, and butter into a dough. Place the chicken back on the stove and return it to a boil, then drop the dumplings in, 1 tablespoon at a time. Cover, lower the heat, and simmer for 15 minutes. Serve hot.

NOTE: If a stewing hen cannot be found, you can use a broiler, but you will need to enrich the broth with the addition of a chicken bouillon cube.

Chicken Croquettes

These chicken croquettes, like their salmon-based cousins, are a testimonial to the African-American way with leftovers. Prepared from cooked chicken with the addition of celery and a bit of onion, and bound with eggs, they could be stretched even farther with the addition of bread crumbs. These unstretched croquettes are for the good times.

SERVES 4

3 cups chopped cooked chicken
1/2 cup minced celery
1/4 cup minced onion
1/4 cup minced green bell pepper
1 egg
2 tablespoons heavy cream
4 tablespoons butter

Mix the chicken, celery, onion, and bell pepper in a medium-sized mixing bowl. In a smaller bowl, beat the egg and heavy cream and fold it into the chicken mixture. You will have a thick mixture. Form it into croquettes about 3 inches in diameter. Heat the butter in a heavy skillet until it is foaming and place the croquettes in the skillet, cooking them for 5 minutes on each side, or until golden brown. Serve hot.

Good bread. Good meat. Good Lord let's eat!

Chicken Yassa

Chicken Yassa, a dish from the southern part of Senegal in West Africa, is one of the first West African dishes that I ever tasted and one that I use to introduce African cooking to friends. It's become a sort of good-luck recipe for me, and I serve it at New Year's or at least once during the holiday season in tribute to the cooks who went before me. What's it doing in an African-American cookbook? It's here for two reasons. First, it's to remind us about the origins of African-American tastes, and secondly, it's to speak of the new African immigrants who daily are expanding our ideas of what African-American food is.

SERVES 6

4 tablespoons fresh lemon juice
3 large onions, sliced
Salt and freshly ground black pepper, to taste
1/8 teaspoon minced habanero chile
5 tablespoons peanut oil
1 frying chicken (2 1/2 to 3 1/2 pounds), cut into serving pieces
1 habanero chile, pricked with a fork
1/2 cup water

In a large nonreactive bowl, prepare a marinade from the lemon juice, onions, salt, pepper, minced chile, and 4 tablespons of the peanut oil. Place the chicken pieces in the marinade, making sure that they are all well covered, and allow them to marinate for at least 2 hours in the refrigerator.

Preheat the broiler. Remove the chicken pieces, reserving the marinade, and place them in a shallow roasting pan. Grill them until they are lightly browned on both sides. Remove the onions from the marinade. Cook them slowly in the remaining oil in a flame-proof 3-quart casserole or Duch oven until tender and translucent. Add the remaining marinade.

When the liquid is thoroughly heated, add the chicken pieces, the pricked chile, and the water. Stir to mix well, then bring the yassa slowly to a boil. Lower the heat and simmer for about 20 minutes, or until the chicken is cooked through. Serve hot over white rice.

Kédjenou

This is a traditional one-pot dish from the Ivory Coast. With the increasing popularity of Kwanzaa, the African-American year-end celebration, more and more of us are looking to the African motherland for holiday celebration dishes, and slow-cooked *kédjenou* is a perfect choice. The dish, which in the Côte d'Ivoire is prepared with everything from guinea hen to lobster, can be made with chicken. Traditionally cooked in a clay pot called a *canari,* which is sealed closed with a banana leaf, kédjenou can also be prepared in a dutch oven or any heavy flameproof casserole that can be tightly sealed. Serve the kédjenou with rice instead of the Ivoirian *attiéké,* a fermented starch.

SERVES 4

1 (2½- to 3-pound) chicken, cut into serving pieces
2 medium-sized onions, sliced
2 tablespoons minced fresh ginger
1 clove garlic, minced
1 bay leaf
Salt and freshly ground black pepper, to taste

Place all of the ingredients into a dutch oven or heavy flameproof casserole, cover tightly, and cook over medum to low heat for 40 minutes. Every 5 minutes or so, shake the casserole to mix the ingredients and make sure that they do not stick to the pot. *Do not uncover the pot while cooking.* When ready, uncover, discard the bay leaf, and serve with white rice.

Moyau

A spiritual says, "Let the circle be unbroken." With the increase in African immigration to the United States, the culinary path is coming full circle, as African dishes direct from the motherland are finding their way onto African-American tables. Kwanzaa is an occasion for feasting and self-examination. It is designed to strengthen the African-American community and to provide a cultural alternative to the commercial frenzy of the Christmas holidays. On the evening of the sixth day of Kwanzaa, December 31, the traditional communal feast of Karamu is held, and those attending bring food in celebration. This dish, which uses smoked chicken and hot chiles, is from Benin, in the area that was once called the Slave Coast because so many of its children were taken into bondage in the New World. Low-sodium soy sauce replaces the often unavailable and extremely salty Maggi sauce that is used in Benin today.

SERVES 4

4 smoked chicken breasts, skinned
6 medium-sized ripe tomatoes, peeled, seeded, and coarsely
*   chopped*
2 medium-sized onions, thinly sliced
¼ cup chicken stock
1 tablespoon peanut oil
2 teaspoons reduced-sodium soy sauce
2 habanero chiles, pricked with a fork

Place the chicken breasts and the remaining ingredients in a wide saucepan or dutch oven. Bring to a boil over medium heat. Reduce the heat to low and simmer uncovered, stirring occasionally, for 25 minutes, or until the flavors have mixed and the onions are tender. Serve hot over rice.

Fried Chicken Livers

Chicken innards are savored by many African-Americans and fried chicken livers are a supreme delicacy. Nowhere are they served better than in the New Orleans restaurant the Praline Connection, located in the Faubourg Marigny. There, in a dish that would give a cardiologist pause, they are accompanied by fried pickles.

SERVES 4

Oil for frying
1 pound chicken livers
1 egg
½ cup milk
½ cup cornmeal
½ cup flour

Heat 2 inches oil to 375 degrees. While the oil is heating, clean the livers and trim off any hard gristly bits. Beat the egg and milk together in a small bowl. Dip the chicken livers into the egg and milk mixture and then into a plate of the cornmeal and flour mixed together, turning them to make sure that they are well coated. Drop them into the hot oil a few at a time and cook for 3 minutes on each side. Serve hot, with Cole Slaw (pages 76 and 77) and fried pickles.

Charisse's No-Pork Gumbo with Turkey Fixings

As I was finishing up this book in the summer of 1993, I was tallying up recipes and looking for just one more gumbo recipe to add. I was introduced to Charisse Lillie from Pennsylvania, and we hit it off instantly. She talked of her Texas origins and spoke of a fantastic gumbo that she makes for her friends. I, who am notoriously bad at remembering names, had created a mnemonic device for hers using the Louisiana sausage, chaurice, I was amazed to discover that her recipe for gumbo used *no pork*. So here's Charisse's no-pork gumbo with turkey fixings. While Charisse's directions were very explicit about quantities of ingredients, she left the seasoning to taste. So, in keeping with her recipe and so that your gumbo will truly be your own, I'll follow her example here and leave the seasoning to taste. Like most gumbos, this one is made in industrial quantity to be frozen for a later date, or simply to be served to hordes of friends at a party. Note that the finished gumbo is left to stand one hour before serving.

SERVES 25

1¹/₂ cups (3 sticks) butter
1 cup diced red bell pepper
1 cup diced yellow bell pepper
1 cup diced green bell pepper
1 cup diced celery, including the leaves
3 large ripe tomatoes, coarsely chopped
1 cup diced onions
2 cloves garlic, diced
1¹/₂ teaspoons fresh basil
1¹/₂ teaspoons oregano, fresh or dried
14 cups water
3 extra-large cans crushed tomatoes
1 pound hot Italian turkey sausage

1 pound smoked turkey kielbasa
1 pound sweet Italian turkey sausage
2 pounds jumbo shrimp
1 pound backfin crabmeat
2 pounds fresh oysters
6 crabs, cleaned, shelled, and cut in half
1 pound okra, topped, tailed, and cut into 1-inch pieces
4 pounds frozen baby shrimp
Tabasco
Gumbo filé
Garlic powder
Celery salt } *to taste*
Onion powder
Lawry's seasoned salt
Old Bay seasoning

Melt the butter in a very large stockpot. Add the bell peppers, celery, fresh tomatoes, onions, garlic, basil, and oregano and sauté until the onions are translucent. Add the water and crushed tomatoes and stir to make sure that the ingredients are well mixed.

In a heavy skillet, sauté the 3 types of sausage until they are cooked through. Cut them into bite-sized pieces and add them and their drippings to the stockpot. Season to taste, bring to a boil, then lower the heat to low and simmer for 1 hour, stirring occasionally.

Clean and devein the jumbo shrimp, cut them in half, and add them to the stockpot along with the crabmeat, oysters, and crabs. Add the okra and the frozen baby shrimp (unthawed) and simmer 15 minutes longer. Season to taste. Allow the gumbo to sit 1 hour before serving. Charisse serves the gumbo hot over a scoop of rice with Tabasco and Ritz crackers on the side.

Basting and checking are essential.

Gumbo Z'Herbes

The food of the Creole world of southern Louisiana, Texas, and the coastal areas of Georgia, South Carolina, and parts of Florida deserves a work of its own. However, suffice it to say here that Creole food is ripe with variations on the gumbo theme. This gumbo is traditionally a Lenten gumbo that is prepared with nine, eleven, or thirteen types of greens.

This one, though, forgets its Lenten origin with the addition of meat. It would be virtually impossible to measure all the greens exactly, so this recipe should be considered, as with all gumbo recipes and indeed all good African-American recipes, a launching pad for individual interpretations.

SERVES 10 TO 12

1 pound collard greens
1/2 pound kale
1/2 pound mustard greens
1/2 pound turnip greens
1/2 pound spinach
1 large bunch watercress
Tops from 1 bunch beets, 1 bunch carrots, 1 bunch radishes
1 medium-sized green cabbage
10 sprigs flat-leaf (Italian) parsley
4 scallions, including green tops
6 chives
1 gallon lightly salted water
3 cups diced cooked ham
1/2 pound veal breast, diced
2 tablespoons bacon drippings
1 large onion, chopped
1 tablespoon chopped parsley
2 bay leaves
4 sprigs fresh thyme
2 whole cloves
3 allspice berries, cracked
1/4 teaspoon minced habanero chile, or to taste
Salt and freshly ground black pepper, to taste

Pick over all the greens, removing any dark or discolored spots. Cut off the fibrous stems and wash the greens well. Tear the greens into large pieces, place them in a large stockpot, and add the salted water. Bring the greens to a boil, then reduce the heat and cook them over low heat for 2 hours. When done, remove the greens, reserving the water. Chop the greens finely and return them to the water.

In a heavy skillet, sauté the ham and the veal in the bacon drippings. Add the onion and the chopped parsley and continue to cook until the onion is lightly browned. Prepare a bouquet garni of the bay leaves, thyme, cloves, and allspice and add it and the minced habanero, along with the contents of the skillet to the greens. Cook over low heat for about 1 hour. Correct seasoning and serve hot in soup bowls.

Fried Butterfish

These sweet fish are available for most of the year in the Northeast. For many African-American families they evoke family memories. My mother tells tales of her parents sitting down to a breakfast of fried butterfish and grits while the children were just served grits; she hoped one day to be old enough to enjoy the butterfish. Well, she is certainly old enough *now* and she enjoys butterfish every chance she gets, catching the elusive silvery fish off a pier in Edgartown, Massachusetts. When she brings them home, we fry them in a simply seasoned flour-and-cornmeal mixture. Delicious!

SERVES 4

8 to 10 medium-sized butterfish
Bacon drippings, lard, or vegetable oil for frying
¼ cup cornmeal
½ cup flour
Salt and freshly ground black pepper, to taste

Have the fishmonger scale and remove the heads from the fish. Wash and clean the fish and pat them dry with paper towels. Preheat 2 inches of oil for frying to 375 degrees in a deep, heavy skillet. While the oil is heating, mix the cornmeal, flour, salt, and pepper and coat both sides of the fish with the mixture.

Place the butterfish in the hot oil and fry for 5 to 8 minutes, turning occasionally so that both sides are well browned. Drain them on paper towels and serve hot. They are as good for breakfast accompanied by grits and biscuits as they are for dinner with Smothered Cabbage (page 134) or collard greens (page 124) and cornbread (pages 185–88).

Salmon Fry

Recipes for salmon cakes and croquettes abound in African-American families; I'm still trying to find a reason for the fascination we have long held for canned salmon. The closest that I can come to an explanation is that it was exotic and inexpensive, which doubled its appeal. Anyhow, my father was a lover of salmon croquettes and my mom always made them using her mother's recipe for salmon pan fry. This recipe can also be used for salmon cakes or salmon croquettes; simply shape the mixture into cakes or ovals and fry on both sides until crisp and brown.

SERVES 4

1 can (1 pound) pink salmon
2 tablespoons minced onion
2 eggs
¼ cup yellow cornmeal
Salt and freshly ground black pepper, to taste
2 tablespoons bacon fat or extra-virgin olive oil

Remove the bones and skin from the salmon, place the salmon meat in a mixing bowl, and break it up with a fork. Add the onion, eggs, cornmeal, salt, and pepper and mix well. Place the bacon fat or oil in a skillet, add the salmon mixture, and cook it until lightly browned on both sides, about 5 minutes each side. Serve hot.

Fried Catfish

Catfish are bottom feeders; they grow and thrive in the most unseemly places. For this reason, for years they were considered not quite the proper eating by many upwardly mobile African-Americans. In truth, catfish are delicious and sweet-tasting, and now that they are farmed, they are increasing in popularity, even with those who eschewed them before. One of the favored ways of serving catfish (and also one of the easiest ways to obtain them for those who are not in the South) is as fillets. The fish are either dipped into a beaten egg mixture before being rolled in cornmeal and deep-fried, or simply rolled directly in the cornmeal mixture. This recipe uses the egg dip method.

SERVES 6

2 teaspoons Louisiana Red hot sauce or Tabasco
Juice of 2 lemons
3 pounds catfish fillets
Oil for deep frying
2 eggs
¹/₄ cup milk
2 cups cornmeal
Salt and freshly ground black pepper, to taste

Mix the hot sauce and the lemon juice together, rub it on the fish fillets and allow them to marinate in the refrigerator for an hour.

Heat 2 inches of oil for frying in a heavy deep skillet or a fryer to 375 degrees. While the oil is heating, beat the eggs and milk together. Dip the fish fillets into the eggs and milk, drain them slightly. Season the cornmeal and roll the fillets in it. Fry them a few at a time in the hot oil for 2 to 3 minutes, or until golden brown. Serve hot with tartar sauce and hot sauce.

In 1972, catfish raised in man-made ponds became an extra crop for southern farmers.

UPI/BETTMANN

Coddies

When crabs became an increasingly expensive luxury, many blacks living on the Eastern shore found that they had to substitute other, less expensive seafood. When codfish was substituted for the crab in crab cakes, coddies were born.

SERVES 6 TO 8

2 pounds codfish fillets
1 cup fresh soft bread crumbs
2 eggs
¹/₃ cup light cream
1 teaspoon finely minced onion
2 teaspoons minced parsley
Dash of hot sauce
Dash of Worcestershire sauce
2 tablespoons butter or olive oil for frying

Mix the codfish with the bread crumbs. Beat the eggs until light while pouring in the cream. Add the egg and cream mixture, the onion, parsley, hot sauce, and Worcestershire sauce to the fish and bread crumbs and mix them together well. Adjust the seasonings and shape the mixture into patties. Heat the butter or oil in a skillet and fry the patties a few at a time for 3 to 5 minutes on each side, or until lightly browned. Serve hot.

Fried Porgies

Porgies play a primary role in African-American cooking history. When Du Boise Heyward wanted to find a name for his male protagonist in a work set in black Charleston, he could find no more evocative name than Porgy. Decades later his *Porgy and Bess* inspired Gershwin's opera. Nina Simone's unforgettable version of "I Loves You Porgy" inevitably comes up every time that porgies are served at my dining table.

Recently, when I mentioned that I was working on this book, a well-known African-American statesman had two questions to ask. "Will the book have cheese grits in it?" and "Can you fry a porgy?" The answer to both questions was affirmative.

12 medium-sized porgies
1 tablespoon Crab Boil (page 97)
$1/2$ cup fresh lemon juice
Oil for frying
$1/3$ cup mayonnaise
$1/4$ cup yellow cornmeal
$1/4$ cup flour
Salt and freshly ground black pepper, to taste

Have the fishmonger clean the porgies and remove the heads and fins. Grind the seafood boil in a spice grinder until it is almost a powder. Place the porgies in a large bowl with the lemon juice and the ground seafood boil and leave them for 1 hour.

When ready to cook, heat 2 inches of oil for frying in a heavy cast-iron skillet. Remove the porgies from the marinade, rinse them briefly, and slather them on both sides with the mayonnaise. Mix the cornmeal, flour, salt, and pepper together in a paper bag and place a few fish in the bag at a time, shaking them so that they are well covered with the mixture. Put a few fish at a time in the hot fat and fry them for 2 to 3 minutes on each side, or until they are golden brown. Drain them on paper towels and keep them warm while repeating the frying process until all of the fish are cooked. Serve hot with Hot Sauce (page 89) and Cole Slaw (pages 76 and 77).

Deep-Fried Soft-Shell Clams

This is an African-American dish from the Chesapeake region. Many years ago black cooks in the region discovered that ordinary pancake mix made a perfect batter for deep-frying crabs and clams. It sounds strange, but it tastes delicious.

SERVES 4 TO 6

Vegetable oil for frying
1 cup commercial pancake mix
$1/2$ teaspoon cayenne, or to taste
Salt and freshly ground black pepper, to taste
1 quart fresh shucked soft-shell clams, drained

Preheat the oil 3 inches deep in a heavy saucepan or fryer to 375 degrees. Place the pancake mix in a brown paper bag and add the cayenne, salt, and pepper. Add the clams a few at a time and toss lightly until they are well coated. Shake off any excess breading, then place the clams a few at a time in the hot oil and fry for 1 to 2 minutes, or until they are golden brown. Continue the process with the remaining clams, draining the cooked ones on paper towels and keeping them warm. Serve the clams hot with Cocktail Sauce (page 94).

NOTE: Use only the pancake mix that requires the addition of an egg and milk or water; the other will not give the same results.

Batter-Fried Soft-Shell Crabs

This typical Maryland dish is another illustration of how local bounty influences the larder in African-American kitchens. Soft-shell crabs are a special seasonal delicacy in the Chesapeake area and are eaten sautéed and pan-fried. Inspired by the use of pancake mix in the recipe for deep-fried soft-shell clams, I tried it with soft-shell crabs with delicious results.

SERVES 6

Oil for deep-frying
One dozen small soft-shell crabs
1 cup commercial pancake mix (see Note above)
1 tablespoon Old Bay seasoning
Salt and freshly ground black pepper, to taste

Heat 2 inches of oil to 350 to 375 degrees in a deep-fat fryer. Clean and prepare the soft-shell crabs. Prepare the pancake mix according to package directions, adding the Old Bay seasoning and salt and pepper. Dip the crabs into the batter and put them in the hot oil. Fry for 3 to 5 minutes, drain, and serve hot.

Scalloped Oysters

This recipe reveals its South Carolina origins in its use of mace as well as in its use of the oysters that are abundant in the Low Country region. These now expensive crustaceans were occasionally available to the enterprising slaves and freedmen, who would catch them and then hawk them on the streets of the city. The oysterman and his cry was so typical of the area that Gershwin incorporated the sound into a memorable scene in *Porgy and Bess.*

SERVES 6

½ loaf white bread, sliced and toasted
½ teaspoon freshly grated nutmeg
⅛ teaspoon ground mace
3 allspice berries, crushed
4 cloves, crushed
Salt, black pepper, and cayenne pepper, to taste
5 tablespoons butter
1 quart drained oysters, liquid reserved
⅓ cup amontillado sherry
¾ reserved liquid from the oysters

Preheat the oven to 350 degrees. Grate the toasted bread until you have 1 cup of freshly prepared toasted bread crumbs. Mix the bread crumbs and the dry ingredients together in a small bowl. Butter the bottom of 1½-quart baking dish and put in a layer of oysters. Top the oysters with a layer of the bread crumb mixture and dot small pieces of butter throughout in the bread and oyster layers. Continue to layer the oysters and the bread crumbs and butter until the baking dish is almost full, ending with a layer of bread crumbs dotted with butter. Mix the sherry and the oyster liquid together and pour them over all. Bake for 45 minutes. Serve hot.

Maryland Crab Cakes

Seafood is the hallmark of coastal African-American cooking. The Chesapeake region is noted for its crabs; shrimp, she-crabs, and oysters turn up in many dishes from the Carolina Low Country, while shrimp and crayfish define the tastes of the Gulf area. They, along with porgies, catfish, mackerel, and other finny creatures, became a part of the culinary habits of African-Americans because they were readily available and cheap, if not free for the fishing.

These Maryland-style crab cakes are Sunday go-to-meeting crab cakes, for they are not stretched with cracker crumbs or with bread crumbs; rather, they are simply bound with an egg and a bit of mayonnaise.

SERVES 4 TO 6

1½ pounds fresh backfin crabmeat
1 egg
2 tablespoons mayonnaise
Dash of Worcestershire sauce
Salt, freshly ground black pepper, and Tabasco, to taste
5 tablespoons butter

Pick over the crab to ensure that there are no pieces of shell or cartilage. Combine the crabmeat, egg, mayonnaise, and seasonings in a bowl and mix well. Form the mixture into small cakes with your hands and refrigerate half of them.

Heat half of the butter in a heavy cast-iron skillet, and when it foams, sauté the crab cakes over medium heat for about 2 minutes on each side, or until golden brown. Remove and keep them warm while repeating the same cooking process with the second batch. Serve hot.

Alternatively, the crab cakes can be deep-fried in peanut or canola oil for 3 to 5 minutes, depending on their size. Drain them on paper towels and serve hot.

Frogmore Stew

The cooking of the Low Country of South Carolina is, in a word, wonderful. It is the cooking of the Creole world, mixing the traditions of Native Americans, Europeans, and Africans with astonishing and delicious results, and is a variation of the same magnificent cooking that has delighted gourmets for centuries in New Orleans. The difference is that in the Low Country it is frequently easier to trace the African influence in dishes such as red rice and Charleston's own variation of gumbo. The names of ingredients also shout

out their African origins: eggplant is known here as guinea squash and sesame seeds are called by their Wolof name, benne.

Frogmore stew is one of the dishes emblematic of the region. According to my friend Hoppin' John Taylor, it is named for the former town center of St. Helena Island. Traditionally, this dish calls for cleaned live crabs, but I have substituted the more readily available fresh crabmeat.

SERVES 8 TO 10

¹/₄ cup Crab Boil (page 97)
2 gallons water
1 dozen ears fresh corn
1¹/₂ pounds hot link sausage, cut into 2-inch pieces
1 pound fresh crabmeat
3 pounds fresh shrimp
Salt and freshly ground black pepper, to taste
Ground hot chile or hot sauce, to taste

Place the crab boil in a large stockpot along with 2 gallons of water and bring to a boil. Shuck the ears of corn, cut them into pieces 2 to 3 inches in length, and add them to the water along with the sausage. Cook for 10 minutes over high heat, then add the crabmeat and shrimp and cook for an additional 4 minutes. Remove the pot from the heat, adjust the seasonings. Lift all the ingredients from the pot with a large slotted spoon, mound them in a big bowl, and serve hot. You may want to serve a small dish of the minced chile or a bottle of hot sauce for those who will want their Frogmore stew truly spicy.

Caribbean Court Bouillon

This is one of those dishes that provides a link between the cultures of the French-speaking Caribbean and that of New Orleans. It's only logical, after all, since they were both a part of the French overseas empire until the early nineteenth century, when the Louisiana territories were purchased by the United States. While the court bouillons of New Orleans and of Martinique and Guadeloupe are startlingly similar, neither of them resembles the classic French court bouillon (which is a clear poaching liquid) in the least. This is a Caribbean version from Carmelita Jeanne from Guadeloupe.

SERVES 6

2 tablespoons vegetable oil
1 teaspoon annatto seeds
3 scallions, minced
4 cloves garlic, peeled
1 tablespoon minced fresh parsley
1 teaspoon minced fresh thyme
Salt and freshly ground black pepper, to taste
2 large ripe tomatoes, peeled, seeded, and coarsely chopped
1½ pounds red snapper fillets, cut into 6 portions
1½ cups boiling water
¼ cup fresh lemon juice
¾ teaspoon minced Scotch bonnet chile

Heat the oil in a heavy skillet over low heat. Add the annatto seeds and sauté them for 2 to 3 minutes or until the oil becomes orange. Transfer the oil to a blender along with the scallions, 3 of the garlic cloves, the parsley, thyme, salt, and pepper. Pulse until the mixture becomes a paste. Return the paste to the skillet, add the tomatoes, and cook over medium heat for 5 minutes, stirring until the mixture is slightly thickened. Add the snapper fillets and continue to cook for 3 minutes. Add the water, reduce the heat to low, and simmer, uncovered, for 5 minutes or until the fish is opaque.

Mince the remaining clove of garlic and mix it with the lemon juice and chile in a small nonreactive bowl. Gently stir this mixture into the sauce, adjust the seasonings, and serve hot with Okra and Rice (page 115).

Bismilliah
—Islamic Blessing

Breads and Baking

Industrial quantities of breads and cakes are baked for holidays.

*Kneading is a must
for good yeast breads.*

"YOU'VE GOT TO HAVE THE FLAVOR"

Vernice Charles is a world traveler whose voice still retains traces of the South, which is surprising since she was born right in New York right near Lincoln Center in what was then called the San Juan Hill section. "I'm a New Yorker born and bred. My mom was from Baltimore and poppa was from Charleston. They got to New York around the turn of the century and were married in 1906; I was born in 1909.

"I grew up in the Yorkville area of New York City. Momma did a lot of cooking in the folks' kitchens, so she didn't cling too much to African-American tradition in the foods we had at home. We didn't have Hoppin' John and we didn't have greens. We had spinach and string beans and lettuce and carrots, and in the winter, she'd make great vegetable soup.

"Poppa maintained a few things from his South Carolina heritage. When he was at home in South Carolina, they had a rice pot and nothing could be cooked in that pot except rice. We ate rice a lot, but momma always saw to it that there were potatoes for variety as well. I also remember that every time that momma went away, poppa would cook steamed onions with frankfurters on top of them. They were delicious and so different from the foods momma made.

"When I married, my husband was from the United States Virgin Islands and we lived there for nine years . . . but down there you had to have a cook, so I really didn't get to do much. I guess I was never a real cook. Over the years, though, I did learn to love Virgin Island dishes like boiled fish and green bananas and to use fresh herbs and spices from the garden. I also learned to love other West Indian dishes like plantains and avocado, peas and rice, and goat meat, and I like cornmeal funghi with okra in it. They took learning to love, but once I acquired a taste for them, they too became part of the foods that are me. I guess the foods that I like are very varied because the folks in my life came from such different backgrounds.

"Now that I've reached my majority," she adds jokingly, "I don't cook too much any more, and when I do I try to stay away from things that I know are bad for me, like chocolate and fatty foods, but I do still have favorites from the past that I like to have every once in a while. I love well-seasoned roast pork with applesauce and gravy; I'm not sure who that comes from. Whenever I go to Baltimore, I have to have crab cakes and steamed crabs. My mother used to love them and to speak fondly of steamed crabs and beer. I go with my relatives and we head to a place where they spread newspaper on the table and we sit and talk and crack crabs and eat and talk and crack crabs and pick out the meat. I also have to have my taste of the islands from time to time.

"I guess that seasoning is the key to African-American food. We use fresh seasonings whenever possible, so that when the food comes to the table it has flavor . . . you've got to have the flavor."

Iron-Skillet White Cornbread

There are many variations on cornbread in the South. The following recipe is the one my mother's side of the family used; the cast-iron pan guarantees a crispy crust. Now, cornbread is a subject that can make for fighting: Some like it to be a bit sweet and don't mind if it's made in muffin tins or cornstick pans. Still others like it better the day after, when it's fried.

SERVES 6 TO 8

1 cup white stone-ground cornmeal
3/4 cup flour
1 tablespoon sugar
1 tablespoon baking powder
1/2 teaspoon salt
3/4 cup evaporated milk
1 egg
3 tablespoons vegetable oil

Preheat the oven to 425 degrees. Place the cornmeal, flour, sugar, baking powder, and salt in a large mixing bowl. Add the milk, egg, and vegetable oil and beat for about 1 minute, or until the mixture is smooth. Pour the mixture into a well-greased, seasoned cast-iron skillet and bake for 20 minutes. Serve hot with butter.

Yellow Cornbread

Even in my urban northern upbringing, when we'd run out of bread, mother would whip up a batch of cornbread. It was also an indispensable accompaniment to certain dishes such as collard greens, where its crumbly consistency is perfect for sopping up the pot likker. Fresh hot out of the oven, slathered with creamy butter, there's nothing that can replace it. While cornbread can be baked in a variety of types of pans, purists insist that it be baked in a square or rectangular one so that there are corner pieces with dark golden brown crust on two sides.

MAKES 12 PIECES

³/₄ cup yellow cornmeal
³/₄ cup flour
2 tablespoons sugar
1 tablespoon baking powder
¹/₂ teaspoon salt
³/₄ cup milk
1 egg
3 tablespoons melted butter

Preheat the oven to 425 degrees. Grease an 8-inch square baking pan. Place the dry ingredients in a large bowl. Add the milk, egg, and melted butter and beat for about 1 minute, or until the mixture is smooth. Pour the batter into the square pan, place in the oven, and bake for 20 minutes, or until the cornbread is lightly browned on the top and a toothpick inserted into it comes out clean.

Fried Cornbread

This is my favorite way with cornbread. In my house, this was a breakfast dish to go with bacon and ham, prepared in the drippings from either. The crispness of the toasted cornbread and the slightly salty, smoky taste of the drippings, coupled with the sweetness of the jam and the melting butter, were truly ambrosial.

SERVES 4

2 tablespoons bacon drippings
4 to 6 pieces leftover cornbread, split
Butter and Blackberry Jam (page 87), to taste

Heat the bacon drippings in a heavy cast-iron skillet over medium heat. Place the split cornbread pieces in the drippings and fry until lightly browned on both sides. Serve hot with butter and jam.

Cracklin Cornbread

Cracklins are the crunchy bits of pork and fat that are left behind when the lard has been rendered from the pig. They are similar to the fried pork rinds that many of us have tasted and loved. Cracklins must be soaked for fifteen minutes or more in water to soften them; otherwise they will be hard and gristly. After they're soaked they should be minced in a meat grinder or food processor.

MAKES 12 PIECES

1 recipe Yellow Cornbread (page 185)
1/2 cup minced pork cracklins

Prepare the cornbread. When the batter is mixed, add the minced pork cracklins and stir them to mix them in well. Bake as the recipe directs. Serve hot.

Jalapeño Cornbread

Unlike cracklin cornbread, jalapeño cornbread is a a modern variation on the theme. The minced jalapeño chiles are added according to personal taste, but I usually find a tablespoon or so does nicely.

MAKES 12 PIECES

1 recipe Yellow Cornbread (page 185)
1 tablespoon finely minced preserved jalapeño chiles

Prepare the recipe for cornbread. When the batter is ready, add the minced jalapeño chile and mix in well. Pour the batter into a greased baking pan and bake as the recipe directs. Serve hot.

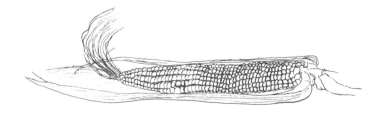

Spoon Bread

Spoon bread can be prepared with either white or yellow cornmeal. This is an old recipe given to me by family friend Alma Whittaker. It calls for white cornmeal, an indication of its Deep South origins.

SERVES 6 TO 8

4 cups milk
1 cup white, water-ground cornmeal
1¹/₂ teaspoons salt
1 tablespoon sugar
5 eggs
3 tablespoons baking powder
4 tablespoons shortening or butter, melted

Preheat the oven to 350 degrees. Grease a 2¹/₂-quart casserole dish and set it aside. In a medium-sized saucepan, heat 2 cups of the milk over low heat. Combine the cornmeal, salt, sugar, and the remaining milk in another saucepan. Gradually add the cold cornmeal-milk mixture to the warm milk and continue to cook over a low flame, stirring constantly to prevent lumping. Cook for 5 to 10 minutes, or until the mixture begins to bubble. Remove from the heat and allow to cool slightly. Add the eggs, one at a time, stirring well after each addition. Stir in the baking powder and the shortening and mix well.

Pour the mixture into the greased casserole and bake for 50 minutes to 1 hour. Serve hot, by heaping spoonfuls.

Cornmeal Mush

Although this is a dish that African-Americans received from the Native Americans, it is also popular in some parts of West Africa and the Caribbean today. Corn, though, is a New World ingredient and was not available in West Africa prior to the Columbian Exchange; even Nigeria's *amala* owes a debt to the corn mushes of Native Americans and, ironically, perhaps even to the corn mushes served on slave ships. Cornmeal porridges are prepared virtually the same way throughout the African diaspora in the New World and have names such as *coo coo* and *funghi*. In the United States, cornmeal mush is served plain as a breakfast dish with milk, syrup, or sugar. Prepared with less water, chilled, cut into slices, and fried in bacon drippings, cornmeal mush becomes a side dish at dinner.

SERVES 2 TO 4

¹/₂ teaspoon salt
2¹/₂ cups water
¹/₂ cup stone-ground yellow cornmeal

Place the salt and water into the top half of a double boiler and bring to a boil directly over medium heat. When the water is boiling, pour in the cornmeal a bit at a time, while stirring constantly. Continue to cook the cornmeal mush over direct heat for 5 minutes, then remove it, add water to the bottom half of the double boiler, and bring it to a boil. Place the top half back on the double boiler and continue to cook until the mush is creamy, about 20 minutes. Serve hot. You may need to add a bit of water to the porridge just prior to serving to "loosen" it a bit.

Hush Puppies

These fried bits of cornmeal are a perfect accompaniment to fried seafood. Depending on the version of the story, they were created to throw to dogs to keep them from barking either while hunting or while the food was being transported from the kitchens to the dining room. Clearly, they're too good to go to the dogs.

SERVES 8

1¹/₂ cups yellow cornmeal
¹/₄ cup flour
1 teaspoon salt
2 teaspoons baking powder
1 egg
1 cup milk
1 large onion, minced
Peanut oil for frying

Mix the dry ingredients in a medium-sized bowl. Beat the egg and milk together in a smaller bowl and add the minced onion. Pour the egg, milk, and onion over the dry ingredients and stir until they are well mixed.

Meanwhile, heat 3 inches of oil in a heavy skillet to 375 degrees. Drop the batter by heaping tablespoonfuls into the oil and fry for 2 to 3 minutes, or until golden brown and slightly puffed, turning them once to brown on both sides. Drain the hush puppies on paper towels and serve them hot with fried fish.

White Cornmeal Hoecakes

Hoecakes are a typical black southern bread. No one seems to be quite certain of the etymology of the word *hoecake*. Some think that it indicated that the bread was originally baked on a hoe. Others decry this idea as mythology and claim that such a thing could not be done. Still others suggest that the word is a corruption of "whole cake."

Hoe or not, in my family the word came to mean the large biscuit that was the traditional portion of the man of the family. I remember how astonished the three of us were when a guest once selected the hoecake and scarfed it down. My father pouted for a full week until he got his hoecake the following Sunday. When my paternal grandmother cooked *these* hoecakes, though, they were not large biscuits, but rather a large piece of skillet cornbread. I never learned how to flip it, so I now get the taste of her hoecake in smaller cakes like these.

MAKES 12 CAKES

1 cup white stone-ground cornmeal
¹/₄ teaspoon salt
1 cup water
6 tablespoons bacon drippings for frying

Place the cornmeal and salt in a medium-sized bowl. Add the water and stir until you have a thick batter. Heat 2 tablespoons of the bacon drippings in a heavy cast-iron skillet for about 2 minutes, then drop in the batter a tablespoon at a time and flatten it with the back of a spoon. Fry the hoecakes for about 1¹/₂ minutes on each side, turning them once. Make sure that they are nicely browned on each side, then transfer them to a heated platter and continue cooking until all the batter has been used. Serve hot with butter and jam or syrup.

Beaten Biscuits

My Gramdmother Harris was a mistress of breakfast breads. Her white cornmeal hoecake was excellent, and anyone who ever tasted her beaten biscuits knew that they had dined on what the angels eat. As a child, though, I didn't realize that Grandma Harris's silky-topped beaten biscuits were a southern tradition. It was only later—*much* later—that I realized that she was a southern holdout in the North.

Beaten biscuits acquire their wonderful sheen and special taste because they are literally beaten with a mallet or potato masher or axe blade until the gluten in the flour develops.

Now, I won't claim that these biscuits are as good as hers, but they're as good as you'll get without her. They're best when sopped in Alaga syrup into which you have cut bits of butter. If you're fancy, try Molasses Butter for a similar taste (page 98).

MAKES ABOUT
12 BISCUITS

2 teaspoons butter
2 cups flour
1¹/₂ teaspoons sugar
¹/₂ teaspoon salt
2 tablespoons lard
¹/₄ cup milk
¹/₄ cup water

Grease a baking sheet with the butter and put it aside. Mix the flour, sugar, and salt in a large mixing bowl and add the lard. Using your fingers, crumble the lard into the other ingredients until the mixture has the consistency of coarse cornmeal. Combine the milk and the water and add them to the mixture slowly, a teaspoon at a time, kneading the dough after each addition so that the liquid is completely absorbed. Continue to knead the dough until it is smooth.

Preheat the oven to 400 degrees. Spread the dough out on a sturdy floured surface and whack at it steadily for 20 to 30 minutes with a mallet or potato masher. You'll be able to tell when it's ready, because the dough will develop a glossy, satiny look. When the dough has been well beaten, form the biscuits. Place them on the greased cookie sheet and bake for 25 minutes. Serve hot and savor.

Biscuits

These are the quintessential African-American breakfast bread. Even today, I marvel at my mother's ability to whip up a batch of biscuits at the drop of a suggestion.

MAKES ABOUT
12 BISCUITS

¹/₄ cup lard
2 cups flour
1 level tablespoon baking powder
1 teaspoon salt
1 tablespoon sugar
³/₄ cup milk

Preheat the oven to 400 degrees. Cut the lard into the dry ingredients with a fork or pastry blender until the mixture resembles coarse cornmeal. Stir in the milk a small bit at a time, adding just enough so that the dough rounds up and leaves the sides of the bowl. Turn the dough out onto a lightly floured surface and roll it out until it is ¹/₂ inch thick. Then with a 2¹/₂-inch biscuit cutter or the edge of a drinking glass, cut out the biscuits and place them on an ungreased baking sheet. Bake for 10 to 15 minutes, or until they are golden brown on top. Serve hot with butter and jam or with syrup.

Angel Biscuits

These biscuits, a cross between baking powder biscuits and hot rolls, are a specialty of my friend Charlotte Lyons, the food editor of *Ebony* magazine. She was happy to give me her recipe.

MAKES ABOUT
3¹/₂ DOZEN BISCUITS

1 package active dry yeast
2 tablespoons warm water (105 to 115 degrees)
1 cup shortening
5 cups self-rising flour
¹/₄ cup sugar
1 teaspoon baking soda
2 cups buttermilk

Dissolve the yeast in the warm water. Cut the shortening into the dry ingredients with a fork or pastry blender until the mixture resembles fine crumbs. Mix the dissolved yeast with the buttermilk. Stir the buttermilk and yeast mixture into the dry ingredients and mix until the dough is soft and sticky and leaves the sides of the bowl.

Turn the dough out onto a generously floured cloth-covered board. Gently roll in flour to coat and shape the dough into a ball. Knead the dough 25 to 30 times, sprinkling with flour if it is too sticky. Place the dough in a lightly greased bowl, cover, and refrigerate for at least 3 hours, but no longer than 3 days. Use as needed.

When ready to bake, roll or pat the dough out until it is ½ inch thick. Cut it into biscuits with a 2-inch biscuit cutter or the edge of a drinking glass and place them about 1 inch apart on a greased baking sheet. Let the biscuits rise in a warm place for about 1 hour, or until they have doubled in size.

Preheat the oven to 400 degrees and bake the biscuits for 12 to 14 minutes, or until they are golden brown. Remove them immediately from the baking sheet and serve piping hot.

Sweet Potato Biscuits

Hot breads for dinner are a way of life in the traditional African-American world, and biscuits appear on the table not only for breakfast, but for lunch and dinner, too. This variation is perfect with a baked ham, and a great way to use up leftover sweet potatoes.

MAKES ABOUT
24 BISCUITS

2 cups leftover mashed sweet potatoes
1 tablespoon butter
2 cups flour
1 tablespoon dark brown sugar
Salt, to taste
¼ teaspoon ground cinnamon
Pinch freshly ground nutmeg
¼ teaspoon baking soda
⅓ cup buttermilk
1 teaspoon fresh lemon juice

Preheat the oven to 375 degrees and lightly butter two baking sheets. In a large bowl, mix the mashed sweet potatoes and butter with the dry ingredients. Slowly pour in the buttermilk and lemon juice until you have a soft, slightly sticky dough. (You may have to use a bit more flour to achieve the right consistency.) Coat the dough lightly with a dusting of flour, working it slightly so that the dough is completely covered.

Roll the dough out on a floured surface until it is about $1/2$ inch thick and cut the biscuits with a biscuit cutter or water glass. Place the biscuits on the baking sheet and bake them for 15 to 17 minutes, or until they are lightly browned on top. Serve hot with butter or with Molasses Butter (page 98).

Johnnycakes

The origin of the name *johnnycake,* as with so many African-American dishes, is shrouded in more than mystery. Some have suggested that the name is a corruption of the term "journey cakes," and hint at a European origin for the dish. Others believe that the word may be a corruption of "Shawnee cake" and be a tribute to the Native Americans who originally prepared it. Still others postulate an African-American birth, giving as their reason the fact that the dish is served under the same name in the African-American South, in Jamaica, and in the Dominican Republic, (where Samana, on the north coast, was home to escaped American slaves).

Whatever the origin of the dish and its name, it has become a traditional African-American one. In the American South, the dish is frequently prepared from cornmeal. However, a flour-based version is also popular, and is the one found in the Caribbean. Johnnycakes are traditionally eaten at breakfast with jam or syrup.

SERVES 6

4 cups flour
2 teaspoons baking powder
1 teaspoon salt
$1/2$ teaspoon freshly ground black pepper
$1/2$ cup lard
$1/4$ cup cold water
Oil for frying

Sift the dry ingredients into a large mixing bowl and cut in the lard until the mixture can be formed into small dough balls. Add the water a bit at a time until the dough has a firm consistency. Knead on a floured surface for 5 minutes.

Fill a heavy cast-iron skillet or a fryer half full of oil and heat it to 375 degrees over medium-high heat. With your thumb and forefinger, pinch off 2-inch balls of dough and flatten them with your hand or the bottom of a plate until they are about ½ inch thick. Fry the cakes a few at a time in the oil for about 3 minutes, or until they puff up slightly and are golden in color. Drain them on paper towels and serve them hot with butter and jam or syrup.

Beignets

In New Orleans, one of the jewels in the African-American culinary crown, the correct brewing of coffee is considered an art form. One of the first people to sell coffee in the French Market was an African-American woman named Tante Rose. She set up her burners and her coffeepots and provided good, hot, black café Creole. *Beignets,* those delectable bits of sugar-dusted fried dough, have over the years become the coffee's traditional accompaniment.

MAKES ABOUT 30

2 tablespoons lard
¼ cup granulated sugar
½ teaspoon salt
½ cup boiling water
½ cup evaporated milk
½ package dry yeast
¼ cup lukewarm water
1 egg, well beaten
3½ cups sifted flour
Butter, softened
Oil for frying
Confectioners' sugar

Mix the lard, granulated sugar, and salt together in a medium-sized mixing bowl and pour the boiling water over them. Add the evaporated milk and place the bowl in the refrigerator until it has cooled to lukewarm. In another bowl, dissolve the yeast in the lukewarm water and add it, along with the beaten egg, to the cooled mixture of milk and lard. Stir 2 cups of the flour into the mixture and beat it well. Gradually add the remaining flour until you have a soft dough. (You may need a bit more flour.) Place the dough in a buttered bowl, rub the top of the dough with butter, cover it with wax paper and a slightly damp cloth, and chill it until you are ready to use it. (This can be done a day ahead.)

When you are ready to prepare the beignets, heat 3 inches of oil in a heavy saucepan or fryer to 375 degrees. Remove the dough from the refrigerator, place it on a lightly floured surface, and roll it about ¼ inch thick. Cut the dough into 2-inch squares and fry them a few at a time until they are golden brown, turning once. Be careful not to let the dough rise before frying. When the beignets are brown, drain them on paper towels and sprinkle them with confectioners' sugar.

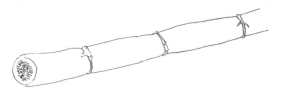

Calas

The *cala,* or deep-fried rice fritter, was for many years a traditional New Orleans delicacy. The African-American *cala* woman was a daily sight in the New Orleans streets until the early 1900s. The rice fritter was a traditional accompaniment to the daily coffee, even though it has been supplanted today by the beignet. Calas, though, seem to have been the exclusive culinary preserve of African-American cooks who peddled them in the French Market and door to door, carrying their covered bowls of calas on their heads. Their cry, *"Belle cala! Tout chauds!"* ("Beautiful rice fritters! Nice and hot!") is all that remains today of the cala.

There are two basic recipes for cala: One calls for baking powder and whole rice while the other calls for yeast and mashed rice. It would seem that the latter is the more authentic. Indeed, the Vai people of Liberia and Sierra Leone, West African rice-growing regions whose people were represented in the southern slave census, make rice fritters; their word for uncooked rice is *kala.* For the Bambara people, the word means the straw or stalk of a cereal, and in the Gullah dialect of Georgia and South Carolina, *kala* means rice. Do note that the dough must rise overnight.

SERVES 6

2¼ cups cold water
¾ cup raw long-grain rice
1½ packages dry yeast
½ cup lukewarm water
4 eggs, well beaten
⅜ cup granulated sugar
¾ teaspoon freshly grated nutmeg
¾ teaspoon salt
2 cups flour
Vegetable oil for frying
Confectioners' sugar

Place the water and rice in a saucepan and bring to a boil. Lower the heat and cook the rice for 25 to 30 minutes or until it is soft and tender. Drain the rice, place it in a mixing bowl, mash it with the back of a spoon, and set it aside to cool. In a separate bowl, dissolve the yeast in the lukewarm water, then add it to the cooled rice. Beat the mixture for 2 minutes, then cover the bowl with a slightly moistened towel and set it in a warm place to rise overnight.

When ready to prepare, add the eggs, granulated sugar, nutmeg, salt, and flour to the mixture, beat it thoroughly, cover it, and set it aside to rise for 30 minutes. Heat 3 inches of oil in a heavy pan to 375 degrees. Drop the batter by the tablespoonful into the hot oil, frying a few at a time until golden brown. Drain on paper towels then dust with confectioners' sugar and serve hot.

Desserts
and Candies

Summer just isn't summer without watermelon.

*Praline ladies are
a New Orleans street tradition.*

COMING TO GRIPS

My uncle, Gregg Jones, is, as he puts it, "the only man in my family for two generations back who isn't a Baptist minister." He's a musician and cabaret artist who left the mainland United States for the nightclubs and hotels of San Juan, Puerto Rico, some twenty years ago. There, he has grown old gracefully with his Danish wife, Mona, and their brood of adopted dogs. Uncle Gregg's tastes of home are the same as my mother's, for they grew up in the same tradition of food. Now his diet is restricted, but memories of delicious meals linger as he works on ingenious ways to create the tastes of the past with the restrictions of the present.

"Before, I used to do a lot of cooking on the grill outside. The weather here lends itself to outdoor cooking and I enjoyed it. I'd grill a leg of lamb stuffed with garlic and rubbed with oregano or barbecue a chicken until the skin got crispy. I'd do slow-cooked vegetables and foods cooked in oil. Now, though, that food is much too greasy for me. I can no longer have the pork, pig's feet, the skin on the chicken, and so forth.

"Instead, I treat myself with ninety percent fat-free Polish sausage. We eat a lot less meat, and when we do have animal protein, it's chicken or fish. We eat a lot more vegetables now, too, and lots of beans to replace the meat protein that we're not getting. I experiment using some of the ingredients that I found in Puerto Rico. For example, when I make meatballs, I'll season them with *adobo criollo*, a Puerto Rican spice mixture, and serve them in a curry gravy instead of in the traditional Italian red sauce. I also approximate the taste of fried fish by breading whitefish fillets in cornmeal and pan-frying them in a low-cholesterol oil. I freeze them first and then fry, so that they don't overcook.

"We cheat with chocolate, but we also enjoy healthier treats like plantains baked in the microwave, or frozen bananas. I've adapted to the restrictions, but this food that I eat daily is as healthy as I'm gonna get."

Watermelon

Outside the window of my home office in Brooklyn, I can see a man with a blue car. He appears virtually every day to open his trunk, remove a large table and a scale, and set up a display of fruits and vegetables that changes with the seasons. In the fall, it's grapes, winter brings yams, and summer's approach is signaled by the arrival of some of the sweetest watermelons in New York City.

Pictures of watermelon have been found in Egyptian tomb drawings. Here in the United States it has become so connected with African-Americans that some of the most vicious culinary stereotypes have been based on our alleged love of the fruit. A little bit of watermelon goes a long way with me. I have to beg friends for their rinds to make the watermelon rind pickles that I adore. However, no African-American cookbook would be complete without the inclusion of this sweet summer fruit. Remember to save the rind afterward for pickling.

SERVES 1

1 large slice of watermelon
Privacy

Chill the watermelon. Sit down on the porch, bite into the fruit, and spit the seeds out as far as you can.

Basic Pie Crust

With all of the pies and cobblers of the African-American dessert experience, there's one recipe that is essential, and that's a "killer" pie crust recipe. This one, which produces a light flaky crust, is my mom's secret weapon. Because it contains lard, the dough must be rolled out quickly after it is removed from the refrigerator or the pastry willl become very soft.

MAKES 1
(8- OR 9-INCH)
SINGLE-CRUST
PIE SHELL

1 cup flour
$^{1}/_{2}$ teaspoon salt
$^{1}/_{3}$ cup chilled lard
2 or 3 tablespoons cold water

Mix the flour and salt in a medium-sized bowl. Cut the lard into the mixture with a pastry blender or 2 knives until it has the consistency of cornmeal. Slowly add 2 tablespoons of the water to the mixture, using a fork to mix it in until it becomes a dough. (If the dough sems too crumbly, add the remaining water a bit at a time.) Flatten the dough into a disk, wrap it in wax paper, and refrigerate for 30 minutes.

Preheat the oven to 350 degrees. Roll out the dough on a floured surface until it is about 10 inches round and $^{1}/_{8}$ inch thick. Fit it evenly into a pie plate without stretching it. Roll up the overhanging pieces and crimp the edges. Prick the bottom of the pastry with a fork and bake it for about 20 minutes or until golden brown. Allow the crust to cool and fill it with one of the pie fillings.

NOTE: Different fillings may necessitate different degrees of doneness for the basic pie crust or even for an unbaked pie crust. Check individual recipe before proceeding.

Chess Pie

This pie is traditional in the Alabama and Mississippi areas. In other parts of the country, it is simply known as a custard pie.

MAKES 1 (9-INCH) PIE

$^{1}/_{4}$ cup unsalted butter, at room temperature
3 cups dark brown sugar
2 tablespoons flour
3 eggs
$^{1}/_{2}$ cup heavy cream
$^{1}/_{2}$ teaspoon salt
$^{1}/_{2}$ teaspoon vanilla extract
$^{1}/_{2}$ teaspoon freshly grated lemon zest
1 9-inch pie shell (page 202), baked for 10 minutes and cooled

Preheat the oven to 400 degrees. In a medium-sized mixing bowl, cream the butter and sugar until smooth. Add the flour and mix well. Beat the eggs and add them to the mixture. Add the cream, salt, vanilla, and lemon zest. Beat the mixture well and pour it into the partially baked pie shell. Bake the pie for 5 minutes at 400 degrees and then reduce the heat to 375 degrees and continue to bake for 20 minutes longer. This pie is best left a bit soft in the center, as otherwise it may be too chewy.

Molasses Pie

This pie is considered by many to be one of the ancestors of today's pecan pie. It can be traced back to slave times, when it was a special Christmas treat. One hint of its slave origins is the use of molasses (the traditional slave sweetener) instead of sugar. The pie has a rich gingerbready taste that is enhanced when served with freshly made whipped cream sweetened with a hint of molasses.

MAKES 1 (9-INCH) PIE

1 unbaked 9-inch pie shell (page 202)
¹/₂ cup flour
¹/₂ teaspoon ground allspice
¹/₂ teaspoon ground cinnamon
¹/₂ teaspoon salt
1 teaspoon baking soda
1 cup sour milk
³/₄ cup molasses
2 eggs
1 teaspoon fresh lemon juice
2 tablespoons melted butter

Preheat the oven to 375 degrees. Sift the flour, allspice, cinnamon, and salt into a bowl. Mix the baking soda, sour milk, and molasses and add to the dry ingredients. Beat the eggs and add them, the lemon juice, and melted butter to the mixture and stir well. Pour the mixture into the pie shell and bake it until the top begins to brown. Lower the heat to 300 degrees and continue baking until the custard is firm. (Traditionally, a broom straw was inserted into the pie and if it came out without any filling sticking to it it was done.)

Bean Pie

A recent addition to the African-American culinary repertoire is the bean pie. This became a common snack in many neighborhoods during the sixties and seventies, when black Muslims with their neat dark suits and their bow ties sold the pies along with copies of the newspaper *Muhammad Speaks*. The bean pies caught on quickly and for many African-Americans are known as Muslim bean pies. Here is an adaptation of the traditional recipe that uses canned Great Northern beans.

MAKES 1 (9-INCH) PIE

1 9-inch pie shell (page 202), baked for 10 minutes and cooled
2 (15-ounce) cans Great Northern beans, drained
3 eggs, slightly beaten
1¼ cups sugar
¼ cup melted unsalted butter
1 teaspoon vanilla extract
1 teaspoon ground cinnamon
1 teaspoon freshly grated nutmeg
½ teaspoon freshly ground allspice
1 teaspoon baking powder
⅓ cup evaporated milk

Preheat the oven to 350 degrees. Place the drained beans in the bowl of an electric mixer and beat them until they are smooth. Add the eggs, sugar, butter, vanilla, and spices. In a separate bowl add the baking powder to the milk and pour it into the bean mixture. Beat the mixture well and then pour it into the partially baked pie crust. Bake the pie for 50 minutes, or until it is firm. Allow the pie to cool before serving.

Fried Pies

Fried fruit pies are a common snack in much of the African-American South. They are small and portable, and can be eaten hot or cold. Hot, though, is definitely better! In the summer months fresh fruits are used, and in the winter, home-canned or home-dried fruits take over. Either way, peaches are a very popular filling.

Fried pies can be made large, like turnovers. Smaller ones, cut out with a biscuit cutter, are almost like cookies.

MAKES ABOUT 12 PIES

¹/₂ pound dried peaches, soaked overnight in 2 cups water
1 cup granulated sugar
Pinch of salt
Oil for frying
Basic Pie Crust (page 202)
Confectioners' sugar for dusting

After the peaches have been soaked overnight in the water, put the peaches and their soaking water in a medium-sized saucepan and bring to a boil over medium heat. Lower the heat and allow them to simmer until all of the water has been absorbed. Place the peaches in a food processor and pulse until they are a thick paste. Return the paste to the saucepan, add the sugar and salt, and cook for 5 minutes, stirring constantly, until the mixture has a marmaladelike texture. Preheat 3 inches of oil to 375 degrees in a heavy saucepan or a deep-fryer. With a biscuit cutter or the edge of a water glass, cut out rounds of dough. Place a tablespoon or two of the peach filling in the center of the dough, wet the edge slightly with water and fold the dough into a turnover shape. Press the edges together with a fork to seal them. Fry the small pies in the hot oil until they are golden brown all over, about 3 minutes per side. Drain on paper towels and dust with confectioners' sugar. Serve hot or cold.

Pecan Pie

This recipe is a southern classic. It mixes the region's favorite, brown sugar, with its preferred nut, the pecan. Some scholars feel that this pie is a descendant of the molasses pie, as they both have the same consistency. To cut the super sweetness of the pie, try serving it in small slivers with a dollop of unsweetened whipped cream on top.

1 9-inch pie shell (page 202), baked for 10 minutes and cooled
1/2 cup pecan halves
1 1/2 cups chopped pecans
1 cup firmly packed light brown sugar
1 cup light corn syrup
2 tablespoons flour
1 teaspoon vanilla extract
1/4 teaspoon salt
3 eggs
2 tablespoons cold butter

Preheat the oven to 350 degrees. Line the pie shell with half of the pecan halves and all of the chopped nuts. In a medium-sized bowl, combine the brown sugar, corn syrup, flour, vanilla, and salt. Beat the eggs and add them gradually, stirring well to make sure that they are well mixed. Pour the mixture into the pie shell. Dot with bits of butter and arrange the remaining pecan halves on the top of the pie. Bake for 1 hour, or until firm. Serve warm.

Peach Cobbler

Deep-dish cobblers are standbys on African-American dessert tables, though the ingredients change with the geography and with the seasons. While blueberry cobblers remind me of cold, stormy summer nights on Martha's Vineyard, the juicy sweetness of a peach cobbler has always made me think of the South, even when I did not known the region at all. There cobblers were prepared when there were bumper crops of peaches, and even in the winter this homey treat could be prepared from peaches that had been put up earlier in the year. I maintain that fresh peach cobblers are better.

We also like our pie à la mode. I will never forget attending an African-American teachers' conference where the gala dinner ended with apple pie. My neighbor looked at the naked pie, then added several dabs of butter and called for a dish of vanilla ice cream.

SERVES 6 TO 8

10 medium-sized ripe peaches
1¼ cups sugar
1 teaspoon fresh lemon juice
1 tablespoon cold butter
1 Basic Pie Crust (page 202)

Wash the peaches, peel them, remove the pits, and slice them lengthwise into ¼-inch slices. Place the peach slices, 1 cup of the sugar, and the lemon juice into a well-buttered 1½-quart baking dish. Dot the peaches with the butter.

Preheat the oven to 375 degrees. Roll the dough out on a floured surface. Cut out a circle the size of the top of the baking dish. Trim the scraps and place them in the peaches, sugar, and lemon juice. Place the crust on top of the peaches, covering the entire top of the baking dish. Bake for 30 minutes, or until the dough is golden brown on the top, and serve hot. Traditionally, the cobbler is served in small bowls with a bit of the crust and the warm peaches in each bowl. It can be served plain or topped with whipped cream or with vanilla or peach ice cream.

Sweet Potato Pie

My mother's sweet potato pie is a classic. In my house, as in most African-American households, my mother reigned supreme in the realm of baking. (Actually *my* father couldn't cook a lick, but in African-American homes where men *do* cook, they tend to have dominion over the barbecue and the grill and only occasionally venture into the area of baking.) This pie, along with molasses pie, is perhaps one of the African-American pies with the longest history. Sweet potatoes were among the foods that the slaves prized as treats, and they were also relatively available. The sweet potato pones of some parts of the African-American South were probably the basis of this dessert, which evolved later when flour became more common in the African-American diet.

MAKES 1 (9-INCH) PIE

4 tablespoons (½ stick) butter, at room temperature
1 cup firmly packed dark brown sugar
1½ cups boiled mashed sweet potatoes
½ cup applesauce

2 eggs, lightly beaten
¹/₃ cup mlk
1 tablespoon fresh lemon juice
1 tablespoon freshly grated lemon zest
1 teaspoon vanilla extract
¹/₂ teaspoon freshly grated nutmeg
¹/₄ teaspoon salt
1 baked, cooled 9-inch pie shell (page 202)

Preheat the oven to 425 degrees. In a deep bowl, cream the butter and brown sugar until light and fluffy. Add the cooked mashed sweet potatoes and the applesauce. Add the eggs and beat vigorously.° Continue to beat while adding the milk, lemon juice, lemon zest, vanilla, nutmeg, and salt. Continue beating until the mixture is creamy and smooth. Pour the sweet potato mixture into the fully baked pie shell and bake for 10 minutes. Then lower the temperature to 325 degrees and bake for 35 minutes longer or until firm (a knife should come out clean when inserted into the center of the pie). Some prefer the pie served at room temperature, but I suggest serving it warm.

° You may wish to push the sweet potato and egg mixture through a sieve for smoothness at this point, as the eggs can be elusive. My mother once found a whole baked egg yolk in one of her pies!

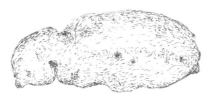

Lemon Meringue Pie

This lemon meringue pie can be found on groaning boards at family reunions and at church teas. The recipe is my mother's and she is so well known for her lemon meringue pies that folk have been known to request one for dessert when invited for dinner. Recently, I attended a gathering where lemon meringue pie was served chilled. It was all right, but at my mother's it's always served at room temperature.

¹/₄ cup cornstarch
5 tablespoons fresh lemon juice
1¹/₂ cups water
1¹/₃ cups sugar
Finely grated zest of 1 large lemon
1 tablespoon unsalted butter
Pinch of salt
2 eggs, separated
1 baked, cooled 8-inch pie shell (page 202)
Pinch of cream of tartar

Preheat the oven to 350 degrees. Combine the cornstarch and lemon juice in a medium-sized nonreactive saucepan and stir until the cornstarch dissolves. Stir in the water, 1 cup of the sugar, the lemon zest, butter, and salt. Bring to a boil over moderate heat, stirring constantly with a wooden spoon.

Place the egg yolks in a medium-sized bowl and gradually whisk in the hot lemon mixture. Allow it to cool slightly and then pour it into the pie shell and set it aside.

In a medium-sized bowl, beat the egg whites with an electric mixer at medium speed or by hand. Add the cream of tartar and continue to beat them for 1 minute, until they are frothy. Add the remaining ¹/₃ cup sugar and continue to beat until the egg whites form stiff peaks, about 2 minutes. Gently dollop the meringue over the top of the lemon filling, using the back of a spoon or a spatula to swirl designs into it. Bake for 25 minutes, or until the meringue is golden brown. Allow the pie to cool slightly. Serve warm.

Pound Cake

Cakes and pies are hallmarks of the African-American dessert table. Not for us the dainty cookies and sweetened breads of other ethnic groups. We want cakes and pies and we want a variety of them. They may have been a luxury in the past, when sugar was something truly special, but now they have become for many a necessity.

SERVES 10

½ pound (2 sticks) butter, softened
3 cups sugar
6 eggs
3 cups sifted flour
½ cup heavy cream
2 tablespoons lemon extract
2 teaspoons vanilla extract
1 teaspoon freshly grated lemon zest
¼ teaspoon freshly grated nutmeg

Preheat the oven to 350 degrees. Butter a 10-inch loaf pan and flour it. In a large mixing bowl, cream the butter and sugar together. Place the eggs in the bowl of an electric mixer and beat them for 2 minutes. Add ⅓ of the eggs and 1 cup of the flour to the butter and sugar and mix them thoroughly. Repeat this twice more with the remaining eggs and flour. Gradually add the remaining ingredients and mix well.

Pour the batter into the loaf pan and bake for 1 hour; the cake should be nicely browned and pull away from the edges of the pan slightly. When done, remove the cake from the oven and allow it to cool for 10 minutes, remove it from the pan and cool on a rack. The cake may be served warm or room temperature.

Leftover pieces of pound cake are wonderful when toasted and served with a topping of ice cream and fruit preserves.

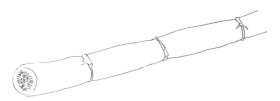

Aunt Zora's Tea Cakes

Tea cakes, which are similar to sugar cookies, were a traditional holiday treat throughout much of the South. I cannot see a recipe for tea cakes without thinking of the wonderful character in Zora Neale Hurston's *Their Eyes Were Watching God* who enables Janie to find herself. For this reason, I have named these Aunt Zora's. I only wish that they were truly her recipe.

MAKES 24 CAKES

3¹/₂ cups flour
1 teaspoon baking soda
¹/₂ teaspoon salt
¹/₄ pound (1 stick) butter, at room temperature
¹/₂ cup firmly packed light brown sugar
¹/₂ cup granulated sugar
2 eggs, lightly beaten
1 teaspoon vanilla extract
¹/₂ teaspoon freshly grated nutmeg
¹/₂ cup thick sour cream
2 tablespoons granulated sugar, 2 tablespoons dark brown sugar,
*   and 1 tablespoon freshly grated nutmeg, mixed, for sprinkling*

Sift the flour and mix it with the baking soda and salt. In another bowl, cream the butter and sugar. Beat in the eggs and add the vanilla and ¹/₂ teaspoon freshly grated nutmeg. Add the flour mixture to the butter mixture and fold in the sour cream, stirring the mixture until it is smooth.

Sprinkle a bit of flour on a flat surface and roll the dough out until it is about ¹/₄ inch thick. Sprinkle it with the mixture of sugars and nutmeg. Place the dough on a well-greased 14-inch baking sheet and bake for about 10 minutes or until nicely browned. Remove and allow to cool. When cooled, cut the cakes into 24 pieces with a knife or a cookie cutter.

Banana Fritters

The fritter tradition harks back to West Africa, where frying in deep oil is one of the major cooking techniques. In the African Atlantic world, fritters can be served as appetizers, as a vegetable, and even as a dessert, as they are here.

My maternal Grandma Jones had a way with fritters. She would prepare them from the overripe bananas that she found at low prices at her local greengrocer's.

SERVES 4

Peanut oil for frying
2 eggs, lightly beaten
¹/₂ cup cold milk
3 tablespoons light brown sugar

1 cup flour
Pinch of baking soda
4 ripe bananas, sliced diagonally into ¼-inch pieces
2 tablespoons confectioners' sugar

Heat 3 inches of oil in a heavy saucepan or deep fryer to 375 degrees. Mix the eggs, milk, brown sugar, flour, and baking soda together in a medium-sized bowl. Add the banana slices a few at a time, coating them well with the batter.

With a long slotted spoon remove the banana slices a few at a time and place them into the oil. Fry the bananas for 2 to 3 minutes, until lightly browned, turning them once. Drain them on paper towels and transfer them to a serving platter. Repeat the process until all of the bananas have been fried. Sprinkle them with the confectioners' sugar and serve warm.

Banana Pudding

Although essentially English in origin, puddings prepared from leftover ingredients are common desserts in the black South and in African-American homes in the North. Banana pudding is perhaps less well known than rice pudding or bread pudding; it is very much like a fruit trifle using leftover cake, a milk custard, and bananas as its main ingredients.

SERVES 6

12 slices leftover Pound Cake (page 210)
6 ripe bananas, sliced into rounds
2 eggs
1 egg yolk
½ cup sugar
1 teaspoon vanilla extract
1 cup milk
½ cup light cream
Freshly grated nutmeg

Preheat the oven to 350 degrees. Butter a medium-sized casserole or ovenproof baking dish. Slice the cake very thin and place a layer at the bottom of the baking dish. Arrange a layer of bananas over the cake slices.

Combine the eggs, egg yolk, sugar, and vanilla in a medium-sized mixing bowl and whisk until they are well blended. Pour the milk and cream into a small saucepan and heat until hot to the touch. (Do not allow the mixture to get too hot, or the eggs will curdle.) Pour the milk mixture into the egg mixture while beating. Continue to stir, over low heat, until the mixture coats a spoon.

Top the layer of cake and sliced bananas with a layer of custard and continue layering in this manner until the ingredients are used up. Sprinkle with a grinding of fresh nutmeg and bake the banana pudding for 30 minutes, or until the top is slightly brown. Remove it from the oven and let it stand at room temperature until cooled. Serve cool, or refrigerate for a few hours and serve cold.

Bread Pudding

In this luscious yet homey treat, stale bread is toasted and torn into bits, and reappears transformed into bread pudding. As with rice pudding, there are those who want raisins in their bread pudding and those for whom raisins in bread pudding are tantamount to treason! Take your pick.

SERVES 6

3 eggs
3 cups milk
1/2 cup sugar
1/2 pound stale white bread
1 cup dark raisins (optional)
1 teaspoon vanilla extract
Bourbon Sauce (page 216)

Preheat the oven to 350 degrees and butter a 1½-quart baking dish or ovenproof casserole. In a medium-sized mixing bowl, beat the eggs until light. Add 2½ cups of the milk, all the sugar, and the vanilla to the eggs. Crumble the bread in a bowl and wet it thoroughly with the remaining ½ cup milk. Add the raisins (if using them) and put the bread mixture in the casserole. Pour the egg mixture over it, making sure that the ingredients are well mixed. Bake for 1 hour, or until lightly browned on top. Serve warm with bourbon sauce.

Rice Pudding

My father's favorite dessert was rice pudding. He was a purist; he liked it *plain* and would brook no adulterations such as coconut or raisins. The true way with rice pudding is a frequent topic of debate when African-American food comes up, as is the question of what really ought to go into potato salad, and the raisins-or-no-raisins-in-bread-pudding debate. As for rice pudding, there are partisans of raisins, those who go for coconut, and those who like both. This is a basic recipe, one of which my father would approve. You may embellish it if you wish.

SERVES 6

4 cups milk
¹/₄ cup uncooked rice
¹/₂ cup sugar
¹/₂ teaspoon salt
1 teaspoon vanilla extract
¹/₄ teaspoon freshly grated nutmeg

Preheat the oven to 300 degrees. Mix the milk, rice, sugar, and salt in a buttered 6-cup casserole or ovenproof baking dish and bake the mixture uncovered for 2 hours, stirring every half hour. After 2 hours, add the vanilla and the nutmeg, stir well, and bake for an additional 30 minutes, or until a crust forms and the rice is tender. Serve the rice pudding warm. If you prefer, it can be allowed to cool, then refrigerated and served cool.

Milk Rice

No African-American cooks are more exacting in their demands for top-quality ingredients than the black Creole cooks of New Orleans, and no African-American cooks are more frugal. This dish is but one example of their creativity.

Called *riz au lait* in New Orleans, this dish can be a breakfast treat as well as a dessert. It can be prepared from uncooked or cooked rice. This recipe calls for cooked rice and is a perfect way to use up leftover rice. It is similar to the rice puddings that are found

in other parts of the African-American South and bears a strong re-
semblance to the rice desserts and side dishes of the French-speaking Caribbean and Brazil.

SERVES 4

2 cups cooked rice
1¹/₂ cups milk
¹/₄ cup granulated sugar
Dash vanilla extract
¹/₄ cup firmly packed light brown sugar
Freshly grated nutmeg

Place the rice, milk, and granulated sugar in a medium-sized
saucepan and bring to a boil. Lower the heat, add the vanilla, and
cook for 2 minutes, stirring occasionally. Place the rice in a serving
dish and allow it to cool, then refrigerate it for 2 hours. Serve cold.
Each diner sprinkles light brown sugar and freshly grated nutmeg
to taste on the top of individual servings.

Bourbon Sauce

Bread pudding and even banana pudding can be dressed up with
the addition of a sweet sauce such as bourbon sauce, which begins
with a caramel base and adds a healthy dose of bourbon.

MAKES ABOUT 2 CUPS

1 cup sugar
³/₄ cup water
¹/₄ cup bourbon
Pinch of ground cloves
¹/₄ teaspoon ground cinnamon
¹/₄ teaspoon freshly grated lemon zest

Place the sugar in a heavy saucepan and let it melt over medium
heat until it is golden. Add the water, bourbon, cloves, cinnamon,
and lemon zest and bring to a boil. Cook for 3 minutes, then allow
the sauce to cool to room temperature.

Benne Seed Wafers

Most South Carolina cookbooks will tell you that *benne* is an African word for sesame. Africa, though, is a continent, home to a multitude of languages, and I had to go to the Caribbean to discover in the work of linguist Maureen Warner-Lewis that *benne* is a word contributed to the African-American culinary lexicon by those of Wolof origin. It is used to mean "sesame" in Trinidad as well as in the Low Country of South Carolina.

This connection becomes even more fascinating when coupled with the knowledge that the Wolof are a major people from the Senegambian region of West Africa. Their *thiébou dienne* is startlingly similar to South Carolina's red rice and their traditional basketwork is closely related to that of the Gullah people of South Carolina's Low Country.

Legend has it that eating sesame brings good luck. Benne seed wafers come both sweet and savory. This is a sweet version.

MAKES ABOUT
2 DOZEN

1 cup sesame seeds
1 cup firmly packed brown sugar
4 tablespoons (¹/₂ stick) unsalted butter, at room temperature
1 egg, lightly beaten
¹/₂ cup flour
¹/₄ teaspoon salt
¹/₈ teaspoon baking powder
1 teaspoon fresh lemon juice
¹/₂ teaspoon vanilla extract

Preheat the oven to 325 degrees. In a heavy medium-sized skillet, toast the sesame seeds over moderate heat until they are golden brown, watching to be sure they don't burn. Cream the brown sugar and butter together in a medium-sized bowl. Add the egg, flour, salt, and baking powder and blend to form a soft dough. Stir in the toasted sesame seeds, lemon juice, and vanilla extract and mix well.

Grease 2 baking sheets and drop the dough onto them by the teaspoonful, leaving space between them for the cookies to spread. Bake the cookies for 15 minutes, or until they are slightly brown at the edges. Let them cool briefly on the baking sheets, then transfer them to a rack to cool completely.

Pralines

This New Orleans confection is another important link in the chain of African-American cooking. Throughout the African diaspora in the New World, women have worked at preparing sugared confections and selling them from door to door in public areas of the city. During the period of enslavement, the money earned from these sales frequently went to the mistress of the house, although on some occasions a portion was given to the woman, who might in this manner one day be able to pay for her freedom. After Emancipation, the selling of sweets became a time-honored way of earning a small but honorable living. The legacy of the slave saleswomen still lives on in Brazil's *baianas de tabuleiro*, in the sweets sellers of the Caribbean, and in the *pralinières* of New Orleans, although there are only a perilous few of them left.

The term *praline* is not an African one, although the similarities of the New Orleans praline with candies from Curaçao, Brazil, Jamaica, Guadeloupe, and other places where Africans have cooked in the New World would startle many a French Quarter shop owner. The name harks back to France and to the Duc du Praslin, who is said to have had a particular fondness for the sugar-coated almonds that bear his name in France. A while back, I was speaking with Leah Chase, the doyenne of African-American Creole cooking of New Orleans, and was startled to hear her recall that the original praline was not the brown sugar pecan confection that is so familiar today, but rather a pink or white coconut patty that is much closer in taste and in form to its Caribbean and Brazilian cousins. Here then are the white and pink coconut versions of this achingly sweet treat.

MAKES ABOUT
A DOZEN PRALINES

1¹/₂ cups sugar
¹/₂ cup evaporated milk
1 teaspoon butter
¹/₂ teaspoon vanilla extract
1 cup freshly grated coconut

Mix the sugar and milk together in a heavy saucepan and cook over medium heat until they reach 236 degrees on a candy thermometer. Remove the mixture from the heat; add the butter and vanilla and beat the mixture until it is creamy with a slight shine, but still thin. Then add the coconut and stir well to make sure that the coconut is evenly distributed. Drop the pralines by the spoonful onto a sheet of greased aluminum foil or a slab of confectioners' marble and allow them to harden. When hardened, they can be stored in tins, if they last that long.

Pink Pralines

These pralines were a traditional Christmas treat for many a Creole child. They were formerly prepared with a red dye prepared from cochineal, but today a few drops of red food coloring added along with the coconut to the above mixture will do the trick nicely.

Benne Pralines

Here is where New Orleans meets Charleston and they both meet the Caribbean. Benne pralines, although less well known than their coconut or pecan counterparts, are also a part of the confectioner's heritage of the African-American South. In this case, a half cup of sesame seeds are toasted in a heavy skillet until they are golden brown and then added to the basic praline mixture instead of the coconut.

Pecan Pralines

Historical pralines notwithstanding, far and away the most popular praline in New Orleans today is the brown sugar pecan variation. Many recipes remind us that these candies hark back to the days before fresh milk was readily available, so they use evaporated milk. However, this more modern version uses light cream to delicious effect.

1 cup firmly packed light brown sugar
1 cup granulated sugar
½ cup light cream
2 tablespoons salted butter
1 cup pecan halves

Place both types of sugar and the cream in a heavy saucepan and bring to a boil over medium heat, stirring constantly. When the temperature reaches 228 degrees on a candy thermometer, stir in the butter and pecans and continue to cook, stirring constantly, until the mixture reaches 236 degrees. Remove the pan from the heat and allow the mixture to cool for 5 minutes.

Beat the mixture with a wooden spoon until the candy coats the pecans but does not lose its gloss. Drop the pralines 1 tablespoon at a time onto a well-greased piece of aluminum foil or a slab of confectioners' marble. Allow the pralines to cool. They can be eaten as is, stored in tins, or crumbled over vanilla ice cream for a New Orleans–style dessert.

Molasses Taffy

Many would say that Louisiana is the true home of molasses taffy, as it is one of the birthplaces of sugar cultivation in the United States. This flavorful candy was a treat for many plantation owners during Christmas festivities, and taffy pulling is frequently described in the literature of the period. Away from the Big House kitchens, where molasses was the only sweetener that was used, molasses taffy was a particular treat. Taffy pulls were common until well into the twentieth century. Again, as with pralines, these molasses candies form a sweet link between parts of the Southern United States and several countries of the Caribbean.

MAKES ABOUT
3 DOZEN
CANDIES

2 cups dark molasses
2 tablespoons unsalted butter
1 teaspoon vanilla extract

Place the molasses in a heavy aluminum or unlined copper saucepan and bring it to a boil over medium heat. Boil until the molasses reaches the hard-ball stage on a candy thermometer (250 to 266 degrees). Remove it from the stove and add the butter and vanilla, stirring to mix them in. Pour the candy out onto a well-greased piece of confectioners' marble or a well-greased heavy platter or baking sheet and allow it to stand until the candy begins to get slightly hard around the edges.

Moisten your hands with ice water. Take a ½-cup-size ball of taffy into both hands and pull it back and forth until the taffy changes color and becomes golden. When the taffy begins to harden, twist it or braid it into sticks, tie it into knots, or shape it as desired.

NOTE: Taffy and indeed most candies are weather-sensitive. Pick a cool, dry day to make this recipe.

Sweet Potato Candy

The sweet potato turns up in almost all courses of the African-American diet. In this unusual recipe, it is transformed into a candy with the addition of brown sugar and lemon juice.

MAKES ABOUT
3 DOZEN CANDIES

3 medium-sized sweet potatoes
1 pound light brown sugar
1 teaspoon fresh lemon juce
Cinnamon, to taste
Granulated sugar

Scrub the unpeeled sweet potatoes and place them in a saucepan with water to cover. Bring them to a boil, lower the heat, and cook until they are fork-tender. Remove them from the water and allow them to cool slightly; peel them and put them through a food mill.

Sift the sugar to remove all the lumps. Place the sweet potato pulp in a heavy saucepan with the brown sugar and lemon juice and cook over low heat until the mixture separates easily from the sides of the pan, about 25 minutes. Allow the mixture to cool, then flavor to taste with the cinnamon. Place it in the refrigerator and allow it to chill for 1 hour. Form each candy by taking a small ball of the sweet potato mixture, rolling it into a 1-inch log, and dusting it with sugar. Wrap each log in waxed paper. They will keep 1 month stored in an airtight container.

Mais Tac Tac

This is a variation on a traditional New Orleans recipe for molasses popcorn. Like the other Creole confections, it was a common sight on the pristine white cloths of the candy ladies who used to sell sweets outside of the local schools and in Jackson Square. These traditional candies, with names such as *la colle* (glue), *pralines aux pistaches* (nut pralines), and *candi tiré* (pulled candy), have all but vanished except in recipe books.

MAKES ABOUT 7 CUPS

¾ cup granulated sugar
½ cup firmly packed dark brown sugar
⅓ cup corn syrup, light or dark
⅓ cup water
½ teaspoon salt
2 tablespoons unsalted butter
½ teaspoon baking soda
½ teaspoon vanilla extract
7 cups popped popcorn

Place the two types of sugar, the syrup, and water in a large, heavy aluminum or unlined copper saucepan and bring to a boil over medium heat, stirring frequently, until the mixture reaches the soft crack stage (270 to 290 degrees). Stir in the salt and continue cooking, watching carefully, until the mixture reaches the hard crack stage (300 to 310 degrees). Remove the pan from the heat, add the butter, baking soda, and vanilla and stir them well to mix them. Slowly add the popped corn and mix it in well.

Pour the mixture out onto a piece of greased confectioners' marble, a chilled heavy greased platter, or a chilled greased baking sheet and spread it out. Allow the mixture to cool and break it into pieces. This candy will keep well in airtight containers for a month and may be frozen in an airtight container indefinitely.

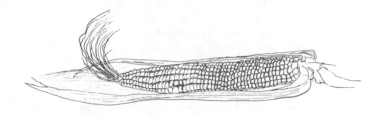

Fast Fudge

No one is sure where fudge originated. Some say that it began in northern girls' colleges, where it was cooked up over gas jets in dormitories. Others say that it began with a baker's error in Philadelphia. However, it has become an undeniable part of an African-American way with candies, which, in the case of fudge, has more to do with *eating* it than *making* it. African-Americans have a legendary sweet tooth that embraces borrowed tastes such as fudge, fondant, and divinity, as well as pralines, peanut patties, and taffy, the latter candies being more directly related to our experiences in this hemisphere.

MAKES ABOUT
24 PIECES

¹/₄ pound (1 stick) butter
¹/₂ cup powdered cocoa
1 egg, separated
¹/₂ cup confectioners' sugar
1 teaspoon vanilla extract
¹/₂ cup minced walnuts (optional)
Walnut halves for decoration (optional)

Melt the butter in the top half of a double boiler set over simmering water. Add the cocoa and stir until you have a smooth paste. Remove the pan from the heat, but keep the hot water in the bottom of the double boiler. Whip the egg white into peaks. In a separate bowl, beat the egg yolk. Add the confectioners' sugar, vanilla, and beaten egg yolk to the butter and cocoa mixture and beat in well. Finally, fold in the whipped egg white, and the nuts, if desired. Pour into a well-buttered 8-inch-square baking pan. Allow to cool, cut into 1-inch squares when firm, and serve. You may decorate each fudge square with a walnut piece, if you like.

Benne Candy

It is thought that sesame seeds were brought to South Carolina's Low Country around 1600 by African slaves. Benne seeds are made into savory appetizer wafers and cookies; they also turn up in candies of all descriptions.

MAKES ABOUT
2 DOZEN CANDIES

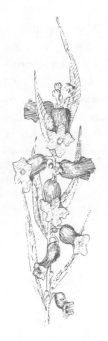

1³/₄ cups sesame seeds
2²/₃ cups firmly packed light brown sugar
1 tablespoon butter
¹/₂ cup half-and-half
1 teaspoon fresh lemon juice
1 teaspooon vanilla extract

Place the sesame seeds in a heavy skillet over medium heat and toast them, watching them carefully so they don't burn, until they turn a golden brown. Put the brown sugar, butter, half-and-half, and lemon juice in a saucepan and cook over medium heat, stirring occasionally, until the mixture reaches the firm ball stage (244 to 248 degrees on a candy thermometer). Remove the mixture from the heat, add the sesame seeds and vanilla, and stir well, until all of the ingredients are well mixed and creamy. Drop the benne candy by the teaspoonfuls onto a slab of confectioners' marble or a buttered heavy platter. Allow the candy to cool. The candy will keep for several weeks in an airtight container.

Beverages

The modern kitchen on the Baltimore and Ohio "Royal Blue" in 1937.

WHAT'S MINE
AND WHAT'S YOURS

June Bobb, a colleague and friend from Queens College, is a lover of the food of African-Americans. In the twenty-four years that she has lived in the United States, she's made many friends and sampled many dishes. They remind her of her home in Guyana, but they're not the same. For her, the tastes of childhood are "peas and rice, pepperpot, curry and roti, Caribbean-style chow mein, mettagee (a boiled vegetable dish), dry food (vegetables with fish on the side), and lots and lots of greens."

These are different tastes from the cornbread, collard greens seasoned with ham hocks, black-eyed peas and rice, barbecued ribs, and sweet potatoes that she associates with the food of Stateside African-Americans. She doesn't miss the tastes of Guyana because she can find them right in Brooklyn, New York, where she lives.

"Formerly we used to be able to get only selected ingredients. Now, though, you can get everything, including special vegetables like bora and callaloo, although you might have to go to a specialty shop for them. Some items like coconuts and plantain chips have now found their ways into the aisles of mainstream supermarkets." As the availability of Caribbean ingredients grows in areas with large numbers of residents from the region, the second beneficiaries are their neighbors, African-Americans, who find that the new items can be used in innovative ways in their own cooking. The tastes are similar, but different.

When asked to find similarities between the cooking of Guyana and the cooking of African-Americans, June Bobb finds several. "We both eat lots of rice, lots of it, and frequently with beans. Up here, folks season with ham hocks. Where I'm from we use pig tails and salt beef to season things. We also use coconut milk for taste, as well. But basically the tastes are the same. We both eat okra, though I only eat it if it's fried dry and cooked with shrimp. Also, when greens are cooked, they're never plain, they always have something added for flavor. The most important similarity, though, is that the food both here and in Guyana is always well seasoned. That's a major point in common. And we both love hot sauces on our foods."

These similarities, along with the multiplicity of cross-cultural friend-ships, is blurring the line between "what's mine" and "what's yours." Sure, there will always be a difference between collards and ham hocks and pigs' tails and callaloo, but in the future, it will all be out on one table.

Bluffs Bloody

My parents were lucky enough to discover Martha's Vineyard over thirty-seven years ago and decided to purchase a summer house there, so I've virtually grown up summering on the island with friends and guests. One of the fixtures of any Oak Bluffs summer is a series of house parties known as "five to sevens," for the hours when they are usually held. These are family parties that have over the years grown into summer events. Some are catered, complete with tents and hired bartenders and servers, while others involve neighbors getting together and cooking their favorite recipes. Parties are invariably multigenerational, with grandparents, parents, and children often at the same one. For years, a hallmark at our house was a Bluffs Bloody, our own special twist on a Bloody Mary.

SERVES 1

1 cup V-8 juice
1 tablespoon fresh lemon juice
Dash of Hot Sauce (page 89), or to taste
Dash of Tabasco, or to taste
2 teaspoons Worcestershire sauce
Pinch of celery salt
Vodka, to taste
1 trimmed scallion, 1 peperoncini, and 1 strip fresh zucchini, for garnish

Mix all of the ingredients together except the garnishes and place them in a large chilled stemmed glass. Add several ice cubes and the garnishes. Serve immediately. These can also be made in quantity in a pitcher or made without the vodka, with each guest adding alcohol (or not) to taste.

Minted Iced Tea

Iced tea is *the* drink of the southern United States. The African-Americans who are descended from the old family retainers that used to serve it on the veranda are now drinking it themselves with a vengeance. At ladies' luncheons or church outings, family dinners and fine restaurants, gallons of the stuff are consumed all year round. My first experiences with iced tea were mostly about not pouring the boiling tea water over the cold ice cubes and breaking the glass pitcher. (A few did break in a tidal wave of tea, ice cubes, and glass.) I've since learned to prepare a strong tea extract, cool it down with ice, and then dilute it to taste.

SERVES 4 TO 6

5 orange pekoe tea bags
8 cups boiling water
8 to 10 sprigs of fresh mint
Cold water
Superfine (not *confectioners'*) *sugar, to taste*

Place the tea bags and the boiling water in a teapot. Bruise four of the mint sprigs and put them in the pot with the tea bags. Allow the minted tea to steep for 15 minutes. Cool it down by adding a few ice cubes to the teapot, then pour the cooled minted tea concentrate into a tall glass pitcher. Add ice cubes, cold water, and superfine sugar to taste, stir to mix well, and serve over ice in tall chilled glasses, garnished with the remaining mint sprigs.

A Cool Drink I

My maternal grandmother, Bertha Philpot Jones, was a wonderful, warm, round dynamo of a grandmother. She had raised ten children during the trials of the Great Depression. She was a minister's wife and a clubwoman par excellence. Dinner at her house was a special treat for me, because she lived a considerable distance away. I can remember being allowed to sit with the grown-ups to get away from my tormenting older cousins. There, I sat quietly and listened to wonderful conversations about family characters, tales, and traditions as the adults picked away at turkey carcasses and ham bones. These family gabfests were always well lubricated, not with alcohol or coffee, but with gallons of what my Virginia grandmother euphemistically called a "cool drink." It was always served in one of her ornate cut-glass pitchers, and could have different hues and tastes depending on what was in season. Here's one variation.

Juice of 10 oranges
Juice of 3 lemons
1 pint water
Sugar, to taste
Ice

Mix all the ingredients together in a large pitcher and serve.

A Cool Drink II

This variation on Grandma Jones's cool drink produces a pretty pink drink that is beautiful when served in crystal glasses.

SERVES 4

¹/₃ cup sugar, or to taste
¹/₂ cup chilled fresh lime juice
1 cup fresh orange juice
3 cups cold water
2 tablespoons grenadine
Ice

Place all of the ingredients in a large pitcher. Stir until the sugar has dissolved and add the ice. Serve in your prettiest glasses.

Creole Café

Long before there was Starbuck's or any of the other coffee emporia that exist today, there were the coffee ladies of New Orleans. The first ladies to sell hot, steaming cups of dark coffee blended with chicory on Jackson Square in front of the cathedral were African-American ladies such as the legendary Tante Zoe, spoken of in the *Picayune Creole Cookbook,* and Rose Nicaud, who sold coffee in the French Market. The Creole have several dicta for coffee making, most of which apply as well today as they did almost a hundred years ago.

- Coffee beans should be parched just prior to making the coffee.
- Coffee should be roasted to a rich, deep brown.
- Coffee should always be made using the drip method.
- The water for the coffee should be boiling before the coffee is made.
- The coffeepot should be kept scrupulously clean.

When the coffee is prepared using these dicta, the only thing that remains to truly take it to the heights is to use it as the basis for preparing Creole Café Brûlot.

Creole Café Brûlot

Imre, my favorite waiter at Galatoire's in New Orleans, makes a wicked café brûlot. It's hot and sweet and aromatic with lemon and orange. The coffee can be prepared in any chafing dish, but traditionally a large silver brûlot bowl and brûlot ladle are used. I have a brûlot bowl at home, but this is as close as I can get to Imre's magic touch. Even so, it makes a wonderful ending to a formal meal.

MAKES ABOUT 4 CUPS

Peel of 2 lemons
Peel of 1 orange
6-inch cinnamon stick, broken in half
10 whole cloves
6 teaspoons sugar
³/₄ cup brandy
¹/₄ cup Mandarine Napoleon liqueur
¹/₄ cup white Curaçao
3 cups hot strong coffee made in the Creole manner

Cut the lemon and orange peel into long strips, removing as much of the white pith as possible. Place the peels, along with the cinnamon, cloves, and sugar, in a brûlot bowl or chafing dish over a lighted alcohol burner. Mash the ingredients with the bowl of a ladle. Then slowly add the brandy and liqueurs, stirring until the sugar dissolves. After the liquid has warmed, carefully light it. Slowly add the hot coffee, stirring constantly until the flame goes out. Serve hot in brûlot cups or demitasse cups.

Mister Good Daddy

Grace Bayles has been a friend of my family for as long as I can remember, and for all of that time she has been a staunch teetotaler. Whenever she comes to a party we always have on hand a nonalcoholic punch that she has baptized "Mister Good Daddy." It's a family joke, though actually the Mister Good Daddy is so good that those who *do* drink alcohol use it as a base for an alcoholic fruit punch.

SERVES 8 TO 10

1 can frozen grape juice, thawed
1 can frozen pink lemonade, thawed
1 quart ginger ale
1 pint water

Mix all of the ingredients in a large pitcher or punch bowl. Add ice and serve.

Corn Liquor

When Joan Baez sang in the sixties, "Get you a copper kettle," she could have been speaking to generations of African-Americans who have enjoyed home-brewed liquors of one type or another. Corn liquor is only one term for the strong beverage, which can have the kick of a country mule.

I made my first acquaintance with corn liquor at Minnie Hester's, a legendary after-hours spot in Durham, North Carolina. There, sitting at a Formica table with a chopped barbecue sandwich on white bread and a paper cup full of the strongest-tasting stuff I'd ever swallowed, I decided that corn liquor was something I could live without. A decade later, a Mississippi friend treated me to another taste of home brew. Either my taste buds had toughened up or the beverage was much smoother; it tasted very much like a smooth Brazilian *cachaça* or a Haitian *clairin*. Corn liquor is still not my favorite tipple by a long shot, but for research purposes, a sip or two a decade has done no harm. If you're near some good moonshine, try it, for a unique taste of the past.

Bourbon

Named for the county in which it was first made, which was named in turn for the last French royal dynasty (high praise indeed), this all-American beverage is the traditional strong drink of choice in much of the black South. Its sweetish taste comes from its preparation, using limestone water and tall corn. For many blacks, the taste for bourbon was a regional, not an African one; a sip or so was given to the slaves at holiday season or on a special occasion. Africanisms survive in the pouring of a small bit of a newly opened bottle as a libation for those who went before. This habit was transformed in the sixties to pouring a bit "for the boys upstate" to express solidarity with African-American political prisoners.

Bourbon may not be African in origin, but those with a finely tuned sense of irony will appreciate the fact that the gentleman who brought quality control to the bourbon makers was named James C. Crow; the beverage Old Crow takes its name from him. And as any self-respecting southern drinker knows, that bird on the bottle has his head turned because "too much Old Crow will make you 'shamed."

Lagniappe

Me, age one.
What's for dinner?

One of my first memories is cooking with my mother in the kitchen of the house where I was born. The house had a large kitchen with a breakfast nook and bright windows that looked out onto the green backyard. As an only child, I had fair run of the kitchen, and often, to keep me amused while she was cooking, my mother would allow me to have a bit of dough or a few vegetables to play with.

On one such day, I pressed and pounded and transformed the bit of dough that she had given me into something that went into a small pie plate to be baked along with her dessert. When it was removed, it was flat, it was crusty, and it was oh-so-very pink (red food coloring must have been one of the ingredients). My mother, always willing to show support, tasted it and it wasn't too bad. We decided, though, that it wasn't a cookie; it wasn't a pie; and it certainly wasn't a cake—so we called it coo-pie-cake. It was my first culinary invention.

Over the years, there have been more inventions and adaptations, both successful and unsuccessful. However, the one that my mother and I always remember laughingly is coo-pie-cake. The taste is long forgotten, but the feeling of accomplishment and the delight in creating something new and different are constantly duplicated each and every time that one of my recipes turns out well, or when I receive a compliment on a homemade chutney or a way with a roast or a twist with an okra stew. Thanks to the experience of coo-pie-cake, I will always cook, and will always enjoy it. The enjoyment of cooking is what my mother passed on to me. With this book I hope that I've passed it on to you.

Menus

Know your ingredients.

A Texas Juneteenth Family Picnic

Deviled Eggs
Mom's Deviled Ham Spread
Cole Slaw
Potato Salad
Iron-Skillet Fried Chicken
Pound Cake

MUSIC: *James Reese Europe Band Music*

Kwaanza Feast

Roasted Peanuts
Pickled Black-eyed peas
Roasted Pumpkin Seeds
Chicken Yassa
Plain White Rice
Cucumber Salad
Salade de Fruits

MUSIC: *Olatunji's Drums of Passion/Youssou N'Dour*

Diaspora Potluck

Yam Chips
Moyau
Plain White Rice
Quick Greens, Brazil Style
Hearts of Palm and Pineapple Salad
Pound Cake

MUSIC: *Brazilian/World Beat*

Chitlin Soirée

Super-rich Virginia Crab Cakes, made the small size
Chitterlings
Southern Succotash
Wilted Dandelion Greens
    with Hot Bacon Dressing
Jalapeño Cornbread
Vintage Champagne

MUSIC: *Anything by Ellington*

I Loves You Porgy Carolina Fish Fry

Fried Porgies
Deviled Eggs
Cole Slaw
Potato Salad
Hush Puppies
Pecan Pie

MUSIC: *Porgy and Bess (Satchmo and Ella or Leontyne and Warfield)*

Maryland Crab Feast

Deviled Crabmeat
Batter-fried Soft-Shell Crabs
Maryland Crab Cakes
Hot Vinegar
Okra and Rice
French-fried Sweet Potatoes

MUSIC: *Cool jazz*

Low Country Luxe

Cheese Straws
Shrimp Fritters
She-Crab Soup
Limpin' Susan
Avocado and Grapefruit Salad
Fresh Ham with Peach-Sage Marinade
Minted Green Peas
Broiled Peaches
Benne Seed Wafers

MUSIC: *Marsalis and Battle "Baroque Duet"*

Palm Sunday Tea

Pound Cake
Pink Pralines
Sweet Potato Pie

MUSIC: *Aretha's "Amazing Grace," James Cleveland's "Peace Be Still," and Al Green's gospel records*

Classic Creole

Fried Eggplant Galatoire Style
Gumbo Z'Herbes
Bread Pudding with Bourbon Sauce
Café Brûlot

MUSIC: *Sweet Emma and the Preservation Hall Jazz Band*

"Sweet Tooth" Dessert Buffet

Molasses Pie
Chess Pie
Fast Fudge
Pralines
Aunt Zora's Tea Cakes
Pound Cake

MUSIC: *Scott Joplin's rags and cakewalks*

Funeral Meats

Macaroni and Cheese
Mixed Greens
Slow-cooked String Beans and Ham
Iron-Skillet Fried Chicken
Baked Ham
Molasses Pie
Pecan Pie
Sweet Potato Pie

MUSIC: *Olympia Brass Band, the Zion Harmonizers*

Motown Munchies

Deviled Eggs
Peanut Soup
Carrot and Raisin Salad
Gospel Bird
Creamed Corn
Quick Greens, Brazil Style
Bean Pie

MUSIC: *Motown classics by the Supremes, Marvin Gaye and Tommi Terrell, and the rest*

Dunbar Food Feast

Roasted Peanuts
Iron-Skillet Fried Chicken
Plain White Rice
Tomato, Cucumber, and Onion Salad
Corn on the Cob
Basic Okra
Fried Pies
Watermelon

MUSIC: *African-American Classics—spirituals, work songs, blues*

Something Special

Jerusalem Artichokes
Wilted Spinach
Milk Rice
Creamed Corn
Grilled Tomatoes
Roast Leg of Lamb
Beaten Biscuits
Lemon Meringue Pie

MUSIC: *Anything by the Neville Brothers*

Nighttime Is the Right Time (Chicken and Waffles Midnight Supper)

Iron-Skillet Fried Chicken
Waffles
Vintage Champagne

MUSIC: *The Platters, The Chantells, The Shirelles, and black music of the fifties and sixties*

Pigfoot and a Bottle of Beer Bash

Spicy Pecans
Deviled Crabmeat
Hot Potato Salad
Pig's Feet
Hot Vinegar
Iron-Skillet White Cornbread
Banana Pudding

MUSIC: *Bessie Smith, Ma Rainey, and the Blues Queens*

North Ca'lina Cue

Chopped barbecue sandwich
Cole Slaw

MUSIC: *Old Rhythm and Blues Tunes*

How I Got Ovah Slave Remembrance Supper

Gospel Bird
Hominy Grits
Mixed Greens
Baked Sweet Potatoes
Iron-Skillet White Cornbread
Molasses Pie

MUSIC: *Fish Jubilee Singers or The soundtrack from "Roots"*

Saturday Night Stomp

Pickled Okra
Fried Chicken Livers
Plain White Rice
Cole Slaw
Biscuits
Banana Fritters

MUSIC: *Jazz by your favorites*

Breakfast Bonanza

Ham with Red-Eye Gravy
Grits
Fried Green Tomatoes
Broiled Peaches

MUSIC: *None, just blissful silence and the sound of quiet chewing*

Appendices

The closet of canned goods and salt pork belonging to a Mississippi Delta family in 1939.

Glossary

From the folks who know how to *nyam*, grease, and grit; who named the chicken the Gospel bird; and know what to do with every part of a pig. Here, then, is a glimpse at the wondrous vocabulary of our culinary universe, from ingredients to eating.

INGREDIENTS

ALAGA SYRUP
The name comes from the ellision of the abbreviations for Alabama, Louisiana, and Georgia, the three states in which this cane syrup is the breakfast syrup of choice.

BACON
The meat from the sides and back of a pig. It is salted, smoked, cut into slices, and fried for breakfast. It also turns up in the cooking of African-Americans as bacon drippings. In years past, a coffee can on the back of the stove was almost a necessity; it caught the bacon drippings when they went into virtually every other dish to add a seasoning hint of smoke and taste. Slab bacon can be purchased in many parts of the country and then cut into the thick slices that are more like the country bacon that would traditionally be used in African-American cooking, but any type of lean smoky bacon is just fine. Streak of lean/streak of fat (a.k.a. "streak o' lean") is not bacon, but salt pork, although the products can be used interchangeably with virtually the same results.

BARBECUE
It is thought that this word comes into the language from the Arawak Indian word *barbacoa* from the Caribbean. There it meant the grill of green wood that served to cook meat. It first came into American usage in the early eighteenth century and was well on its way to being as popular as it is today by the time the country became independent. Barbecuing involves either marinating a piece of meat, grilling it over a wood fire, and serving it with a sauce, or basting it while it's cooking and serving it with a sauce. The two basic types of sauces seem to be red tomato-based ones and vinegar and molasses–based ones. Meats range from pork in various forms

to beef (in Texas), and even to lamb. Chicken, while it can be cooked on a barbecue grill, really doesn't make it to barbecue heaven. There are several basic types of barbecue: North Carolina barbecue, Texas barbecue, and Georgia barbecue.

Now if I haven't mentioned your favorite type of barbecue, please don't blame me. The subject is vast and the African-American contribution is frequently undocumented or unmentioned even in the few works that have been published. African-American barbecue merits a treatise of its own, and the African-American pit masters (mainly men) deserve a statue in the town square of more than one southern city. Perhaps, someone wiser in the ways of the pit masters than I will heed the call!

BARBECUE SAUCE

Most of the barbecue sauces on the market are the tomato-based variations on the barbecue theme. If you want to purchase one, try the next best thing to your own, one of the sauces from Ken Davis from the list of mail-order sources.

BAY LEAF
(*Laurus nobilis*)

The leaves of the laurel tree. (Yes, that's what it is! Roman heroes were simply crowned with wreaths of bay leaves.) Bay leaves are among the few herbs traditionally used in African-American cooking. They are purchased dried and are best when purchased loose, so that you can choose them for their medium size and be sure that they are whole and without any broken bits which might get lost when cooking. They are usually removed from a dish prior to serving.

BEANS
(*Phaseolidae* sp.)

There are over a thousand types of beans. Indeed, research shows that many types were eaten in Africa prior to the Columbian Exchange and therefore were a part of the original African diet. In the South, the lima or butter bean reigns supreme and turns up in southern succotashes and in soups and stews. They are best when bought fresh, and shelled. However, beans are also just fine, thank you, when purchased dry, and they are among the few vegetables than stand up reasonably well to canning.

BENNE
(*Sesamum indicum*)

A South Carolina term for sesame seeds, which came to the United States from Africa. The word is a corruption of *bene,* the term for sesame among the Wolof people of the Senegambia region. In Charleston, the seeds can be found as ingredients in benne seed wafers and benne seed candy, and are thought to bring good luck.

Sesame seeds can be purchased in most health food stores and can be toasted for greater flavor. They will keep indefinitely when stored in the refrigerator, but should be used immediately after toasting.

BLACK-EYED PEAS
(cowpea, field pea)

A larger cousin of the COWPEA.

BLACKSTRAP MOLASSES

A very dark type of molasses. Traditionally it was used in much African-American cooking. It can be replaced with any type of molasses.

BLACK WALNUTS
(*Juglans nigra*)

Almost impossible to crack, these strong-flavored nuts grow wild in the Ozarks and throughout the central and eastern parts of the country. They should be purchased in small quantities and stored in the refrigerator, because they do not keep well (the oil goes rancid rapidly). When you find black walnuts that are unshelled, pass them by unless you have a sledgehammer and some time. They're really hard nuts to crack. You can buy them already cracked from the mail order source listed on page 271.

BOLOGNA
(Baloney)

A mild sausage that allegedly comes from Italy (although I'll wager that today's American version has little to do with the city of the same name). The sausage is popular in African-American communities for its price as much as for its taste, and in the bad old days, many recipes for pork or beef were created with bologna as a substitute. Today, the sausage turns up in sandwiches and occasionally fried on the breakfast table as a breakfast meat.

BOURBON

This spirit, named for the royal house of France, is as American as the flag. The beverage must be produced from a femented mash of which at least 51 percent is corn. It must, by law, be aged in new, charred, white oak barrels for at least two years. The results are ambrosial, and aside from white lightning (see listing) perhaps the drink most emblematic of the southern United States. For decades this was the legal spirit of preference of African-Americans. (Corn liquor just usually didn't come with a revenue stamp.)

BROWN SUGAR

This sugar gives an extra touch to much African-American baking and canning. However, be cautious when adding it, as it will color foods.

BUTTERMILK

This tart milk is a treat that comes from the churn as butter is being prepared. It is best served chilled, and is also used as an ingredient in biscuits and in some cakes. African-American etiquette disagrees as to whether cornbread should be dunked in the buttermilk or crumbled into it. Both methods are used in regions of the South.

CATFISH
(*Ictaluridae*)

This scavenger fish is one of the delicacies of African-American eating. The fish generally have two to four pairs of long whiskerlike barbels, big, *big* mouths (earning them the appellation "lawyer fish" in some parts), strong spines, and no scales. They love the muddy bottoms of rivers and canals and feed in the muck. For this reason, they were disdained by more proper southerners and left to those who didn't let environment and eating habits influence their ideas of what made good food. Traditionally the fish is dipped in a cornmeal batter and fried to a crispy turn at summer fish fries. Catfish is now farmed, so that those who shunned its alleged "muddy" taste can now enjoy it. The fish are available fresh, both whole and filleted, in fishmongers', and frozen in many supermarkets.

CHILES
(*Capsicum* sp.)

The African taste for the spicy edge of culinary life has followed her descendants to just about everywhere we are in the world. Whether they're called hot peppers or chiles, these are the little red, green, and yellow "devils" that add spice to much of our cooking. Many lovers of soul food would no more think of eating without their thin bottles of hot stuff than they would of having biscuits without sopping the gravy.

Chiles are best purchased fresh and without blemishes. They can be refrigerated and will keep for a week or longer. To preserve them, try grinding them and freezing the paste, or whipping up one of the numerous hot sauce, hot vinegar, or hot condiment recipes that exist. (See Condiment chapter.)

CHITTERLINGS
(**CHITLINS**)

There's no polite way to describe chitterlings, or chitlins, as they're more frequently called. They're the small intestines of a pig. For this reason they must be scrupulously cleaned before cooking, no matter what it says on the box or tub in which they're purchased.

Chitlins can be purchased at butcher shops and supermarkets in most African-American neighborhoods. When ready to cook them, be aware that they have a powerfully strong smell that is unpleasant to almost everyone except the most dedicated chitlin lover. Warn your neighbors and then proceed.

CLABBER

Between buttermilk and butter lurks clabber. It's a thickened buttermilk.

COCONUT
(*Cocus nucifera*)

While the coconut is used in virtually every course of the meal in Africa, Brazil, and the Caribbean, for most African-Americans coconut means dessert. Grated coconut is an ingredient in everything from fruit salads to the icing for towering cakes.

While grated coconut can be purchased canned or packaged, this is usually sweetened. Unsweetened coconut can be found at health or natural food stores. It cannot, however, compare in taste with home-toasted, freshly grated coconut.

COLLARDS
(*Cruciferae* sp.)

These are one of the types of leafy greens traditionally eaten in the South. While the greens are not African-American in origin (the name collard is a corruption of the Old English *colewort*), the habit of eating them cooked "down to a low gravy" and drinking the pot likker is African in origin.

Fresh collards are available in vegetable markets in African-American neighborhoods almost year-round. They're best, though, in the fall and winter after they've been kissed by the first frost.

Canned and frozen collard greens are readily available. Other greens are mustards, turnips, kale, or a mixture of several.

CORN
(Zea mays)

One of the New World's gifts to the cooking of the world, corn is a vegetable that Africans adopted even before they became African-Americans. Corn on the cob, though, is a fairly recent development, and references are found back only as far as the nineteenth century.

In the years of enslavement, corn usually meant cornmeal to most African-Americans. The cornmeal was then transformed into all types of pones, breads, hominies, cakes, and porridges, which were virtually the staff of life. The great North-South cornmeal debate rages on. Southerners from the deep South prefer white cornmeal and those from the North and those with "high falutin'" notions prefer yellow. My paternal grandmother always made her cornbread in a skillet on the top of the stove with white cornmeal. My maternal grandmother used yellow meal and baked hers.

CORN LIQUOR

Home-brewed liquor prepared from a mash that is mostly corn. It packs the proverbial kick of a country mule or can be smooth. It's also known as white lightning.

CORNMEAL

See CORN.

COWPEAS and FIELD PEAS
(Vigna sinensis)

Native to Africa, the cowpea may owe its cultivation in this world to Thomas Jefferson, who admonished an overseer at Monticello to plant a field with them as they were dying out in the neighborhood. Although many would confuse them with beans, these often used legumes are truly peas. In fact, they're one of the most frequently used legumes in African and African-American cooking. Eaten in Hoppin' John on New Year's Day, they're thought to bring good luck for the year. Cowpeas are sometimes called field peas, since they were at one time planted around the edges of fields. A larger cousin is known as the black-eyed pea. These are available virtually everywhere dried or canned, and can occasionally be found fresh seasonally in farmers' markets and African-American vegetable stores.

CRAB
(Decapoda sp.)

There are over 4,400 species of crab, and all true crabs are edible. For most African-Americans, though, the crabs that count are those found on the eastern seaboard of the United States, notably the blue crab (*Callinectes sapidus*). In their moulting season, these also turn up as the famous soft-shell crabs.

Crabmeat is best fresh, naturally, but is available frozen at fishmongers'.

CRACKLINS

See FATBACK.

CRAYFISH
(crawfish or crawdaddys)
(*Decapoda* sp.)

These freshwater crustaceans are also known as *mudbugs* because of their penchant for burrowing in the mud of rivers and canals. The Louisiana type are some of the smallest and tastiest of the species.

Crayfish are growing in popularity and can occasionally be found at fishmongers' outside of the Louisiana, Texas, Mississippi area where they are virtually totemic. For the rest of us not fortunate enough to live within crayfish territory, they can be ordered. (See mail order sources.)

DANDELION
(*Taraxacum officinale*)

These are indeed the same plants that are yanked up from grass lawns to the accompaniment of muttered curses. However, in the kitchen, they are revered indeed as good eating. They can be added to a pot of mixed greens or gumbo z'herbes, tossed in a salad with a hot bacon vinegar, or even transformed into dandelion wine.

Dandelion greens are only delicious during the brief period of their youth in the spring; after that, they are too tough and bitter.

Dandelion leaves are available virtually everywhere on the lawn. *Wash, wash, wash* to avoid pesticides. They can also be purchased at fairly great expense in fancy greengrocers'.

FATBACK

The clear fat from the back of a loin of pork. It is salted and/or smoked and appears as an ingredient in many southern recipes. When fatback is cut into small pieces and fried, it becomes cracklings or cracklins and is used in such dishes as cracklin cornbread. Rendered fatback is called lard, and is traditionally used as a fat for frying chicken or fish.

FILÉ
(Powdered Sassafrass)
(*Sassafras albidum*)

This condiment is also used as a thickener in many Creole gumbos. The powdered sassafrass is an addition brought to the dish by the Choctaw Indians, who used to sell their filé in the French Market in New Orleans.

GREENS

The West African habit of eating a wide variety of leafy greens made into soupy stews is translated by one word in the African-American culinary lexicon—greens. These greens may be collards, mustard, turnip, kale, or any variety of wild greens. Traditionally they were (and are) stewed down to a "low gravy" with a seasoning piece of fatback. If the times were good, they were cooked with a leftover ham bone or a seasoning piece of smoked ham hock. Today, with the new emphasis on healthy eating, the greens are cooked for less time and may even be stir-fried in a bit of oil and garlic and served with an accompanying hot sauce.

GRITS

Introduced to American colonists by Native Americans, grits are simply a term for a pounded form of dried corn. However, in the nineteenth century corn began to be processed and hominy grits were developed, thereby confusing the world. Hominy grits are prepared from corn that has been soaked in a weak lye solution and hulled. Readily available, hominy grits have become an integral part of a traditional southern breakfast. They are eaten with sausage in most of the South, with shrimp in South Carolina's Low Country, and in soufflés in the North. Large-kernel hominy, similar to Mexican *pozole*, is called "samp" and eaten as a breakfast food as well. True grits are still around, but usually only when someone takes the trouble to pound the corn himself.

For special stone-ground hominy grits, see mail order sources.

HAM
(Calas, Virginia, Smithfield)

The smoked or cured thigh of the hind leg of the hog, this is the king of the African-American and indeed the southern table. Hams may be country hams preserved in the styles of varying southern states. These are the royalty of the ham world, of which the emperor, for some tastes, is the Smithfield ham from Smithfield, Virginia, which is aged for as long as twelve months. Hams such as country hams and Smithfield hams are expensive indeed, and in flavor are deserving of the royal treatment.

Hams are available from a variety of sources. Next time your budget permits, bypass the mundane supermarket ham and try a country ham. (See mail order sources.)

HEAD CHEESE

A sausage prepared from the head of a pig or a calf; the head cheese is pickled and then served in its own flavored jelly. Head cheese is available by the slab at butchers' shops in African-American neighborhoods.

HOG MAWS

These are just what they say they are—the maw or stomach of the hog. Like chitlins, they must be cleaned scrupulously before they are cooked, and like chitlins, they are an acquired taste.

HOG'S HEAD CHEESE

See HEAD CHEESE.

HOMINY

See GRITS.

HOT SAUCE

Traditional African-American restaurants around the country would as soon be caught without cornbread as without a tall thin bottle of hot sauce as a tabletop condiment along with the salt and pepper. Hot sauces under a variety of names are a hallmark of African-American cooking. Try preparing your own, or order one of the more common varieties by mail (see mail order sources). If that fails, your local supermarket will always yield Tabasco.

KALE
(*Cruciferae* sp.)

It is interesting to note that for some people this appellation also covers collard greens, but they are most assuredly not kale. When in doubt, remember: Collards are straighter and smoother than kale, which is curly. Kale appears among the mixed greens of the African-American South, but it has not attained the popularity of collards or turnip or mustard greens. However, because it is also popular in Northern European cooking, it is more readily available.

Kale is best purchased fresh when the leaves are green and curled. Kale can also be purchased canned and frozen, but if you must, the frozen kind is preferable.

KARO SYRUP

This corn syrup is somewhere in taste between the lightness of maple syrup and the thick dark taste of molasses. It is a substitute for Alaga syrup on many northern African-American tables. Any corn syrup will do, though.

LARD

See FATBACK.

MAYONNAISE

Prepared from egg yolks, oil, lemon juice or vinegar, and other seasonings, this condiment is essential in such African-American delights as potato salad and shrimp salad. Homemade is still the best.

MOLASSES

A by-product of sugar production, molasses was a typical way of sweetening things for many slave families. In fact, it was the most popular sweetener in the country in the eighteenth century. Molasses played an even more important role in the lives of most African-Americans, for the infamous triangular trade that traded molasses for rum for slaves was how many of us came to the hemisphere.

Molasses in several forms is readily available in most supermarkets and is used because the taste for it lingers on in some of the baking of African-Americans.

MUSTARD GREENS
(*Cruciferae* sp.)

Another of the leafy greens that Africans found so delicious, mustard greens are sometimes called Indian mustard. Like other greens, they are served slow-cooked and stewed, and are frequently mixed with other greens.

OKRA
(*Hibiscus esculentus*)

These small pods are among the most maligned vegetables in the western world. However, in African and African-inspired cooking, okra comes into its own. The word *okra* comes from *nkruma*, the term for the vegetable in the Twi language of Ghana. In the Bantu languages, one of the words used is *quingombo*, from which we get our "gumbo." Okra pods are valued because of their thickening properties, and are used in soups, stews, and sauces. The vegetable is also prized for itself and eaten simply boiled and served with a pat of butter. A few drops of vinegar or lemon juice in the cooking water will cut the slime.

Okra is available fresh in vegetable markets and can be readily found canned and frozen. If fresh is unavailable, substitute frozen (avoid the canned!). The trick is that the more it is cut or cooked, the slimier it becomes.

| OLD BAY SEASONING | This seasoning mix with a faint taste of celery is one of the crab boil seasonings that is popular with natives of the Chesapeake region. It can be purchased in many fish markets and specialty shops or can be mail-ordered (see mail order sources). |

PEANUTS
(Arachis hypogaea)

A quintessential New World snack, peanuts appear in almost all courses of African and African-inspired cooking. Ironically, peanuts originated in South America, found their way to Africa with the Portuguese, and only returned to the northern part of the hemisphere with slaves. Despite George Washington Carver's attempts to demonstrate their versatility, for most African-Americans the nut is eaten as a snack food. It turns up in brittles, as snacks, and even raw and boiled.

Roasted peanuts are found everywhere. However, for raw ones, African-American vegetable markets are the best source in the North. They can be mail-ordered (see mail order sources).

PECANS
(Carya illinoinensis)

This nut comes from the tall hickory tree native to the United States and grows all the way from Illinois to Mexico. The name seems to come from one of the languages of the southeastern Indians, either the Algonkian *paccan* or the Cree *pakan*. A classic nut of the American South, pecans make tabletop appearences in pies, chopped on salads, and in pralines from New Orleans.

The nuts are readily available shelled and unshelled. Purchase them in places that have a good turnover to be sure they are fresh. They can also be mail-ordered.

PIG AND PIG PARTS

Although not indigenous to the hemisphere, pigs took to the wide open spaces of the New World with a vengeance. The result is that up until well into the nineteenth century, pork was the most popular meat in this country and it is arguably still the most popular among African-Americans. (This, though, is changing with new health-consciousness and with religious and dietary restrictions.)

Head for a butcher shop in an African-American neighboroood; if you can't find one, try a butcher shop in a German neighborhood and make special requests.

PORGIES
(Sparidae family)

These marine fish are prized as a sweet white meat fish. They are relatively easy to catch, as they inhabit sandy bottoms. The fish is known as sea bream outside of the United States. In the African-American tradition they are most frequently served fried.

They are available virtually year-round in fish markets on the east coast.

PORK RINDS

The crispy fried rinds of fatback that has been rendered into lard. They are available packaged in the South and in African-American and Hispanic neighborhoods.

POSSUM or OPOSSUM
(*Didelphis virginiana*)

The name of this nocturnal marsupial comes from the Algonquin for "white animal." As most slaves were able to hunt only at night, if at all, the nocturnal possum was fair game. The animals were usually caught live, then purged and cooked. Possum is traditionally stewed or roasted.

Possum is difficult to obtain unless you have friends who are hunters.

POULTRY SEASONING

This prepared seasoning is usually a mixture of sage, thyme, celery, and other herbs and spices. It is used in such dishes as cornmeal stuffing and roast chicken. It is a recent addition to African-American culinary habits. Not all brands are created equal; my paternal grandmother swore by her Bell's and so do I. It's readily available at many supermarkets.

RABBIT
(*Leporidae* sp.)

As fewer African-Americans are hunters, rabbits are not on everyone's menu. When they are, they're likely to be stewed or roasted, or even turn up in a Brunswick stew. They can be raised domestically and are available in specialty meat markets.

RACCOON (COON)
(*Procyon lotor*)

The masked marauder of the animal world can only be eaten if you've got a friend who hunts; raccoons are almost never available commercially. In years past, they were considered a delicacy by African-Americans and were served up roasted and stewed. They are reputed to go particularly well with sweet potatoes.

RICE
(*Oryza sativa*)

South Carolina is conceded the honor of being the home of rice growing in the United States and that state's rice comes from Madagascar, an island off the coast of East Africa. There was also a West African variant of rice, and Africans from rice-growing regions of West Africa were brought to the southern United States to work in the rice plantations of South Carolina. Folks both black and white from the Low Country have been known to eat rice at all three daily meals.

Rice is readily available in supermarkets. The brand you select will depend on your method of cooking.

RUTABAGAS
(*Brassica napobrassica*)

Also called swede turnips, these root vegetables are popular in many African-American households, perhaps because they kept well for long periods of time without refrigeration.

They are readily available in greengrocers' and in supermarkets. They should be firm and without blemishes.

SAGE
(*Salvia officinalis*)

This herb is a genus of the mint family. The leaves are the only part used for seasoning. Sage goes particularly well with pork and with chicken.

It is readily available both fresh and dried. If dried, it, like all herbs, should be purchased in small quantities and used rapidly, as it will lose its pungency.

SALMON
(*Salmonidae* sp.)

Canned salmon was a staple in many African-American households well up into the 1960s, when the prices began to rise drastically. The fact that canned salmon was inexpensive accounts for the numerous salmon croquette and salmon-and-egg recipes that are plentiful in African-American cooking and are never prepared with fresh salmon.

Canned salmon is still readily available in supermarkets; it's just gone up in price.

SALT and
SALT SUBSTITUTES

Salt mines have been known in the area that is Mauritania since the sixth century, there were salt mines at Taoudini in Mali, and the Saharan salt trade thrived for centuries. Salt was originally used for the most part as a preservative and not primarily as a seasoning; the seasoning was a residual effect of the preservation process.

SEVEN STEAK

This particular type of steak is much used by Creole cooks in New Orleans. According to Leah Chase it gets its name from the shape of the bone in the cut, which resembles the number 7.

SHRIMP
(*Decapoda* sp.)

Shrimp's tendency to spoil rapidly kept its consumption to areas in which it was fished, and many of these areas were those where urban slavery allowed slaves limited liberty of movement. In cities such as Charleston, South Carolina, and New Orleans, Louisiana, African-American shrimp fishermen would hawk their wares through the streets, proclaiming their freshness. Shrimp boils are as emblematic of these areas as crab boils are of the Chesapeake and clambakes are of the Northeast. In the African-American tradition, shrimp are usually served in a salad, boiled (hot or chilled as shrimp cocktail), in the Creole styles of New Orleans, and deep-fried.

Shrimp (usually frozen and thawed) are readily available today at fishmongers' and in supermarkets.

SMOKED TURKEY WINGS

These are frequently substituted for smoked pork by those with dietary or religious restrictions. The taste is similar, although the richness of the pork is not there.

Smoked turkey wings are available at many supermarkets.

SORGHUM
(*Sorghum vulgare*)

This plant is African in origin; evidence of its use has been found in tombs in Egypt that go back eight thousand years. Used in the South by all peoples as a sweetener until cane sugar became affordable following World War I, sweet sorghum produces a syrup that is thinner than molasses and lighter in taste.

Sorghum syrup is available in health food stores. Sorghum, the grain, is never used in traditional African-American cooking.

SOUSE MEAT

This pickled pig meat may be found in the form of a jellied slablike sausage or in a more terrinlike variation. It is an American variation on the souses of the Caribbean. Souse is frequently confused with head cheese; they are similar in ingredients and in taste.

Souse meat is available at butcher shops in African-American neighborhoods.

SQUIRREL
(*Sciuridae* sp.)

One of the original ingredients called for in Brunswick stew, squirrel is another of the game meats that will be tasted only by those with friends who hunt.

SUGAR

The African-American sweet tooth is legendary; one has only to sample the difference between the traditional baking of African-Americans and that of other groups to appreciate this. Over the centuries, this sweet tooth has been served by molasses, sorghum, muscovado (unrefined brown sugar), and more recently white sugar.

All of these sweeteners, from refined white sugar to molasses, are readily available in supermarkets. For sorghum or more intensely flavored brown sugar, try a health food store.

SWEET POTATOES
(*Ipomoea batata*)

The confusion between sweet potatoes and yams still persists in the southern United States. Botanically, and elsewhere in the world, a yam is a hairy, frequently white-fleshed tuber of the *Dioscorea* family. So please note, whatever you choose to call them, Louisiana yams and all other southern yams are members of the *Ipomoea batata* species and really sweet potatoes.

Whether they're called sweet potatoes or yams, these tubers are the basis for some very famous African-American pies and vegetable dishes. They were eaten by slaves as treats simply baked in the ashes of the cabin's fireplaces or roasted in cast-iron pots set in the coals with ashes placed on top of them.

The tubers, a cold weather treat, should be purchased when firm and free from blemishes. Use sweet potatoes relatively rapidly, as they spoil more readily than white potatoes.

TERRAPIN
(*Emydidae* and *Testudinae* sp.)

The most treasured and the rarest of the edible turtles, the terrapin was prized in the nineteenth century as an ingredient in rich soups and stews. It was so sought after that it became virtually extinct. Today, turtle is found rarely and only in canned or frozen form. It also makes an appearence in canned turtle soups.

TURNIPS
(*Brassica rapa*)

This northern European vegetable is prized not only for its tasty roots but also for its leafy greens, which can be cooked separately or along with the turnips.

Turnips are readily available in the autumn and winter and best when small and blemish-free.

WATERMELON
(*Citrullus vulgaris*)

Come summertime, many African-American neighborhoods blossom with trucks of watermelon vendors selling what has become a traditional summer dessert or snack. The melon is thought to have originated in West Africa. Today's varieties have sweet flesh that can range in hue from deep red to light yellowish orange. Although many of the current varieties are grown for a thin rind, the rind makes excellent pickles.

Watermelons are frequently plugged by adept salesmen who will let you sample to know that you're getting the sweetest melon. They're best as a summer fruit, but are increasingly available year-round.

EATING

AKKRA

This bean fritter harks all the way back to the Nigerian people of West Africa. It is well preserved in the cooking of Brazil and the Caribbean, and occasionally turns up as a black-eyed pea fritter in the States, though the West African tradition of fritter-making is more evident in sweet fritters such as New Orleans's calas.

ASHCAKE

A treat from the time of slavery onward, ashcake is a cornmeal mixture baked in the ashes or embers of an open fire. The bread is washed after cooking to remove the ashes and served with molasses.

BISCUIT

If it's the South, if it's breakfast time, and if it's a round, individual-sized bread, what you're looking at on the plate is probably a biscuit. There are many different types of biscuits: buttermilk biscuits, sweet potato biscuits, beaten biscuits, and ham biscuits, to name a few. They should be light and fluffy and butter should melt into delicious yellow puddles when added. BEATEN BISCUITS: This form of biscuit is prepared by beating until the flour breaks down and produces a silky dough that makes a biscuit with a well-browned top and a soft middle. It is delicious with melted butter.

CALAS

In New Orleans, these rice fritters were traditionally hawked on the streets by African-American women whose street cry was, *"Bels calas, bels calas tout chaud!"*

COBBLER

A deep-dish fruit pie with a top crust (or occasionally both top and bottom crusts) is a cobbler. Blueberry and peach are prime fruits for cobbler-making, but almost any pie-making fruit may turn up. They are usually served warm.

CRITTERS

This term applies to any form of wild game that shows up on the table.

FRITTERS

From West Africa to the New World, African-Americans love to nibble, and one of the prime nibbles are fritters, batter-dipped morsels fried to a crispy texture. Fritters can be sweet or savory.

They can be dipped in sauces or eaten alone or even sprinkled with powdered sugar and served as desserts. Corn fritters, banana fritters, and New Orleans's calas are all part of this tradition.

GOSPEL BIRD

If it's Sunday and it's chicken, it's the gospel bird. If it's Saturday and it's chicken or any other day of the week and it's chicken, it's still the gospel bird, so called because chicken was the traditional Sunday dinner.

GUMBO

This dish went from Africa to Louisiana with only a slight name change. *Quingombo* is the name for okra, gumbo's main ingredient, in one of the Bantu languages. The dish, which is based on the traditional African concept of a thick soupy stew served over a starch, can have many ingredients and is a classic of Louisiana's Creole cookery. There are other types of regional gumbos:

CREOLE GUMBO

This is New Orleans's finest, be it filé gumbo thickened with filé powder or fevi gumbo thickened with okra or the traditional Lenten gumbo z'herbes.

CHARLESTON GUMBO

South Carolina got into the gumbo game, too, with its own variation of the New Orleans stew. In Charleston, the gumbo is prepared without a roux.

PHILADELPHIA GUMBO

Although it is no longer called Philadelphia gumbo by most folk, Philadelphia's pepperpot, which made Bookbinder's restaurant famous, is a descendant of the street food that used to be sold by African-American women.

GULF COAST GUMBO

This is a soupy stew prepared by the Conchs or African-Americans of Bahamian origin who live on Florida's Gulf Coast. It, too, like almost all of the other gumbos mentioned, has okra as one of its main ingredients.

HOECAKE

Originally this seems to have been a cornbread that the slaves baked over open fires in the fields on the blade of a hoe. Today, the term can also be applied to a large biscuit that is traditionally baked and saved for the man of the house.

HOPPIN' JOHN

There are many theories as to how the dish got its name. However, no one disputes the fact that this dish of rice and black-eyed peas, or cow peas, is traditionally eaten by many African-Americans on New Year's Day to bring good luck during the rest of the year.

ICED TEA

This is the wine of the South. It's also one of the cool drinks that quench the thirst of teetotaling African-Americans.

JOE FROGGERS

These are molasses cookies from Marblehead, Massachusetts, that are named for an African-American man, Joe Frogger. Frogger, according to legend, lived on the edge of the town's pond and baked fantastic molasses cookies.

LIMPIN' SUSAN Cousin to South Carolina's Hoppin' John, Limpin' Susan is an okra pilau that turns up on tables throughout the Low Country.

PEPPERPOT The rich tripe-based soupy stew is traditional in Philadelphia, where it used to go under the name of Philadelphia gumbo. The dish was hawked as a restorative by African-American women whose cry was "Peppery pot! Nice and hot! Makes backs strong, makes lives long!"

PONE A porridgelike mixture, traditionally prepared from cornbread that is then baked or fried. There are also sweet potato pones.

POT LIKKER When greens have been cooked down to "a low gravy" the cooking liquid that has absorbed all of the nutrients is the pot likker (a corruption of pot liquor). The African habit of consuming the pot likker provided the extra nutrients that saved the lives of many, slave and master alike, during the antebellum period.

PRALINES New Orleans's gift to the world of African-American confections, pralines are more kin to their Caribbean and Brazilian relatives than to their North American cousins. The classic pralines were white or pink coconut or pecan candies; today's brown sugar praline is a newcomer. Like many traditional African-American foods of the urban South and North, pralines were sold by African-American women in the streets.

RED-EYE GRAVY This very special gravy is prepared when a thick slab of country ham has been one of the breakfast meats. The pan juices from the ham are transformed into gravy with the addition of a bit of the breakfast coffee.

SOP It's not really a culinary term but a technique of dipping bread into the sauces and juices that are so much a part of African-American cooking. Biscuits are sopped in molasses at breakfast and cornbread is sopped in pot likker at dinner. It's all a part of the savoring of every morsel.

COOKING STYLES

BULL ROAST This is a Maryland term for a big barbecue that features everything from roast crabs to the steer that at one time gave the feast its name (although true "bull" roasts are very rare).

CREOLE FOOD The debate about who is a Creole is not likely to be solved in my lifetime. If you don't believe me, ask a black and a white Creole from New Orleans. One thing on which they both will undoubtedly agree is on the wonderfulness of Creole food, which historically owes much to the wizardry of African-American cooks from Louisiana and from the Caribbean.

CRITTER FRY This is an African-American term used in the South for a meal that is prepared when hunters return with a mess of different kinds of game that is too diverse for any one dish.

DOCTORIN' IT UP This is a hallmark of African-American cooking: It's what all good African-American cooks do with any recipe that they receive. Somehow we seem virtually incapable of following a straight recipe without adding a little twist here and a little twist there. Today, when time counts, many a cook takes a cake mix or another prepackaged item and adds a bit of this and that to it. That's also "doctorin' it up."

DUNBAR FOOD Ishmael Reed, no slouch at food history himself (read *The Last Days of Louisiana Red*), has baptized what was called soul food by many in the sixties and seventies "Dunbar food" in honor of the great African-American dialect poet Paul Lawrence Dunbar.

FATHER DIVINE FOOD In the depth of the Great Depression, Father Divine was an African-American prophet whose followers provided free home-cooked meals for all at a ridiculously low price. The only true payment demanded was that the diner end his meal with Father Divine's slogan, "Peace: It's Truly Wonderful!" A small payment indeed for wonderful food.

FIDDLIN' See DOCTORIN' IT UP.

FISH FRY When you get together a group of people and fry up a mess of fish and serve them with hush puppies, cole slaw, potato salad, good liquor, and good conversation, you've got a fish fry.

FROM SCRATCH When a dish is prepared from its basic ingredients, as in all of the recipes in this book, it is prepared from scratch.

MAROON FOOD This is the food that evolved from the mixing of the foodways of escaped slaves with those of Native Americans. Examples are some of the foods of the Choctaw and Seminole and the foods of the black Cherokee.

MUSLIM FOOD When the African-American community at large became acquainted with Islam, through the Black Muslim movement and later through contact with many elements in the Islamic world, Islamic dietary rules became important. This is the period that saw the birth of the classic Muslim bean pie.

NYAM, GREASE, AND GRIT	All terms for eating in the African-American culinary world.
PREACHER'S PARTS	When the preacher came to Sunday dinner, as he did in some houses with astonishing frequency, and gospel bird was served, he always laid claim to the preacher's parts (the best parts of the chicken). He inevitably left the bony parts to the family of the house.
SOUL FOOD	This term came into being in the sixties, but as far as I can tell, it was not really a term given to African-American food by African-Americans. It came from outside. We simply called it dinner.

A Cook's Dozen:

Some of my favorite African-American cookbooks

Big Mama's Old Black Pot. Self-published.

Burton, Nathaniel, and Rudy Lombard. *Creole Feast: Fifteen Master Chefs of New Orleans Reveal Their Secrets.* New York: Random House, 1978.
> Edited by Toni Morrison, this is a tribute to the Creole food of New Orleans by the African-American chefs who were and are the unsung heroes of the kitchen.

Butler, Cleora. *Cleora's Kitchens: The Memoir of a Cook and Eight Decades of Great American Food.* 2d ed. Tulsa, OK: Council Oak Books, 1990.
> A life of over eight decades of food in the kitchens of the Midwest in stories, menus, and recipes.

Chase, Leah. *The Dooky Chase Cookbook.* Gretna, LA: Pelican Publishing Company, 1990.
> She calls me "smart mouth" and I call her "Aunt Leah." Her compendium of remembrances and recipes is like sitting down for a conversation with the doyenne of black Creole cooking.

Ferguson, Sheila. *Soul Food: Classic Cuisine from the Deep South.* New York: Grove/Atlantic, 1993
> The former lead singer of the Three Degrees recalls growing up in Philadelphia and cooking with various relatives. The photographs are almost as evocative as the recipes.

Harris, Jessica B. *Iron Pots and Wooden Spoons: Africa's Gifts to New World Cooking.* New York: Ballantine Books, 1991
> A look at the culinary continuum between Africa and the Americas. I wrote it; I like it. 'Nuff said!

Jean, Norma, and Carole Darden. *Spoonbread and Strawberry Wine: Recipes and Reminiscences of a Family*. New York: Doubleday, 1994.
> This book that is treasured by many is a family album with recipes.

Lewis, Edna. *The Taste of Country Cooking*. New York: Knopf, 1976.
> A moving testimonial to the seasonal table of the African-American South by the lady who is one of our culinary foremothers.

Mendes, Helen. *The African Heritage Cookbook*. New York: Macmillan, 1971.
> Published in 1971, this was one of the first works to trace the culinary links between Africa and America. It still makes fascinating reading.

Nash, Jonell. *The Essence of Great Cooking*. New York: Amistad Press, 1993.
> This new collection of recipes from the food editor of the major African-American women's magazine places the accent on healthy eating

National Council of Negro Women. *Black Family Reunion Cookbook*. New York: Fireside Books, Simon & Schuster, 1993.
> A celebration of recipes and food memories from some of the women who constitute the group.

Pinderhughes, John. *Family of the Spirit Cookbook*. New York: Simon & Schuster, 1990.
> John Pinderhughes brings readers into the culinary world of his extended African-American family with recipes and remembrances.

Smart-Grosvenor, Vertamae. *Vibration Cooking: Or the Travel Notes of a Geechee Girl*. New York: Ballantine Books, 1992
> The wit and recipes of the National Public Radio host sum up all of the improvisational glee inherent in any good African-American kitchen.

Woods, Sylvia, and Christopher Styler. *Sylvia's Soul Food: Recipes from Harlem's World-Famous Restaurant*. New York: Hearst Books, 1992.
> Recipes from the "Queen of Soul Food," whose Harlem restaurant is a New York landmark.

and

_____ by _____

(You fill in the blank here with the name of the one favorite that I forgot.)

There are, naturally, more, many more, but these are the ones that I turn to most often for sustenance, both mental and physical.

African-American Restaurants Around the Country

These are some of the places around the country where you can find good traditional African-American cooking, but frankly this is cooking that is best sampled in a friend's house, or better yet at a friend's mother's or grandmother's home. These entries come from friends' recommendations, chamber of commerce listings, years of clipped newspaper and magazine articles, and personal experiences. The restaurants reflect the wide diversity of the African-American dining experience and range from the sweet Savannah chic of trendy Georgia on Los Angeles's Melrose Avenue to the funky uptown down-home cooking of New York's La Famille, with every possible variation in between.

I have not included any of the numerous African, Brazilian, or Caribbean restaurants around the country unless their menus reflect the diversity of African-American dining. Whenever possible, phone numbers have been included along with an *amuse-gueule* of information to whet your palate. Restaurants change owners and menus faster than a chameleon changes colors, so call to make sure that they're still serving what you want—and that they're still there! They are listed in alphabetical order according to their state.

ALABAMA

Birmingham
RIB IT UP
830 First Avenue North
(205) 328-7427
Just what it says!

CALIFORNIA

Los Angeles
GEORGIA
7250 Melrose Avenue
(213) 933-8420
Sophisticated soul and L.A. people-watching go hand in hand

HAROLD AND BELLE'S
2920 W. Jefferson Boulevard
(213) 735-9023
Louisiana's Creole best

Marina del Rey
AUNT KIZZY'S BACK PORCH
4325 Glencoe Avenue
Dunbar food (aka soul food)

San Francisco
DOUG'S TEXAS STYLE BARBECUE
36th and San Pablo (off Interstate
    500)
(510) 695-9048
*Turkey, goat, lamb, and even head
cheese or New Orleans boudin over rice*

THE GINGERBREAD HOUSE
741 5th Street
(510) 444-7373
*Dunbar food meets up with Louisiana
Creole in a gingerbread house.*

POWELL'S PLACE
511 Hayes Street
(415) 863-1404
Sophisticated Soul

GEORGIA

Athens
WEAVER D'S
1016 East Broad Street
(706) 353-7797
Specializing in Dunbar food

Atlanta
ALCEK'S BARBECUE HEAVEN
783 Martin Luther King Jr. Drive
(404) 525-2062
*Dunbar food, including ribs and
Brunswick stew*

AUBURN AVENUE RIB SHACK
302 Auburn Avenue NE
(404) 523-8315
No decor, but great ribs

BLALOCK'S RESTAURANT
476 Edgewood Avenue
(404) 577-2890
*Dunbar food with a special banana
pudding*

CHANTRELLE'S CAFE AND CATERING
646 Evans Street SW
(404) 758-0909
*Eclectic menu with traditional favorites
such as black-eyed peas and sweet
potato pie*

CRICKET'S
2348 Cascade Road SE, and 3
other locations
(404) 753-5191
*The slogan, "Chicken is chicken but the
wing's the thing," says it all.*

DEACON BURTON'S SOUL FOOD
1029 Edgewood Avenue SE
(404) 525-3415
*Iron-skillet fried chicken and peach
cobbler are don't-miss Atlanta favorites
at this restaurant that has become a
piece of civil rights history.*

PASCHAL'S
830 Martin Luther King Jr. Drive
   SW
(404) 577-3150
Civil rights leaders also gathered here to
strategize and savor the fried chicken
and biscuits that are legendary

ILLINOIS

Calumet Park
GULFPORT CAFE AND DINER
12401 South Ashland Avenue
(708) 385-3100

Chicago
ARMY AND LOU'S AWARD WINNING
RESTAURANT
420 E. 75th Street
(312) 483-3100
Catfish, pork chops, chicken, and
people-watching on the South Side

GLADYS' LUNCHEONETTE
4527 So. Indiana
(312) 548-4566
Simple food well done

THE NET 1
200 W. 83d Street
(312) 874-6381
Seafood with a soul twist

NEW QUEEN OF THE SEA
RESTAURANT
8701 South Stony Island Avenue
(312) 221-3711
The restaurant is noted for its soul food
buffet.

NIDA'S OLD WORLD SMOKEHOUSE
1513 W. Irving Park Road
(312) 868-4700
Smoked barbecue, including turkey to
eat in or take out

THE RETREAT
605 111th Street
Pullman Historical District
(312) 568-6000

THE RIB JOINT
432 E. 87th Street
(312) 651-4108
Just what it says!

KANSAS

Kansas City
GATES BAR-BE-CUE
1411 Swope Parkway
(816) 923-0900
Barbecue—what the city's noted for!

ARTHUR BRYANT'S BAR-B-QUE
1727 Brooklyn Avenue
(816) 231-1123
More barbecue!

Overland Park
HAYWARD'S
11051 Antioch Road
(913) 451-8080
Founded over twenty years ago by
Hayward Spears, another man from
Hope, Arkansas. Again, barbecue is the
thing.

MARYLAND

Baltimore
FIVE MILE HOUSE
5302 Reisterstown Road
(410) 541-4895
Crab soup, crab cakes and a take-out menu

MICHA'S CAFETERIA
5401 Reisterstown Road NW
(410) 486-9626
Dunbar food at a cafeteria run by a church

RESTAURANT 2110
2110 N. Charles Street
Cajun rockfish, Maryland crab soup, salmon with Champagne sauce, and an African-American chef, Benjamin Gordon, who is one of the youngest people ever to win the Chaine des Rotisseurs award for fine dining. 'Nuff said!

YELLOWBOWL
1234 N. Greenmount
(410) 685-2932
No decor, but crab cakes and pan-fried trout

MASSACHUSETTS

Boston
BLACK CROW
2 Perkins Street, in Jamaica Plains
(617) 983-9231
Sophisticated dining with a Dunbar je ne sais quoi results in gourmet pizzas and sweet potato soups

BOB THE CHEF'S
640 Columbus Avenue
(617) 536-6204
Chicken and waffles on weekends and ribs and porgies during the week

JIMMY MAC'S BARBECUE
300 Beacon Street, in Somerville
(617) 491-1004
Ribs, dirty rice, and french-fried sweet potatoes are some of the accompaniments to go with a delicious pulled pork

Oak Bluffs (Martha's Vineyard)
LOBSTER IN THE BLUFFS
155 Circuit Avenue
(508) 693-0944
Chef Marvin Jones prepares shore dinners with a touch of soul. Succulent mussels in a spicy tomato sauce, a New England bouillabaisse, and, of course, lobster.

MICHIGAN

Detroit
STEVE'S SOUL FOOD
8443 Grand River
(313) 898-9777
Just what it says.

NEW YORK

Brooklyn
GAGE AND TOLLNER
374 Fulton Street
(718) 875-5181
Although this restaurant is not owned by African-Americans, it merits inclusion as one of the places where the ambrosial dishes of Edna Lewis can be sampled.

McDONALD'S DINING ROOM
327 Stuyvesant Avenue
(718) 574-3728
Church ladies, heaping plates, and good African-American Southern food

RENCHER'S CRAB INN
407 Myrtle Avenue
(718) 403-0944
Maryland-style crabs in Brooklyn

Harlem

COPELAND'S
547 W. 145th Street
(212) 234-2357
This restaurant is where Harlem insiders dine on superb African-American food.

LA FAMILLE
2017 Fifth Avenue
(212) 29-6899
Located upstairs, this small place is the lunch spot for folk from the Studio Museum and others in the know. The greens are delicious.

RENCHER'S CRAB INN
5–15 W. 125th Street
Maryland-style crabs in Manhattan

SYLVIA'S
328 Lenox Avenue
(212) 996-0660
Harlem's best-known soul food restaurant attracts everyone from neighborhood folk to busloads of Japanese tourists.

WELLS
2247 Adam Clayton Powell Boulevard
(212) 234-0700
This landmark has been known for over fifty years for its food, including its famous chicken and waffles.

Other Manhattan Places

B. SMITH'S
771 Eighth Avenue
(212) 247-2222
Sophisticated Dunbar food presided over by former model Barbara Smith.

CAFÉ BEULAH
39 E. 19th Street
(212) 777-9700
One of the newest additions to New York's Dunbar food scene

KWANZAA
19 Cleveland Place
(between Spring Street and Kenmare Street)
(212) 941-6095
This new restaurant celebrates the glories of pan-African foods from Jamaica, West Indies, to Jamaica, New York.

MR. LEO'S SOUTHERN CUISINE
17 W. 27th Street
(212) 532-6673
Off the path in a wholesale sundry district, the restaurant is known for its ribs and its Champagne chitterlings.

MO'BETTER
570 Amsterdam Avenue
(212) 580-7755
Buppies and biscuits

THE PINK TEA CUP
42 Grove Street
(212) 807-6755
In the West Village for over thirty-five years, this unpretentious restaurant is the place for an African-American Southern-style breakfast, or any other meal, for that matter.

THE SHARK BAR
307 Amsterdam Avenue
(212) 874-8500
More buppies and biscuits

OHIO

Cleveland
ART'S SEAFOOD
16402 Euclid Avenue
(216) 681-2787
Seafood with jazz on Saturday and gospel on Sunday morning

EVERYTHING AND THEN SOME
("EATS")
16405 Euclid Avenue
(216) 421-4779
Dunbar food with big-screen television

PENNSYLVANIA

Philadelphia
ZANZIBAR BLUE
305 S. 11th Street
(215) 829-0300
Sophisticated entrées range in style from North African to Caribbean and pass through the entire African diaspora. For dessert there's jazz next door in the club.

OLD BOOKBINDER'S
1985 74th Avenue
(215) 925-7027
No, it's not black-owned, but there's definitely an African-American touch in the pepperpot that comes steaming from the kitchen.

SOUTH CAROLINA

St. Helena Island
THE GULLAH HOUSE RESTAURANT
761 Sea Island Parkway
St. Helena Island
(803) 838-2402
Sweet potato pie, fresh, fresh seafood, and Miss Hannah's casserole, a dish of shrimp, cheese, and grits, are among some of the lures of this restaurant. They also offer occasional cooking classes. Call.

TENNESSEE

Memphis
COZY CORNER
745 N. Parkway
(901) 527-9158
Barbecue

NEELY'S INTERSTATE BBQ
2265 S. 3rd Street
(901) 775-2304
Barbecue

PAYNE'S
1762 Lamar
(901) 272-1523
And more barbecue!

TEXAS

Dallas/Fort Worth

CATFISH SMITH'S
2715 Martin Luther King Boulevard
and three other locations
(214) 426-5409
Fried catfish and all the fixings

DINING TABLE
1409 Ferndale, in Oakcliff
(214) 224-8378
Nouvelle southern with several heart-smart dishes

Houston

ELDORADO
2210 Riverside
(713) 528-8471
Chittlins, fresh-squeezed lemonade, and desserts are free!

RJ'S RIB JOINT
2515 Riverside
(713) 521-9601
Babyback ribs, sliced beef, and more

WASHINGTON, D.C.

FRENCH'S FINE SOUTHERN CUISINE
1365 H Street NE
(202) 396-0991
Dunbar food at its best

JOPLIN'S
225 Georgia Avenue
(202) 462-5401
Located in the Howard Inn, near the university of the same name, the restaurant offers soul food served on white linen.

Local and Mail Order Sources

ANDOUILLE AND OTHER SAUSAGES

Bruce Aidells
1320 Solano Avenue
Albany, CA 94507
(415) 285-6660

BARBECUE SAUCES

Wass Dis Here Sauce
Douglass Enterprises
P.O. Box 13366
Baltimore, MD 21203
Who needs Worcestershire sauce when you've got Wass Dis Here? The barbecuelike sauce comes in mild, medium, and hot.

Ken Davis Barbecue Sauce
Ken Davis Products, Inc.
4210 Park Glen Road
Minneapolis, MN 55416
(612) 922-5556
A wonderful barbecue sauce that comes in several varieties, including low-sodium

BEANS
(Red Beans)

Gazin's
P.O. Box 19221
New Orleans, LA 70179-0221
(800) 262-6410 or (504) 482-0302
Catalog available

BLACK-EYED PEAS

Uncle Wiley's
P.O. Box 91
Tuscumbia, AL 35674
These canned "peas" have a twist of jalapeño chiles.

BLACK WALNUTS

Missouri Dandy Pantry
212 Hammons Drive East
Stockton, MO 65785
(800) 872-6879, or
(800) 872-6880 in Missouri
Catalog available

CANE SYRUP

Golden Kentucky Products
P.O. Box 246
Livingston, KY 40445
(606) 453-9800

CHILES

CHILE TODAY HOT TAMALE
Commerce Center
2227 U.S. Highway 1 #139
North Brunswick, NJ 08902
(908) 360-0036

CORNMEAL
(White Cornmeal)

HOPPIN' JOHN TAYLOR
30 Pinckney Street
Charleston, SC 29401
(803) 577-6404

CRACKLINS
(Cracklins)

POCHE'S MEAT MARKET AND
   RESTAURANT
Route 2, Box 415
Breaux Bridge, LA 70517
(318) 332-2108

CRAWFISH
(Soft-shell Crawfish)

HANDY SOFT-SHELL CRAWFISH
10557 Cherry Hill Avenue
Baton Rouge, LA 70816
(504) 292-4552
FAX (504) 292-5191

FLOUR

WHITE LILY FLOURS
The White Lily Foods Company
P.O. Box 871
Knoxville, TN 37901
(615) 546-5511
*Made from soft red winter wheat, this is
the baking flour of preference for most
of the South, and that includes biscuits!*

HAMS

GWALTNEY GENUINE SMITHFIELD
HAM
Gwaltney of Smithfield
P.O. Box 489
Smithfield, VA 23430
(800) 678-0770
Catalog available

Country Ham

HOPPIN' JOHN TAYLOR
See cornmeal listing

HERBS

WILTON'S ORGANIC PLANTS
357 Harlem and Catherine Avenues
Pasadena, MD 21122
(410) 647-1561
*For those who want to grow their own
herbs and vegetable plants indoors and
out*

HOMINY GRITS

HOPPIN' JOHN TAYLOR
See cornmeal listing

Samp

Goya Products sells white hominy in both dried and canned forms; they are readily available in many supermarkets particularly in black, Hispanic, and Latino areas.

HOT SAUCES
(Red Devil Louisiana Hot Sauce, and the hotter Trappey's Pepper Sauce)

TRAPPEY'S FINE FOODS, INC.
P.O. Box 13610
New Iberia, LA 70562-3610
(800) 365-8727 or (318) 365-8281

COYOTE CAFÉ GENERAL STORE
132 West Water Street
Santa Fe, NM 87501
(505) 982-2454
Mark Miller of Washington's Red Sage and Santa Fe's Coyote Café offers an international array of dried chiles and hot sauces via mail.

PEANUTS
Boiled Peanuts

W. B. RODENBERRY CO., INC.
P.O. Box 60
Cairo, GA 31728
(912) 377-1431

Hot, Spicy Peanuts in the Shell

THE NEW ORLEANS SCHOOL OF COOKING AND LOUISIANA GENERAL STORE
620 Decatur Street
New Orleans, LA 70130
(800) 237-4841 or (504) 482-3632
FAX (504) 483-3922
Catalog available. Peanuts plus everything from CDs of New Orleans jazz and gospel to cast-iron skillets.

PECANS

SUNNYLAND FARMS
P.O. 8200
Albany, GA 31706-8200
(912) 883-3085
Catalog available

RICE

HOPPIN' JOHN TAYLOR
See cornmeal listing

SOUTH CAROLINA SEASONINGS AND DRIED BEAN MIXES

VIRGINIA SMALLS
1091 Greenhill Road
Charleston, SC 29412
Ms. Smalls grows, packages, and sells her own spices and dried bean and rice mixtures at Charleston's Marketplace. She'll send them to you via the mail.

SPRING WATER

MOTHERLAND NATURAL SPRING WATER
199019 Linden Boulevard
St. Albans, NY 11412
(718) 712-2300
Spring water with a soul twist!

Index

akkra, about, 257
Alaga syrup, about, 245, 252
angel biscuits, 192
appetizers, 37–56
   blue cheese straws, 45
   cheese straws, 45
   classic head cheese, 47
   deviled crabmeat, 48
   deviled eggs, 56
   fried eggplant Galatoire style, 44
   ham biscuits, 54
   mom's deviled ham spread, 55
   pickled black-eyed peas, 46
   pickled shrimp I, 50
   pickled shrimp II, 50
   roasted peanuts, 41
   roasted pumpkin seeds, 42
   shrimp fritters, 52
   shrimp spread, 51
   smoked bluefish spread, 53
   spicy pecans, 41
   super-rich Virginia crab cakes, 49
   yam chips, 43
apples, fried, 142
artichokes, Jerusalem, 135
ashcake, about, 257
aspic, tomato, 70
Aunt Zora's tea cakes, 211
avocado and grapefruit salad, 71

bacon:
   about, 245
   Charleston red rice, 109
   dressing, hot, wilted dandelion greens
     with, 73
   hot potato salad, 76

Limpin' Susan, 112
   mixed greens, 124
   okra soup, 62
   rutabagas, 136
   turnip greens with turnips,
     125
baked:
   ham, 151
   okra purloo, 114
   pineapple, 141
   sweet potatoes, 127
   tomatoes, 130
baloney:
   about, 247
   fried, 158
banana:
   fritters, 212
   pudding, 213
barbecue:
   about, 245
   fast cheatin', 157
   sauce, 246
basic okra, 113
basic pie crust, 202
basic vinaigrette, 93
batter-fried soft-shell crabs,
   176
bay leaf, about, 246
bean(s):
   about, 246
   butter, 132
   pie, 205
   red, and rice, 107
beaten biscuits, 191
beef, in cowboy stew, 160
beignets, 195

bell peppers:
    Charisse's no-pork gumbo with turkey
      fixings, 168
    chicken croquettes, 164
    cole slaw II, 77
    deviled crabmeat, 48
    dirty rice I, 110
    dirty rice II, 111
    fried corn II, 121
    ham salad, 79
    maquechou, 123
    pickled black-eyed peas, 46
    shrimp spread, 51
    smothered pork chops, 155
benne:
    about, 246
    candy, 223
    pralines, 219
    seed wafers, 217
beverages, 225–34
    Bluffs Bloody, 229
    bourbon, about, 234
    cool drink I, 230
    cool drink II, 231
    corn liquor, about, 233
    Creole café, 231
    Creole café brûlot, 232
    minted iced tea, 229
    Mister Good Daddy, 233
biscuits, 192
    about, 257
    angel, 192
    beaten, 191
    ham, 54
    sweet potato, 193
blackberry jam, 87
black-eyed peas, 105
    about, 246
    pickled, 46
    soup, 63
blackstrap molasses, about, 247
black walnuts, about, 247
blue cheese straws, 45
bluefish spread, smoked, 53
Bluffs Bloody, 229
boil, crab, 97
boiled crayfish, 53
bologna, about, 247
bouillon, Caribbean court,
    179

bourbon:
    about, 234, 247
    sauce, 216
breaded pork chops, 156
bread pudding, 214
breads, 181–97
    angel biscuits, 192
    beaten biscuits, 191
    beignets, 195
    biscuits, *see* biscuits
    calas, 196
    cornmeal mush, 188
    cracklin cornbread, 187
    fried cornbread, 186
    ham biscuits, 54
    hush puppies, 189
    johnnycakes, 194
    jalapeño cornbread, 187
    iron-skillet white cornbread, 185
    spoon, 188
    sweet potato biscuits, 193
    white cornmeal hoecakes, 190
    yellow cornbread, 185
Breakfast Bonanza menu, 241
broiled peaches, 141
brown sugar, about, 247
Brunswick stew, about, 149
bull roast, about, 259
butter:
    molasses, 98
    pecan, 99
butter beans, 132
butterfish, fried, 171
buttermilk, about, 247

cabbage:
    cole slaw I, 76
    cole slaw II, 77
    gumbo z'herbes, 170
    smothered, 134
cakes:
    Aunt Zora's tea, 211
    crab, *see* crab(s)
    pound, 210
calas, 196
    about, 257
callaloo, 65
candy, 220–24
    benne, 223
    fast fudge, 223

mais tac tac, 222
molasses taffy, 220
sweet potato, 221
Caribbean court bouillon, 179
carrot(s):
    gumbo z'herbes, 170
    and raisin salad, 73
    stoup, 64
catfish:
    about, 247–48
    fried, 172
celery:
    boiled crayfish, 53
    Brunswick stew, 149
    Charisse's no-pork gumbo with turkey
        fixings, 168
    chicken and dumplings, 163
    chicken croquettes, 164
    chicken salad I, 78
    chicken salad II, 79
    classic head cheese, 47
    cole slaw II, 77
    cornmeal stuffing, 98
    dirty rice I, 110
    ham salad, 79
    hot potato salad, 76
    peanut soup, 61
    potato salad I, 74
    quick seafood gumbo, 67
    shrimp salad, 80
    tomato aspic, 70
Charisse's no-pork gumbo with turkey
    fixings, 168
Charleston red rice, 109
cheese:
    blue, straws, 45
    classic head, 47
    grits, 139
    head, 47, 251
    macaroni and, 137
    pepper, grits soufflé, 140
    straws, 45
chess pie, 203
chicken:
    Brunswick stew, 149
    croquettes, 164
    dirty rice I, 110
    dirty rice II, 111
    and dumplings, 163
    gospel bird, 161, 258

kedjenou, 166
livers, fried, 167
moyau, 166
quick seafood gumbo, 67
salad I, 78
salad II, 79
and waffles midnight supper, 240
Yassa, 165
chicken, fried:
    gravy for, 162
    iron-skillet, 161
Chicken and Waffles Midnight Supper
    menu, 240
chiles, about, 248
Chitlin Soirée menu, 238
chitterlings (chitlins), 154
    about, 248
chutney:
    peach, 85
    peach kumquat, 86
    tomato, 87
clabber, about, 248
clams, soft shell, deep-fried, 175
Classic Creole menu, 239
classic head cheese, 47
cobbler:
    about, 257
    peach, 207
cocktail sauce, 94
coconut, about, 248
coddies, 174
coffee:
    Creole café, 231
    Creole café brûlot, 232
    ham with red-eye gravy, 156
cole slaw:
    I, 76
    II, 77
collards, about, 248–49
condiments, 81
    basic vinaigrette, 93
    blackberry jam, 87
    cocktail sauce, 94
    cornmeal stuffing, 98
    crab boil, 97
    Creole seasoning, 95
    garlic spiced oil, 90
    garlic thyme vinegar, 92
    hot sauce, 89
    hot vinegar, 91

condiments, *continued*
    lamb rub, 95
    mayonnaise, 93
    molasses butter, 98
    peach chutney, 85
    peach kumquat chutney, 86
    pecan butter, 99
    peppercorn mixture, 96
    pickled okra, 88
    pickled peaches, 85
    thyme oil, 91
    tomato chutney, 87
    watermelon rind pickle, 84
cookbooks, 262–63
cool drinks:
    I, 230
    II, 231
coosh coosh, 122
corn:
    about, 249
    Brunswick stew, 149
    creamed, 120
    fried I, 121
    fried II, 121
    fritters I, 118
    fritters II, 119
    Frogmore stew, 178
    liquor, about, 233, 249
    maquechou, 123
    okra, and tomatoes, 116
    on the cob, 118
    rabbit stew, 148
cornbread:
    cracklin, 187
    fried, 186
    iron-skillet white, 185
    jalapeño, 187
    yellow, 185
cornmeal:
    about, 249
    hoecakes, white, 190
    mush, 188
    stuffing, 98
cowboy stew, 160
cowpeas, about, 249
crab(s):
    about, 249
    batter-fried soft-shell, 176
    boil, 97
    cakes, Maryland, 177

cakes, super-rich Virginia, 49
Charisse's no-pork gumbo with turkey
    fixings, 168
Frogmore stew, 178
meat, deviled, 48
quick seafood gumbo, 67
she-, soup, 66
crayfish:
    about, 250
    boiled, 53
creamed:
    corn, 120
    onions, 132
Creole:
    café, 231
    café brûlot, 232
    classic, 239
    food, about, 259–60
    seasoning, 95
    tomato salad, 69
critter(s):
    about, 257
    fry, about, 260
croquettes, chicken, 164
crust, pie, 202
cucumber:
    chicken salad II, 79
    salad, 71
    tomato, and onion salad, 68

dandelion:
    about, 250
    greens, wilted, with hot bacon
        dressing, 73
deep-fried soft-shell clams, 175
desserts, 199–220
    Aunt Zora's tea cakes, 211
    banana fritters, 212
    banana pudding, 213
    bean pie, 205
    benne pralines, 219
    benne seed wafers, 217
    bourbon sauce, 216
    bread pudding, 214
    buffet, "sweet tooth," 239
    chess pie, 203
    fried pies, 205
    lemon meringue, 209
    milk rice, 215
    molasses, 204

peach cobbler, 207
pecan pie, 206
pecan pralines, 219
pink pralines, 219
pound cakes, 210
pralines, 218
rice pudding, 215
sweet potato, 208
watermelon, 202
see also candy
deviled crabmeat, 48
deviled eggs, 56
Diaspora Potluck menu, 238
dirty rice I, 110
dirty rice II, 111
doctorin' it up, 260
dumplings, chicken and, 163
Dunbar food, about, 260
Dunbar Food Feast menu, 240

Eggplant, fried, Galatoire style, 44
eggs:
    deviled, 56
    potato salad II, 75
    salmon fry, 172

fast fudge, 223
fatback, about, 250
Father Divine food, 260
field peas, about, 249
filé, about, 250
fish:
    coddies, 174
    fried butterfish, 171
    fried catfish, 172
    fried porgies, 174
    fry, about, 260
    porgies, about, 253
    salmon fry, 172
    smoked bluefish spread, 53
    see also shellfish
french-fried sweet potatoes, 127
fresh ham with peach-sage marinade,
    150
fried:
    apples, 142
    baloney, 158
    butterfish, 171
    catfish, 172
    chicken, iron-skillet, 161

chicken livers, 167
cornbread, 186
corn I, 121
corn II, 121
eggplant Galatoire style, 44
green tomatoes, 129
grits, 139
okra, 113
pies, 205
porgies, 174
salmon, 172
soft-shell clams, deep-, 175
soft-shell crabs, batter-, 176
fritters:
    about, 257–58
    akkra, about, 257
    banana, 212
    calas, 196
    corn I, 118
    corn II, 119
    okra, 116
    shrimp, 52
Frogmore stew, 178
fudge, fast, 223
Funeral Meats menu, 239

garlic:
    spiced oil, 90
    thyme vinegar, 92
glossary, 245–62
gospel bird, 161
    about, 258
grapefruit and avocado salad, 71
gravy:
    for fried chicken, 162
    red-eye, about, 259
    red-eye, ham with, 156
grease, about, 261
green peas, minted, 133
greens:
    about, 250
    collards, about, 248
    dandelion, wilted, with hot bacon
        dressing, 73
    gumbo z'herbes, 170
    mixed, 124
    mustard, 252
    quick, Brazil style, 125
    quick pork and, 152
    turnip, with turnips, 125

grilled tomatoes, 131
grit, about, 261
grits:
    about, 250–51
    cheese, 139
    fried, 139
    hominy, 138
    pepper cheese, soufflé, 140
gumbo:
    about, 258
    Charisse's no-pork, with turkey
        fixings, 168
    quick seafood, 67
    z'herbes, 170

ham:
    about, 251
    baked, 151
    biscuits, 54
    black-eyed pea soup, 63
    callaloo, 65
    Charleston red rice, 109
    dirty rice II, 111
    fresh, with peach-sage marinade,
        150
    gumbo z'herbes, 170
    red beans and rice, 107
    with red-eye gravy, 156
    salad, 79
    slow-cooked string beans, 134
    spread, mom's deviled, 55
    turnip greens with turnips,
        125
head cheese:
    about, 251
    classic, 47
hearts of palm and pineapple salad,
    72
hoecakes, about, 258
    white cornmeal, 190
hog maws, about, 251
hominy grits, 138
Hoppin' John, 105
    about, 258
hot potato salad, 76
hot sauce, 89
    about, 251
hot vinegar, 91
How I Got Ovah Slave Remembrance
    Supper menu, 240
hush puppies, 189

iced tea:
    about, 258
    minted, 229
I Loves You Porgy Carolina Fish Fry
    menu, 238
iron-skillet:
    fried chicken, 161
    white cornbread, 185

jalapeño cornbread, 187
jam, blackberry, 87
Jerusalem artichokes, 135
Joe Froggers, about, 258
johnnycakes, 194

kale, about, 251
karo syrup, about, 252
kédjenou, 166
kumquat chutney, peach, 86
Kwaanza Feast menu, 238

lamb:
    roast leg of, 159
    rub, 96
lemon meringue pie, 209
Limpin' Susan, 112
livers, chicken:
    dirty rice I, 110
    dirty rice II, 111
    fried, 167
Low Country Luxe menu, 239

macaroni and cheese, 137
mail order sources, 271–73
main dishes, 143–80
    baked ham, 151
    batter-fried soft-shell crabs, 176
    breaded pork chops, 156
    Brunswick stew, 149
    Caribbean court bouillon, 179
    Charisse's no-pork gumbo with
        turkey fixings, 168
    chicken and dumplings, 163
    chicken croquettes, 164
    chicken Yassa, 165
    chitterlings, 154
    coddies, 174
    cowboy stew, 160
    deep-fried soft-shell clams,
        175
    fast, cheatin' barbecue, 157

fresh ham with peach-sage marinade, 150
fried baloney, 158
fried butterfish, 171
fried catfish, 172
fried chicken livers, 167
fried porgies, 174
Frogmore stew, 178
gospel bird, 161
gumbo z'herbes, 170
ham with red-eye gravy, 156
iron-skillet fried chicken, 161
kédjenou, 166
Maryland crab cakes, 177
moyau, 166
neckbones, 158
pig's feet, 153
possum, 147
quick pork and greens, 152
rabbit stew, 148
roast leg of lamb, 159
salmon fry, 172
scalloped oysters, 177
smothered pork chops, 155
mais tac tac, 222
maquechou, 123
marinade, peach-sage, fresh ham with, 150
maroon food, about, 260
Maryland crab cakes, 177
Maryland Crab Feast menu, 238
mashed sweet potatoes, 129
maws, hog, about, 251
mayonnaise, 93
about, 252
menus, 237–41
Breakfast Bonanza, 241
Chicken and Waffles Midnight Supper menu, 240
Chitlin Soirée, 238
Classic Creole, 239
Diaspora Potluck, 238
Dunbar Food Feast, 240
Funeral Meats, 239
How I Got Ovah Slave Remembrance Supper, 240
I Loves You Porgy Carolina Fish Fry, 238
Kwaanza Feast, 238
Low Country Luxe, 239
Maryland Crab Feast, 238
Motown Munchies, 239
Nighttime Is the Right Time, 240
North Ca'lina Cue, 240
Palm Sunday Tea, 239
Pigfoot and a Bottle of Beer Bash, 240
Saturday Night Stomp, 241
Something Special, 240
"Sweet Tooth" Dessert Buffet, 239
Texas Juneteenth Family Picnic, 238
milk rice, 215
minted:
green peas, 133
iced tea, 229
Mister Good Daddy, 233
mixed greens, 124
molasses:
about, 252
blackstrap, 247
butter, 98
pie, 204
taffy, 220
Motown Munchies menu, 239
moyau, 166
mush, cornmeal, 188
Muslim food, about, 260
mustard greens, about, 252

neckbones, 158
Nighttime Is the Right Time menu, 240
North Ca'lina Cue menu, 240
nyam, about, 261

oil:
garlic spiced, 90
thyme, 91
okra:
about, 252
basic, 113
Brunswick stew, 149
callaloo, 65
Charisse's no-pork gumbo with turkey fixings, 168
corn, and tomatoes, 116
fried, 113
fritters, 116
Limpin' Susan, 112
pickled, 88

okra, *continued*
    purloo, 114
    quick seafood gumbo, 67
    and rice, 115
    soup, 62
    Southern succotash, 117
Old Bay seasoning, about, 253
onion(s):
    creamed, 132
    tomato, and cucumber salad, 68
oysters:
    Charisse's no-pork gumbo with turkey
        fixings, 168
    quick seafood gumbo, 67
    scalloped, 177

Palm Sunday Tea menu, 239
peach(es):
    baked ham, 151
    broiled, 141
    chutney, 85
    cobbler, 207
    fried pies, 205
    kumquat chutney, 86
    pickled, 85
    -sage marinade, fresh ham with,
        150
peanut(s):
    about, 253
    roasted, 41
    soup, 61
pecan(s):
    about, 253
    butter, 99
    chicken salad II, 79
    pie, 206
    pralines, 219
    spicy, 41
pepper cheese grits soufflé, 140
peppercorn mixture, 96
pepperpot, 259
pickled:
    black-eyed peas, 46
    okra, 88
    peaches, 85
    shrimp I, 50
    shrimp II, 50
    watermelon rind, 84
pie(s):
    basic crust for, 202

bean, 205
chess, 203
fried, 205
lemon meringue, 209
molasses, 204
peach cobbler, 207
pecan, 206
sweet potato, 208
Pigfoot and a Bottle of Beer Bash menu,
    240
pig's feet, 153
pineapple:
    baked, 141
    and hearts of palm salad, 72
pink pralines, 219
plain white rice, 108
pone:
    about, 259
    sweet potato, 128
porgies:
    about, 253
    fried, 174
pork:
    about, 253
    Brunswick stew, 149
    chops, breaded, 156
    chops, smothered, 155
    classic head cheese, 47
    cracklin cornbread, 187
    fast, cheatin' barbecue, 157
    fried corn II, 121
    and greens, quick, 152
    pig's feet, 153
    rinds, about, 253
    see also bacon; ham
possum, 147
    about, 254
potato(es):
    Brunswick stew, 149
    cowboy stew, 160
    neckbones, 158
    rabbit stew, 148
    rutabagas, 136
    salad, hot, 76
    salad I, 74
    salad II, 75
    slow-cooked string beans and ham,
        134
    stoup, 64
    sweet, *see* sweet potatoes

pot likker:
  about, 259
poultry seasoning:
  about, 254
pound cake, 210
pralines:
  about, 259
  benne, 219
  pecan, 219
  pink, 219
preacher's parts, about, 261
pudding:
  banana, 213
  bread, 214
  rice, 215
pumpkin seeds, roasted, 42
purloo, okra, 114

rabbit:
  about, 254
  stew, 148
raccoon, about, 254
raisin(s):
  and carrot salad, 73
  peach chutney, 85
  tomato chutney, 87
red beans and rice, 107
red-eye gravy:
  about, 259
  ham with, 156
restaurants, 264–70
rice:
  about, 254
  calas, 196
  Charleston red, 109
  dirty I, 110
  dirty II, 111
  Hoppin' John, 105
  Limpin' Susan, 112
  milk, 215
  okra and, 115
  okra purloo, 114
  plain white, 108
  pudding, 215
  red beans and, 107
roasted:
  leg of lamb, 159
  peanuts, 41
  pumpkin seeds, 42
rub, lamb, 96

rutabagas, 136
  about, 254
  stoup, 64

sage, 254
  -peach marinade, fresh ham with,
    150
salads, 68–80
  avocado and grapefruit, 71
  carrot and raisin, 73
  chicken I, 78
  chicken II, 79
  cole slaw I, 76
  cole slaw II, 77
  Creole tomato, 69
  cucumber, 71
  ham, 79
  hearts of palm and pineapple, 72
  hot potato, 76
  potato I, 74
  potato II, 75
  shrimp, 80
  tomato, 68
  tomato, cucumber, and onion, 68
  tomato aspic, 70
  wilted dandelion greens with hot
    bacon dressing, 73
salmon:
  about, 255
  fry, 172
salt, about, 255
Saturday Night Stomp menu, 241
sauces:
  barbecue, 246
  bourbon, 216
  cocktail, 94
  hot, 89, 251
scalloped oysters, 177
seasoning, Creole, 95
sesame, see benne
seven steak, about, 255
she-crab soup, 66
shellfish:
  batter-fried softshell crab, 176
  boiled crayfish, 53
  Charisse's no-pork gumbo with turkey
    fixings, 168
  deep-fried soft-shell clams, 175
  quick seafood gumbo, 67
  scalloped oysters, 177

shellfish, *continued*
  she-crab soup, 66
  see also crab(s); shrimp
shrimp:
  about, 255
  Charisse's no-pork gumbo with turkey
    fixings, 168
  fritters, 52
  Frogmore stew, 178
  pickled I, 50
  pickled II, 50
  quick seafood gumbo, 67
  salad, 80
  spread, 51
side dishes, 101–42
  baked peaches, 141
  baked sweet potatoes, 127
  baked tomatoes, 130
  basic okra, 113
  black-eyed peas, 105
  broiled peaches, 141
  butter beans, 132
  Charleston red rice, 109
  cheese grits, 139
  coosh coosh, 122
  corn fritters I, 118
  corn fritters II, 119
  corn on the cob, 118
  creamed corn, 120
  creamed onions, 132
  dirty rice I, 110
  dirty rice II, 111
  french-fried sweet potatoes, 127
  fried apples, 142
  fried corn I, 121
  fried corn II, 121
  fried green tomatoes, 129
  fried grits, 139
  fried okra, 113
  grilled tomatoes, 131
  hominy grits, 138
  Hoppin' John, 105
  Jerusalem artichokes, 135
  Limpin' Susan, 112
  macaroni and cheese, 137
  maquechou, 123
  mashed sweet potatoes, 129
  minted green peas, 133
  mixed greens, 124
  okra, corn, and tomatoes, 116

  okra fritters, 116
  okra and rice, 115
  okra purloo, 114
  pepper cheese grits soufflé, 140
  plain white rice, 108
  quick greens, Brazil style, 125
  red beans and rice, 107
  rutabagas, 136
  slow-cooked string beans and ham,
    134
  smothered cabbage, 134
  Southern succotash, 117
  sweet potato pone, 128
  turnip greens with turnips, 125
  wilted spinach, 126
slow-cooked string beans and ham, 134
smoked:
  bluefish spread, 53
  turkey wings, about, 255
smothered:
  cabbage, 134
  pork chops, 155
soft-shell clams, deep-fried, 175
soft-shell crabs, batter-fried, 176
Something Special menu, 240
sop, about, 259
sorghum, about, 255
soufflé, pepper cheese grits, 140
soul food, 261
soups, 57–67
  black-eyed pea, 63
  callaloo, 65
  okra, 62
  peanut, 61
  quick seafood gumbo, 67
  she-crab, 66
  stoup, 64
souse meat, about, 255
Southern succotash, 117
spiced oil, garlic, 90
spicy pecans, 41
spinach:
  callaloo, 65
  gumbo z'herbes, 170
  wilted, 126
spoon bread, 188
spread:
  mom's deviled ham, 55
  shrimp, 51
  smoked bluefish, 53

squirrel, about, 256
steak, seven, about, 255
stews:
    Brunswick, 149
    cowboy, 160
    Frogmore, 178
    rabbit, 148
stoup, 64
string beans and ham, slow-cooked, 134
stuffing, cornmeal, 98
succotash, Southern, 117
sugar:
    about, 257
    brown, about, 247
super-rich Virginia crab cakes, 49
sweet potato(es):
    about, 256
    baked, 127
    biscuits, 193
    candy, 221
    french-fried, 127
    mashed, 129
    pie, 208
    pone, 128
    possum, 147
    yam chips, 43
"Sweet Tooth" Dessert Buffet menu, 239
syrup:
    about, 252
    Alaga, about, 245

taffy, molasses, 220
terrapin, about, 256
Texas Juneteenth Family Picnic menu, 238
thyme:
    garlic spiced oil, 90
    oil, 91
    vinegar, garlic, 92
tomato(es):
    aspic, 70
    baked, 130
    Brunswick stew, 149
    Caribbean court bouillon, 179
    Charisse's no-pork gumbo with turkey fixings, 168
    Charleston red rice, 109
    chicken salad I, 78
    chutney, 87
    cocktail sauce, 94
    cowboy stew, 160
    Creole, salad, 69
    cucumber, and onion salad, 68
    fried green, 129
    grilled, 131
    maquechou, 123
    moyau, 166
    okra, corn and, 116
    okra purloo, 114
    okra soup, 62
    quick seafood gumbo, 67
    rabbit stew, 148
    salady, 68
    smothered pork chops, 155
    Southern succotash, 117
turkey:
    fixings, Charisse's no-pork gumbo with, 168
    mom's deviled ham spread, 55
    wings, smoked, 255
turnips:
    about, 256
    turnip greens with, 125

vinaigrette, basic, 93
vinegar:
    classic head cheese, 47
    garlic thyme, 92
    hot, 91
Virginia crab cakes, super-rich, 49

wafers, benne seed, 217
Waffles and Chicken Midnight Supper menu, 240
walnuts, black, about, 247
watermelon, 202
    about, 256
    rind pickle, 84
white cornbread, iron-skillet, 185
white cornmeal hoecakes, 190
wilted dandelion greens with hot bacon dressing, 73

yam chips, 43
Yassa, chicken, 165
yellow cornbread, 185

z'herbes, gumbo, 170